COLM MURPHY

50 GREAT IRISH ATHLETES

The Men and Women who did Ireland proud in the athletics stadia of the world.

First published in Great Britain in 2024

Copyright © Colm Murphy
The moral right of the author has been asserted.
All rights reserved.

No part of this publication may be reproduced, stored in a retrieval system, or transmitted, in any form or by any means, without the prior permission in writing of the publisher, nor be otherwise circulated in any form of binding or cover other than that in which it is published and without a similar condition including this condition being imposed on the subsequent purchaser.

Design, typesetting and publishing by UK Book Publishing.
www.ukbookpublishing.com

ISBN: 978-1-916572-87-4

CONTENTS

Introduction	1
Tim Ahearne – With Winged Feet	3
William 'Jumbo' James Murphy Barry – A Renaissance Man	9
Mike Bull – The Sky's the Limit	15
Mark Carroll – King of Distance	21
Eamonn Coghlan – Chairman of the Boards	27
Tommy Conneff – The Little IRISH Wonder	33
Neil Cusack – Boston Winner in a Dunnes Stores Vest	39
John Joseph Daly – The Tough of the Track	45
Maurice Davin – Father of Irish Athletics	51
Pat Davin – Record-breaking All-Rounder	57
Ronnie Delany – Mining for Gold in Melbourne	63
John Flanagan – Putting Hammer Throwing on the Map	69
Ray Flynn – Mighty Miler and Meet Director	75
David Gillick – Masterchef of the 400m	81
Mary Heath – Pioneering Athlete Flying High	87
Rob Heffernan – Walking with the Elite	93
Jim Hogan – The Irishman who Ran for Great Britain	99
Thelma Hopkins – Jumping for Joy	105
Denis Horgan – Shot-Putting Pocket Dynamo	111
Robert (Bobby) Kerr – The Shamrock and the Maple	117
Tom Kiely – The Champion	123
Maeve Kyle – Suffragette of Irish Athletics	129

Con Leahy – The All-Round Jumper	135
Pat Leahy – Jumping with Style	144
Olive Loughnane – World Champion Walker	149
Ken McArthur – 'I Came Here to Win or to Die'	155
Pat McDonald – All-Round Weight Thrower	161
John McGough – 'The Runner' McGough	167
Matt McGrath – Prince of Whales	173
Terry McHugh – Evergreen Olympian	179
Catherina McKiernan – Marathon Supremo	185
James Mitchell – Simply the Best	191
Walter J. Newburn – First Twenty-four Footer	197
Pat 'The Doc' O'Callaghan – The Great All-Rounder	203
Peter O'Connor – Ireland's Peerless Grasshopper	209
Frank O'Mara – World Indoors Double	215
Derval O'Rourke – Queen of the Hurdles	221
Gillian O'Sullivan – World Champion Race Walker	227
Marcus O'Sullivan – Sub-Four Minute Mile Centurion	232
Sonia O'Sullivan – Queen of Distance	238
Mary Peters – Golden Girl of Munich 1972	244
Mary Purcell – 'I Always Wanted to Do Better, Be Better.'	250
Paddy Ryan – The Late Developer	256
Martin Sheridan – Bohola's Hero	262
Jason Smyth – The Usain Bolt of the Paralympics	268
Tim Smythe – Cross-Country Supremo	274
Robert 'Bob' Tisdall – The Irish Wonder	280
John Treacy – Deise Distance King	286
Claire Walsh – A Trail-Blazer and 'Morton Marvel'	292
Appendix 1 – Pen-pictures of the seven authors	298

Colm Murphy RIP

In late October 2022, during a tour of wartime battlefields and sites, Colm Murphy died suddenly doing what he loved, teaching history to school children. He left behind Catherine his beloved wife, and his family, and a wide circle of colleagues and friends. He also left behind a great legacy of teaching and writing, not least of writing about the great days and heroes of Irish athletics.

What many people would not have known is that Colm was at that time the guiding light, editor-in-chief and any other leadership term you wish to use, on a collaboration between seven of us to identify and produce a book dedicated to '50 Great Irish Athletes'. Colm was our referee, our guide and above all our inspiration as we worked on our individual chapters, isolated by distance and Covid 19.

Colm's sudden death left all of us in shock but, after an appropriate interval, we were able to contact Catherine in Kent. We were thrilled that she was able to help us in locating the different versions and drafts of the book, much of which she had worked on herself with Colm as an extra pair of eyes.

Since the end of 2022, a sub-team of our remaining six has worked on proofreading and adjusting the draft. In late April 2023, Colm's ashes were laid to rest in the beautiful countryside around Donoughmore, Co. Cork, overseen by his good friend and fellow athletics enthusiast, Fr Liam Kelleher. From that day, we girded our loins for one last push and the result is the book you hold in your hands.

We have made every possible effort to remain true to Colm's vision for the book. The introduction which follows is exactly as Colm had worded it before his death. He had anticipated, and indeed looked forward to, the many arguments about who was included and who was not, who was 'the greatest' and even who might be in 'volume 2'.

For now, we leave you, the reader, with this book, as a tribute to our friend and mentor, Colm Murphy, and as a reminder of the many, many great athletic heroes produced on the island of Ireland.

(in alphabetical order)
Tom Hunt
Kevin McCarthy
Malcolm McCausland
Lindie Naughton
Pierce O'Callaghan
Cyril Smyth

INTRODUCTION

The concept of this book took shape back in 2019 following a conversation with Pierce O'Callaghan. Having created the Irish Athletics History Facebook page, Pierce was keen to develop the concept of a book on Irish athletes. The 2020s provide a myriad Irish athletics' anniversaries – the 150th anniversary of the National Championships and of the first Irish University Championships, and the centenaries of the National Athletics and Cycling Association of Ireland (NACAI) and of Ireland's first official appearance at an Olympic Games. A book on Irish athletes would complement these many anniversaries.

The task of selecting the athletes to write about would not be easy, and neither would be the writing of the biographies. It was obvious that a select team of biographers would solve both problems to an extent. There would, no doubt, still be many questions on the athletes selected and those not! The team eventually created included respected and renowned authorities on athletics and sport in Ireland – Tom Hunt, Kevin McCarthy, Malcolm McCausland, Lindie Naughton and Cyril Smyth, in addition to Pierce and me.

Whittling down the many deserving athletes took quite some time, argument and thought – the number initially settled at a hundred but eventually brought back to fifty. The criteria used for selection were simple - athletes either born on the island or readily associated with Ireland.

There was also the need to have a balanced selection of athletes from the 150-year period, with no period dominating. We did, however, agree that we would stick to retired athletes, since making any sort of judgement on athletes still in mid-career would have been unfair. Their day would come, perhaps in a Volume 2 someday. The evolution of the sport is noted with women athletes only emerging in the second half of the 20th century despite one notable exception in Mary Heath; an unfortunate situation but one which mirrored the reality of the time.

The history of Ireland and of Irish sport since the 1870s is evident in many biographies, as are the differing views on how athletics on this island should be governed. Nonetheless, the many biographies provide a celebration of sporting achievement, honour and distinction with much humour thrown in and, unfortunately, the odd sad story of glory – Olympic and otherwise – denied.

The main aim of the book is to introduce athletes that may not be well known both to the public and to the athletics enthusiast. Athletics is no different to any other sport in that 'stars' of the present quickly fade from the limelight once their careers are over. The intention with this book is to re-introduce several long-forgotten figures from the mists of time. No doubt the book will provoke much comment and conversation.

That is the intention!

Colm Murphy

TIM AHEARNE
With Winged Feet

In the early decades of the 20th century, Tim Ahearne was one of two brothers who achieved phenomenal marks as long and triple jumpers. While Tim's brother Dan has not made our initial list of fifty athletes, partly because his exploits mainly occurred abroad, he was nonetheless an extraordinary athlete. He won eight American hop, step and jump championships (now called the 'triple' jump) in nine attempts and in 1909, broke the world record with a mighty leap of 50 feet 11 inches (15.52m); a record that stood for fifteen years.

Disappointingly, at the Antwerp Olympics of 1920, Dan only finished sixth in the Olympic triple jump. At those Games he appears to have helped organise the first ever athletes' strike at an Olympics in protest at the living conditions assigned to the American athletes in a city still cleaning up the rubble after the recent world war.

As children, Tim, born 17 August 1885 and Dan, born 12 April 1888, would jump across a river that passed near the family home at Dirreen, Athea in County Limerick; that river was twenty feet wide. At St. Michael's College in Listowel, their sporting skills were fine-tuned, with the brothers also playing Gaelic football for Athea. After winning two jumping events at Listowel Sports as an eighteen-year-old in 1903, Tim began taking part in local competitions. At the age of twenty-two he burst on the Irish athletics scene at national level, winning the 1907 GAA long jump and triple jump titles and tying for the title in the high jump. He was also the all-round champion of Munster, a title he won in Fermoy.

In the following year Tim Ahearne transferred from the GAA to the Irish Amateur Athletic Association (IAAA). By that time, tightened regulations and the enforcement of the GAA ban meant that athletes could no longer compete at the championships run by both associations. There was also a growing belief among press commentators that the GAA was losing interest in athletics and concentrating more on hurling and football. Because the GAA was not recognised internationally and did not encourage its athletes to compete in 'foreign' championships, Ahearne may have decided that IAAA membership would give him greater opportunities for international competition, including the forthcoming London Olympic Games.

In 1908, Tim Ahearne won the IAAA 120 yard hurdles and long jump titles and was second in the high jump behind the great Con Leahy at the RDS Showgrounds in Ballsbridge, Dublin on 8 June six weeks before the London Olympics. Also that year, Ahearne was just two inches shy of Peter O'Connor's world long jump record with a 25' 11" (7.60m) effort. In 1909, he won the IAAA titles in all three of these events. That meant that in just three years, he had won eight Irish senior titles, and only failed to win once in nine title attempts at national championships.

The international opportunities which IAAA affiliation afforded Ahearne came initially in the form of the annual Ireland v Scotland matches. In two years at these contests, Ahearne won one 120 yard hurdles event, one high jump and both long jump competitions. At the 1909 English AAA championships, he won the long jump and was second in the high jump. It was the only time he competed at those championships.

Despite his successes, Ahearne had precious little opportunity to participate at the highest level in his best event: the triple jump. Neither the IAAA nor the English AAA championships featured the triple jump at all. Yet the event had been standardised as a hop, a step and a jump internationally, with old anomalies, like athletes taking two hops and a jump or even two steps and a jump, outlawed by the time of the 1900 Olympics in Paris.

Because triple jump was not included in either the Irish or British championships, there was no English or Irish champion to represent Great Britain and Ireland at the 1908 London Olympic Games, held at the newly erected 'White City' stadium in Shepherd's Bush. London had only been awarded the Games after Rome, the originally selected city, pulled out due to various difficulties, including the eruption of Mount Vesuvius in 1906. With the London organisers determined to see the 'home countries' competing in every event, Tim Ahearne, who was already entered in the long jump, the 120 yard hurdles and the 'standing' long jump, was one of four Irish-born athletes persuaded to enter the triple jump as well. As it turned out, these Irish entrants were the only representatives of Great Britain and Ireland competing in the triple jump. As representatives of Great Britain and Ireland, all the Irish athletes wore circular badges depicting the emblems of England, Ireland, Scotland and Wales on their vests. If you look closely at photos of Tim Ahearne in London, you will see him wearing this badge but with the IAAA logo of three entwined shamrocks clearly visible on his singlet underneath.

Between 20 and 22 July 1908, at London, Ahearne finished eighth in the long jump, but failed to get through the qualifying rounds of the standing long jump and hurdles. If he was going to win any medal in London, it would all come down to the hop, step and jump on 25 July. Even though he was unknown outside Ireland in this event, Ahearne had been within ten centimetres of America's Edward Bloss's world record of 14.78m in 1907 when winning his only GAA 'hop, step and jump' title. There was also a belief that he had gone over 14.80m in another competition in Ireland although the distance and conditions had not been ratified. Ahearne's 1907 GAA mark would have won the title at each of the first three modern Olympic Games.

In London, on 25 July, the nineteen triple jump competitors representing seven countries were divided into three qualifying groups on the morning of 25 July, with the top three in each group then qualifying to take three further jumps. Two other Irishmen had entered – Martin Dineen representing Great Britain and Martin Sheridan the USA. A fierce competition resulted, with Ahearne and the Canadian J. Garfield McDonald battling it out for victory and breaking the old Olympic record distance five times.

Edvard Larsen of Norway, who had been favourite to take the title, was a relatively distant third. Not until his very last jump did Ahearne strike the decisive blow, setting a new Olympic record of 14.92m; not far off Dan Shanahan's world record of 15.25m. When McDonald failed to get anywhere near that with his last effort, the Limerick man was crowned Olympic champion. At twenty-two years old, he was the youngest gold medal winner of the 1908 Games.

As younger sons of a large family, prospects were not great for the jumping Ahearne brothers in Ireland, and within a year of the London Olympics both had emigrated to the USA. Dropping an 'e' from the surname, apparently because of a misspelling by an immigration official, the (now) Ahearn brothers continued to dominate triple jump competitions in the USA, with Dan, as mentioned earlier, winning a remarkable eight AAU championships. Tim placed second at the same championships in 1911, 1913, 1914, and 1916, and won a couple of national indoor titles as well as the Canadian long jump title in 1911. In May 1911, Dan broke his brother's world record with a jump of 15.52 m in New York, also jumping that distance at the American championships in 1915. Since he was not an American citizen at the time, he missed out on the 1912 Stockholm Olympics, as did Tim, who decided not to defend his title.

After retiring from athletics, Tim Ahearn(e) appears to have worked as a tester for the fire department. According to the *Dictionary of Irish Biography*, he later returned to his rural roots and settled on a farm in upstate New York, where he raised prize-winning pedigree cattle. He died in November

1968 aged eighty-three. Dan had died much earlier at the age of fifty-seven in Chicago, having worked in a variety of jobs, including selling insurance and as a policeman.

For a time in the USA, Tim Ahearn(e) represented the New York Athletic Club while Dan was with the Irish-American Athletic Club (I-AAC) in Long Island City. Eventually, both brothers became I-AAC members and contributed to the club's dominance in US athletics for many years. When the people of his hometown of Athea chose a motif for the memorial to the Ahearne brothers, they decided on two winged feet, nicely symbolising the jumping feats of the brothers. This was entirely appropriate, as the New York AC logo has one winged foot while the I-AAC had a winged fist. In many respects, the pair of winged feet was the best way of capturing the brilliance of the pair of flying brothers from nearby Dirreen.

WILLIAM 'JUMBO' JAMES MURPHY BARRY

A Renaissance Man

According to a journal called the *Quarryman in* April 1914, W.J.M. Barry was not only 'the most famous athlete that Queen's College, Cork ever produced' but the equal of any of the throwing greats of his generation and, indeed, of all time.

PJD wrote of Barry in the *Sport* newspaper of March 1926:

'Being an athletic model ... the popular title...was no misnomer. He was a man of heroic build but void of any trace of flaccid muscle or flesh. His presence in an arena was at once arresting and commanding, and his poise with the shot was reproduced as a model by an English authoritative work upon field events. Those who had the privilege of his acquaintance and friendship will remember him as a warm-hearted, impulsive Irishman; modest, but not indifferent to his gifts, and jovial on all occasions and in every circumstance.'

Born in September 1865 in St Luke's, Cork, he was the son of Patrick and Anne Barry of Hill View, Cork. His father was a building contractor and died in 1885. His younger brother was Redmond John Barry, a lawyer and judge who became Lord Chancellor of Ireland; his promising career was cut short by his early death in 1913.

When still a boy, Barry's physique was already remarkable, a fact which earned him the nickname 'Jumbo'. He was educated at St Vincent's, now Christian Brothers' College, and in 1879 enrolled for medicine at Queen's College, Cork.

Barry's frame marked him out immediately as a thrower. He would become proficient in the shot, hammer and the 56lbs for distance events. When beaten into second place in both the hammer and the 56lbs weight by Owen O'Dowd and Owen Harte respectively, it is said he ruefully remarked after the hammer that he would not be beaten in that event again.

Of the three weight events, the shot was his worst, despite his two national and three AAA titles. His best mark, 13.00m, was achieved at the 1889 Queen's College Cork meeting. This was a foot shy of James O'Brien's 'World Record' of 13.33m.

Few athletes could match him with the 'half hundred' – at slinging the fifty-six pounds weight from between the legs, with or without follow, while in throwing the 16lbs hammer he was on a level with the best men in the world in the middle of the 1880s. He threw the weight a phenomenal 8.28m at Mallow in 1885 and though initially queried it was subsequently accepted as a record. There was an 8.65m mark for the 56lbs with follow at the Queen's College Cork sports that same year.

Barry won his first national titles when just eighteen years old – the hammer and the 56lbs distance – and his performances with the primitive implements then in vogue were an earnest of the feats that were to follow. He won the hammer at the inaugural IAAA Championships in 1885, throwing 116 feet 10 inches (35.61m), the first of his 'World Records'.

The hammer remained his true forte. In June 1886, he was the first athlete to better the 40m mark when he threw 40.62m in Limerick. Four national and five AAA hammer titles were to follow – of his second AAA win in 1889 it was noted that: 'He was the finest athlete that ever donned athletic clothing'. Barry enjoyed a double championship victory that year when he tied with R.A. Greene in the shot.

It was also reported by the *London Illustrated News* that: 'He fairly broke the ladies' hearts – few of them had ever seen a finer man than this genial giant of an Irishman.'

Barry's record hammer from a seven foot circle, with a hammer that had a four foot wooden handle and an iron head of 41.98m, stood until 1896 when Tom Kiely threw 42.72m. Barry's best with any hammer was at Sunderland – a 42.25m effort.

In 1887, Barry was based in New York and as secretary of the Manhattan Athletic Club, was among those welcoming the athletes who were part of the 'GAA Invasion' of 1888. Among the tourists was John Daly, a fellow clubman at Queen's College Cork. The tussles between the two in the many and varied throwing disciplines became a feature of the athletics season in North America.

Barry was no stranger to athletics administration, serving several years on the Cork College committee and elected a vice-president of the fledging GAA in 1885. Although he attended the second meeting of the organisation at the Victoria Hotel in Cork, he never took an active part nor competed in any competition under its rules.

Barry also acted as a judge on many occasions, and not without controversy. At the Queen's College Cork sports in 1889, he oversaw the long jump. A foul was called, and the athlete concerned disputed the call, advising Barry that 'he knew nothing of it'. Barry immediately 'disqualified the jumper which gave rise to much comment'.

His final foray as an athlete was at his old stomping ground – the annual Cork College meeting at the Cork County Cricket Club grounds, where he had the satisfaction of winning both the hammer and 56lbs distance.

Barry was not only the ultimate thrower, he was also quite the all-round sportsman. He excelled at rugby playing for the Cork College 1st XV. He was also adept at cricket and a competitive swimmer. As a boxer, he won the heavyweight championship of Edinburgh University and later took amateur titles both in the United States and in Australia. In 1888 in New York, he was touted as a possible world heavyweight contender. Barry's prowess as a swimmer saw him claim the 100 yards championship of the United States and Canada.

His academic career was as extraordinary as his sporting activities. Despite spending many years at Cork College, he never sat an examination and temporarily abandoned his studies. He eventually opted to complete his medical studies at Edinburgh. There he broke all records by qualifying within twelve months. He was admitted a Licentiate of the Royal College of Surgeons, Edinburgh in 1891 and enlisted in the 3rd Volunteer Battalion, the King's Liverpool Regiment.

With the rank of Surgeon-Lieutenant he joined the Trans-Himalayan Expedition which surveyed and studied the spread and control of malaria in that part of India. On return from the subcontinent, he resigned his commission as Surgeon-Lieutenant on 25 September 1895.

On the death of his first wife, Margaret Chambers in 1896, Barry took up a position with the Port of Cardiff Authority as a ship's surgeon on transatlantic voyages. In February 1901, the press was reporting on the first appearance on a London stage of the American star Trixie Friganza (born Delia O'Callaghan) who had a star role in *The Belle of Bohemia* at the Apollo Theatre. The excitement was added to by the romantic story behind her voyage on on the SS Bohemian. She had fallen in love with the ship's surgeon, none other than Doctor Barry himself, and they married on arrival in London. In the early 1920s, Trixie moved into the movies mostly playing quirky and comedic characters and after acting in over thirty films, retired in 1940 due to health concerns. During the height of her career, she used her fame to promote social, civic, and political issues such as self-love and the suffragist movement. The couple subsequently divorced and in 1916, Barry married his third wife Mary Jenkins in Cardiff.

Barry was awarded a medical degree with honours from Brussels University in 1897. In 1911 he was admitted as a fellow of the Royal College of Surgeons, Edinburgh and in June 1912 the degree of Doctor of Medicine was conferred on him by Durham University.

He continued his involvement in sport as president of the Welsh Tailteann Games organising and selection committee.

In that capacity he presided at the athletics and boxing trials at the Sophia Gardens, Cardiff facilities in July 1924. Two years earlier, in August 1922, Barry presented two 25 guinea cups, to be awarded to the winners of the hammer and the weight at the Welsh AAA Championships.

Barry died on 25 March 1926 in Southport. PJD wrote in the *Sport* newspaper of March 1926:

'His death at the age of sixty removes one of the few remaining athletic stars of a great galaxy. He brought fame from the world-arena to his country, and his performances will remain in the native athletic annals as the feats of a splendid type of the men who put high standards of achievement for all who might succeed them.'

'Jumbo' Barry's athletics legacy may well be unique. As well as the championship victories and world rankings, which he topped on three occasions, he extended the world record in the hammer from the mid-30 metres to the low 40 metres. His career began with the shafted hammer thrown from a stand and he was among those leading the evolution from the shafted hammer to the implement used today – a metal ball attached by a steel wire to a grip. That evolution would start in Ireland in the 1880s with Barry to the fore developing the technique necessary for throwing the modified implement.

MIKE BULL
The Sky's the Limit

Doctor Michael Anthony Bull OBE was born on 11 September 1946 in Belfast and was one of the first of the generation dubbed the 'Baby Boomers' to arrive after the Second World War. His father John Bull had met his mother Anne, who had been widowed following the death of her paratrooper husband during the early part of the war leaving her to bring up three children on her own. John Bull, as his name might suggest was English, born in Bristol. He was a former Chief Petty Officer in the Royal Navy, and with seafaring links all the way back to Captain Cook.

Initially based at Eglinton, near Derry/Londonderry, where John was a fitness instructor in the military camp, the family moved back to the Ballysillan area of north Belfast. Bull attended the St. Malachy's College where past pupils include actor Ciarán Hinds, broadcaster Eamonn Holmes and football manager Martin O'Neill as well as athletes Gareth Turnbull, Colm McClean and Joe McAlister.

Bulls's father encouraged him into sport from an early age and in his autobiography *Mike Bull: An Olympian's Story*, he relates being carried on his father's shoulders to rugby training and matches at North RFC where John Bull was captain of the first fifteen. He also accompanied him to playing fields where his father practised throwing the hammer. At fourteen, Mike stood just over six foot (1.83m) and weighed in at a muscular fourteen stone (89kg), making him a natural for most sports.

While Bull shone at both athletics and soccer, where he was already sought by Bristol Rovers as a promising young goalkeeper, the sport in which he excelled was swimming. Competing in the annual school gala in the Falls Road Baths, he regularly won five of the six events, setting long-standing freestyle sprint records. His road to Damascus in swimming came at age fifteen when he swam against Scotland's future Olympic silver medallist Bobby McGregor, who finished half the length of the pool in front of Bull. After that he resolved to stick to athletics.

While enjoying success in the pool, on the track and various sports fields, Bull's idols were not the sportsmen of the day but bodybuilders such as Steve Reeves and Reg Park. At twelve, his father had enrolled him in Buster McShane's Health Studio on top of an old linen factory on Belfast's Corporation Street. McShane would later achieve fame as coach and mentor to Munich pentathlon gold medal winner Mary Peters. But in the meantime, Bull and a few friends lifted weights in McShane's gym every Monday, Wednesday and Friday. He described it in his book as a 'very Irish gym, and the craic was always good.'

News that Reg Park was coming to Belfast excited the young Bull but the five shillings entry fee, the cost of two weeks training at the gym, proved a temporary obstacle. He and his friend Danny Farrell came up with a plan. They would enter the under-16 event which would not only gain them free entry but also the opportunity to meet one of their heroes. He and his friend competed and, despite using improvised and unrehearsed routines, Danny won the competition while Mike was third. All that paled in comparison to the fact that Reg Parks came next on stage after them to perform his outstanding routine to the theme music from the film *Exodus* which was popular at the time.

It was around that time that Mick McCormick, a PE teacher at St. Malachy's, introduced Bull's class to the gravity-defying skill of pole-vaulting in a highly unconventional manner. McCormick stood at one end of the school gym holding an old metal pole lodged in a pile of old-style gym mats. The boys lined up at the other end, full of trepidation, and one by one would sprint down the hall and grab the end of the pole which the teacher would then catapult to the vertical, propelling the fortunate or unfortunate pupil through the air and hopefully landing all limbs intact on the mats.

In this way, McCormick talent-spotted a lengthy line of exponents who carried the St. Malachy's name with success through many years of schools' competition. Bull grabbed the pole as if it were the most natural thing in the world and from that day, had found his sporting vocation. He was sent from the gym to practice on the grass pitches where the landing was a little more inviting, but not much. Such was his progress that in 1964 he was able to set an Irish junior record of 3.76m at the St. Malachy's school sports. He improved this later in the year at Dublin's Santry Stadium, becoming the first Irish pole vaulter to clear 13 feet (3.96m) and then soaring over 3.98m when winning the Catholic Student Games in Girona, Spain.

After Bull became the youngest ever winner of the Northern Ireland decathlon championship, he was picked to represent Ireland at senior international matches against Belgium and Scotland in Brussels, and against England at the then 'new' Crystal Palace. The summer climaxed with yet another Irish record of 4.06m in Dublin where he competed against the reigning world record holder Fred Hansen from Texas. At this meeting, he met a visiting American coach, Lew Harzog, who offered him a scholarship to Southern Illinois University in Carbondale.

This was to be a chastening experience for the Belfast boy wonder. Instead of dominating the headlines as he had done at home, he found that practically every university on the ultra-competitive college circuit had a pole-vaulter better than him. Nonetheless, the experience proved beneficial and, on his return, the following summer, he achieved his ambition of gaining a British vest for a match against Poland on 14 August 1965. It would be the first of a record sixty-nine British international caps for Bull.

The following year Bull would upset the odds when he took a silver medal at the 1966 British Empire and Commonwealth Games in Kingston, Jamaica. Despite having to train in a converted timber shed on the site of Belfast's Harland and Wolff shipyard, where the famous yellow cranes that dominate the city's skyline now stand, that silver medal would kick off a career-long association for Bull with the Commonwealth Games.

Four years later he would take the gold medal at the Edinburgh celebration and, in 1974 had his most successful Commonwealth outing, winning the decathlon and taking the pole vault silver medal in Christchurch, New Zealand. Unfortunately, his Commonwealth adventures ended not with a bang, but with a whimper when he no-heighted in the pole vault at the 1978 Games in Edmonton, Canada, and was eliminated from the competition.

Bull represented Great Britain and Northern Ireland at two Olympic Games. In Mexico 1968 he finished thirteenth with a 5.0m leap and in Munich 1972 he could manage only 4.80m and finished joint sixteenth. He represented his country at numerous European indoor and outdoor championships. During his career he broke the British pole vault record twenty-five times, achieving a best of 5.25m at the Crystal Palace on 22 September 1973. That remained the Northern Ireland and Ulster record almost fifty years later.

It was not all sport with Bull, who was awarded a PhD from Queen's University in 1974. After he retired from professional athletics, he lectured in sports studies and did some commentary work for UTV (Ulster Television). For many years he ran his own business, Mike Bull's Health Gym in Bangor, County Down and was a fitness coach to both the Ulster and Irish Rugby Football Unions.

In 2012, Bull was awarded the OBE by the Queen for services to sport and charity. Two years later he was named 'Britain's Greatest Ever Pole-vaulter' in the world-renowned magazine *Athletics Weekly* by the leading writer and statistician Mel Watman. In 2019, following the death of his wife, he decided to sell his gym and house in Bangor and relocate to Málaga in Spain's Andalucía region.

More recently he made a return to pole-vaulting after an absence of three decades when the Northern Ireland national coach for the event suggested he should come along and observe a training session. Unable to resist having a go, Bull was once more on the runway and clearing heights athletes half his years could not manage. He is now back in weekly training and, in the over 75 age category, continues competing at masters' level having won the over-40 world title in Finland as far back as 1991.

MARK CARROLL
King of Distance

Mark Carroll, born on 15 January 1972, and a native of Knocknaheeny in Cork's northside, was introduced to athletics while a student at the North Monastery Christian Brothers School where he was coached by Brother John Dooley. Recognising his potential, Declan O'Callaghan, who captained the North Mon athletics team, encouraged Carroll to join Leevale Athletic Club. Very soon the run from Carroll's house in Knocknaheeny to O'Callaghan's home in Gurranabraher, and from there to the Leevale clubhouse in Dalton's Avenue to join Der O'Donovan's distance running group, became part of the Carroll routine. The runs became extra special when the group was joined by US scholarship athletes:

'These stories held our attention, made things go fast and lit a fire in many of us to follow in their footsteps to the US,' Carroll explained in the book *Leevale: Home of Champions*.

Carroll first made an impression as a cross-country runner, with a second in the All-Ireland Junior Cross-Country Championships at Killenaule in early 1989. That run won him a place on the Irish team for the World Cross-

Country in Stavanger Norway, a somewhat overwhelming experience for the seventeen-year-old Carroll.

His breakthrough came the following season with Victory in the BLOE U17 Championships and a win in the junior race at the Inter-Counties in Dundalk. His total mileage for the month was 185 miles. In February 1990, he again finished second in the junior race at the National Cross-Country and followed that up with victory in the All-Ireland Schools' championships in Boyle before heading for Aix-les-Bains, France, for the World Cross-Country Championships.

There he finished a respectable 19th in the junior race. He had hoped to make the 5000m qualifying time for the World Juniors, but injury punctuated his track season forcing him to take a long break and he only returned to light training in December. In early 1991, he again finished second in the National Junior Cross-Country in Limerick and in Mallusk a few weeks later, won the All Ireland Schools title for a second year. In the junior race at the World Cross-Country, he ran cautiously and finished 35th. At the Penn Relays in April, Carroll ran the anchor leg for North Mon in the High School Medley Relay, bringing the team from fifth to third place.

In the summer, Carroll returned to the track with a bang, finished second behind Frank O'Mara in the 1500m with a time of 3 mins 43.36 secs at the National Track and Field Championships at Santry. He followed that up with 8:09.43 for 3000m at the British AAA championships where he finished fourth. At the European Under-20 Athletics Championships held in Thessaloniki, Greece, in August of that year, he made a sensational international track debut when he won the men's 5000m in a time of 14:19.48 after a last lap charge. It was only the second time an Irish athlete had won a European junior title and the first time any such title, junior or senior, was won by an Ireland-based athlete. In recognition of his achievements, Carroll was chosen as the 1991 EBS Young Athlete of the Year.

Keeping a close eye on Carroll's progress was Waterford man Ray Treacy, the older brother of John and a former Irish cross-country international himself. In August 1991, Carroll took up a sports scholarship at Providence College, Rhode Island where Treacy was head coach. At the Cork City Sports on 9 July 1993, Carroll broke four minutes for the mile when he finished third behind Marcus O'Sullivan and Niall Bruton in a time of 3:58.64. At Providence, he won the 1995 NCAA indoor 5000m becoming one of only a handful of Irish athletes to have won an NCAA title. In cross-country, he finished third in the 1992 NCAA Championships and was runner-up in 1995. He was named the Providence College Athlete of the Year in 1995 and 1996.

After graduating from Providence in 1995, Carroll turned professional. At the World Championships in Gothenburg, Sweden, he finished twelfth in the 5000m final. Injury woes forced him out of the Atlanta Olympic Games a year later.

Over a few weeks in August and early September 1998, Carroll was at his brilliant best. At the European Championships in Budapest, Hungary, he finished third with a time of 13:38.15 in a tactical 5000m. On 28 August, he smashed Eamonn Coghlan's eighteen-year-old Irish 3,000m record when running 7:33.84 in Brussels,

Belgium. Four days later, on 1 September in Berlin, Germany, he smashed the 5,000m national record with a phenomenal time of 13:03.93, which was over nine seconds faster than Frank O'Mara's record of 13:13.02 set in Oslo in 1987. Less than twelve months later, on 4 August 1999, Carroll broke his own Irish 3,000m record in Monaco when, in possibly his best race, he ran an extraordinary time of 7:30.36 while mixing with the best of the Kenyan athletes.

Carroll struggled in 1999, but still qualified for the final of the 5,000m at the World Championships in Seville, where he finished fourteenth. When he later discovered that he was suffering from anaemia he took another break from the sport.

Rested and restored to full health, in 2000, Carroll began the indoor season in style by setting a new venue mile record of 3:54.98 for the New Balance Track and Field Centre at The Armory in New York. On 4 February, at the Millrose Games, he joined the select list of Irish Wanamaker Mile winners with a brilliant display delay over the final two laps to win in a time of 3:58.19. In both 1996 and 1997, he had won the 3,000m at the same event. Travelling to Ghent in Belgium for the European Indoor Championships, he powered to victory in the 3,000m with a time of 7:49.24 winning Ireland's first European indoor title since Eamonn Coghlan's 1500m victory in 1979.

Carroll continued his assault on the Irish national record book and surpassed John Treacy's twenty-year-old 10,000m time of 27:48.7 on 5 May at Stanford, California when, in his debut at the distance, he crossed the line in a time of 27:46.82. He followed his record-breaking run with several exceptional performances prior to the Sydney Olympic Games in 2000. He secured Olympic qualification at 5,000m with a comfortable 13:21.24 in Boston. Setting his sights on Ray Flynn's records, at Raleigh, North Carolina he ran his fastest 1,500m time of 3:34.91. He crowned his pre-Olympic outdoor season at the Bislett Games in Oslo, Norway, on 13 July when he ran 3:50.62 in the mile – the second fastest mile by an Irish athlete at the time. Within a few days, he ran two 5,000m races, in Stockholm where his time was 13:09.64, and in Zurich where he clocked 13:12.79.

Unfortunately for Carroll, the 2000 Olympics in Sydney, where the top six in two 5000m semi-finals and the three fastest losers would qualify for the fifteen-man final, proved a crushing disappointment. Carroll's form abandoned him and a seventh place in the second semi-final in 13:30.6 saw him eliminated.

Carroll continued to compete over 5,000m at the highest level after Sydney with mixed results. At the World Championships in Edmonton in 2001, he failed to progress from his first-round heat. In the following season, he finished sixth at the 2002 European Championships in Munich, after undergoing knee surgery in January. In 2004, he qualified for the Olympic Games in Athens but was eliminated in the first round, finishing fifteenth in 13:46.81.

By then, Carroll had turned to road racing and in 2002 made his marathon debut in New York where he finished sixth in a time of 2 hrs 10 mins 54 secs; only John Treacy's 2:09:18 was faster as an Irish time. In preparation for the race, he had run a 63:11 half marathon time also in New York. Injuries limited his marathon adventures to just a single race over the distance.

He returned to the track and in 2005, finished ninth in the 3000m at the European Indoors, held in Madrid, Spain. Now in his mid-thirties, he ran several road races, with a best of 28:30 for a 10km in Canton Massachusetts in September 2006. He occasionally ran in Ireland, lining out in the annual Armagh International 5km in both 2008 and 2009 and for the Great Ireland Run 10km in Dublin's Phoenix Park in April 2009.

In 2009, Carroll was appointed head cross-country coach at Auburn University in Alabama and in June 2017, moved to Drake University in Des Moines, Iowa, where he is director of track and field and cross-country. His wife, the former American international athlete Amy Rudolph, coaches the women's cross-country team at the college.

EAMONN COGHLAN
Chairman of the Boards

In any list of Irish athletes, Eamonn Coghlan rates highly as one of the true legends and all-time greats. Olympic glory may have eluded him not once, but three times, and in 1983, a nation celebrated wildly when at last the lad from Drimnagh in Dublin took gold in the 5000m at the inaugural World Championships in Helsinki.

In a sparkling career, Coghlan would clock up seventy-eight sub-four-minute miles, the most stirring of these coming in Boston when he ran a time of 3 mins 58.15 secs and became the fastest man over forty in history to break the four-minute barrier.

As a youngster, Coghlan, born 21 November 1952, and growing up on Cooley Road, in Drimnagh, was something of a teenage terror. One day he was 'scutting' a lorry when he was spotted by a garda. Coghlan swiftly dropped off the back of the lorry and made good his escape – or so he thought. A few days later, the garda knocked on the door of the family home and told Eamonn's father Bill the story.

'Is that your lad?' he asked Bill, who admitted that it was. 'Well, he's a bloody fast runner. If I were you, I'd send him down to his local athletics club immediately.'

And so Eamonn, just a month shy of his twelfth birthday, was packed off to join Celtic AC, based in the Phoenix Park and had his first experience of running and racing.

When Celtic AC broke up, Coghlan joined Metropolitan Harriers based in Islandbridge where Gerry Farnan was coach.

In 1967, he won the Dublin U15 cross-country and made an impression on the track at 800m, 1500m and the mile. By 1970, when he won the Leinster 5000m and was second in the All Ireland Schools 1500m, the American universities were hovering. The following year, Coghlan won both the 1500m and 5000m at the All Ireland Schools Championships and a few months later he was off to Villanova College in the USA, where the coach was Jumbo Elliott.

No longer Eamonn Coghlan, juvenile superstar, he hated it. By Christmas he had enough. His body ached, he couldn't keep up with his studies and he missed his family and his girlfriend, Yvonne. He came home and got himself a job with PMPA Insurance and a 50cc motorbike.

However, Elliott was not prepared to let his talented recruit go, and with Yvonne reluctant to take the blame for ending a promising athletics career, Coghlan returned to Villanova in September 1972, 'with a completely different and more mature attitude' as he wrote in his 2008 autobiography, *Chairman of the Boards, Master of the Mile.*

The following spring, in 1973, he represented Villanova in the Penn Relays for the first time. He would go on to represent Villanova over several distances from 880 yards to three miles reducing his best mile time to 4 mins 00.9 secs in 1974. He returned to Ireland for the summer and joined Donore Harriers. After winning his first national title in the 800m, he was selected to run the 5000m at the European Championships in Rome, Italy that September. He went out in the heats.

Coghlan's arrival as a world class athlete was announced over the space of a week in May 1975. At Pittsburgh on 10 May, he ran his first sub-4-minute mile clocking 3:56.2 secs. A week later, at the Dream Mile in Kingston, Jamaica, his time of 3:53.3 smashed Michel Jazy's European record.

Back at Villanova, Coghlan ended the 1975 college season by adding the NCAA outdoor mile title to the indoor title he won earlier in the season. In his final race for Villanova, he retained his NCAA 1500m title running a new NCAA and Irish record time of 3:37.01. He followed this up at Los Angeles by becoming the first Irish athlete to win the American AAU 1,500m championship.

With Bayi and other African athletes boycotting the Montreal Olympics, Coghlan's chances of winning a medal were improved. Unfortunately, after winning his heat and semi-final easily, doubts began to haunt Coghlan in the twenty-four hours before the final. A decision to shave his legs to improve aerodynamic efficiency resulted in discomfort and a sleepless night. In a telephone conversation, Jumbo Elliott warned Coghlan of the danger of a slow-paced race with several fast half-milers in the field. After a pedestrian opening lap, Elliott's warning panicked Coghlan into accelerating through the field and holding the lead until the bell for the final lap, New Zealand's John Walker, the

Belgian Ivo van Damme and Paul-Heinz Wellman from the Federal Republic of Germany all streamed past relegating Coghlan to the worst place of all – fourth.

After graduating from Villanova, Coghlan renewed his relationship with Gerry Farnan. In 1977, he won the 1500m at the one-day World Games of Helsinki in Finland also winning the AAA title over the same distance. His dominance of indoor racing in America had begun early in the year when he won the first of his seven Wanamaker Mile titles, also winning the prestigious title in 1979, 1980, 1981, 1983, 1985 and 1987. At the European Championships in Prague, Coghlan found himself boxed with 200 metres to go, before passing British athlete Dave Moorcroft to finish second behind Steve Ovett, also representing Britain, in a new Irish record of 3:36.6.

Another hectic indoor season followed in 1979 highlighted by a new world best time on 16 February in San Diego when he won the mile in 3:52.6 breaking the existing record of 3:55.0 On 25 February 1979, at the European Indoors in Vienna, Coghlan won his only European indoor championship medal when taking the 1500m title in 3:41.8. His good form continued during the summer months when he not only lowered his Irish mile record to 3:52.88 and then 3:52.45, but also reduced the 3,000m record to 7:39.08 and the 5,000m best to 13:23.54.

Coghlan raced sparingly in the lead-up to Moscow Olympic Games where the 5,000m was his target. Both Coghlan and John Treacy qualified for the final – the only time Ireland has had two athletes running in the same Olympic final. The final developed into a near perfect race for Coghlan. In the final push for the line, Ethiopia's Miruts Yifter raced clear. When Coghlan was also passed by Suleiman Nyambui of Tanzania and the Finnish athlete Kaarlo Maaninka, he found himself finishing fourth in a second Olympic Games.

Although Coghlan missed the 1982 season due to injury, there was some consolation when he was voted the greatest indoor miler in history. Although he had run fifteen of the twenty fastest indoor miles ever, he had not raced indoors for twenty-two months. The best was yet to come. On 27 February 1983, Coghlan lined out for the Vitalis Olympic Invitational Mile in Meadowlands, New Jersey determined to do justice to the memory of his coaches Jumbo Elliott and Gerry Farman who had both died in 1982. A fortnight before the New Jersey race, his father Bill had passed away in his sleep at Coghlan's American home after witnessing his son win the Wanamaker Mile for the fifth time. After sprinting through the final two laps, Coghlan crossed the line in a new world indoor record time of 3:49.78. 'This is for you guys', Coghlan had said to himself on the final lap. The record would endure for forty-one years.

Later that year came perhaps Coghlan's finest moment. Helsinki in Finland was the venue for the inaugural World Athletics Championships and on 14 August in the 5000m final, Coghlan sprinted past a fading Dmitriy Dmitriyev of the Soviet Union, punching the air in delight as he raced home for victory in 13:28.53.

Age was creeping up on Coghlan and injuries meant he would miss the 1984 Los Angeles Olympics Games and most of the 1985 summer season. In his final Olympic appearance at the Seoul 1988 Games, Coghlan, now aged 36, finished fifteenth and last in the 5000m semi-final.

After Coghlan retired, he returned to Ireland after nineteen years living in the USA. On 1 January 1991, he was appointed chief executive officer of BLE, the Irish Athletics Association. After 144 days in the post, he resigned. He returned to running with a new objective: to become the first man over 40 to run a sub-4-minute mile. In the meantime, he ran the 1991 New York Marathon with his time of 2:25:14 good enough for 41st place.

Despite setting four masters world best times in 1993, the sub-4-minute mile proved elusive it would take another year. At the Harvard College track on 20 February 1994, Coghlan once again created history when he crossed the line in a time of 3:58.15 becoming the first athlete over forty years of age to break four minutes for the distance. An appropriate ending to a career of unsurpassed brilliance.

TOMMY CONNEFF
The Little Irish Wonder

Mentioned as a hero of Ireland in James Joyce's *Ulysses*, Thomas Conneff was born on 10 December 1867 in the townland of Kilmurry near Clane in County Kildare. He never put on a running shoe until he was in his sixteenth year. Even as an adult he only stood a little over 1.65m and weighed 59kg, and as a teenager would have appeared a lightweight in the cut and thrust of handicap running at local sports.

Starting as a sprinter in 1884, but without success, he quickly graduated to 440 yards and 880 yards winning over both distances at Carbury and over the mile in Kilcock that same year. But the first signs of his future greatness came at Monasterevin in September 1885 when he finished runner-up to Irish champion J.J. Manning in both the half mile and mile.

Conneff announced his presence on the national stage the following year of 1886 when he won both the 880 yards and mile at the Caledonian Games Meeting at Ballsbridge on Whit Monday. A feature of both races was Conneff's strong finish. Now running in the colours of Haddington Harriers, he picked up his first Irish Amateur Athletic Association (IAAA) titles a month later in July, taking both 880 yards and mile distances with consummate ease with the strong finishes that were to become his trademark.

After Conneff's failure to win a medal in either the 880 yards or mile at the 1887 AAA Championships in England, doubts were expressed in the contemporary press about his stamina. These were quickly dispelled at the IAAA 4-miles championship later that July when it was reported: 'the little Kildare man ran and won in such a style as to place it beyond doubt that he is the most marvellous exponent of distance running yet developed in Irish athletics.'

Buoyed by a return to form, Conneff decided to enter the Northern Counties Championships in England knowing that he would face, among others, E. C. Carter, the long distance champion of America and England. The diminutive Kildare man lined up in front of a crowd of 42,000 to take on the mighty Carter as well as Farrell of Birchfield Harriers and Mills of Coventry. Farrell made the early pace in the two-mile contest before Mills took over and it was the Coventry athlete who led into the last lap. Up to this point Conneff had appeared to be asleep but he quickly cast off his slumbers and caught his rivals on the penultimate bend, before racing away to win in 9 mins 44.6 secs.

Carter, who finished a beaten third, immediately challenged Conneff to a return match. Arrangements were quickly finalised for a race over four miles at Ballsbridge on 20 August 1887, the prize being a special gold medal costing twenty guineas and sponsored by the *Sport* newspaper. The distance suited the Anglo-American who had won the English championship over that distance and at 10 miles that year. Over 20,000 spectators turned out at Ballsbridge to see it and, although not the favourite, Conneff won, much to the delight of the home crowd.

Accepting an invitation from the Manhattan Athletic Club, Conneff sailed to America in January 1888 to further his career. He quickly made his mark winning the American title for 5-Miles, retaining it the following three years as well as taking the 2-Miles and 10-Miles titles. In 1890, he won the US 15km road race and the Canadian 2-Miles in record time.

Conneff came home to Ireland on 19 December 1891 suffering from typhoid fever. He was observed stepping off the SS *Umbria* from New York 'looking pale and thin and limped as he walked to the Custom House in Queenstown from the tender.' He would spend a month in the Richmond Hospital, Dublin, followed by a lengthy period of convalescence in his native Clane.

During his stay in Ireland, he entered a match of three races against the Salford Harrier W. H. Morton. Conneff failed to reach halfway in the first match over ten miles in Manchester and pulled out of the return five-miles event in Dublin at the last minute due to illness. He took the SS *Umbria* back to the USA on 22 May 1892. He failed to find his form at either the Canadian or American championships later that year, with a third place in the mile at the latter his best result.

The following year, 1893, saw a change in fortunes when Conneff set his first amateur mile world record on 26 August 1893 at Cambridge. Unlike Walter George, who had the competition from rival William Snook to push him to the existing record of 4:18.4 nine years earlier, the Kildare man had no-one to draw him out. Indeed, contemporary reports describe his opposition as 'a pack of pot-hunting mud horses.'

By the end of the first quarter reached in fifty-nine seconds, he had disposed of most of his opponents The half-mile mark was reached in a swift two minutes, and he reached the three-quarter mark in 3:07, a world best. He ploughed on with 'his teeth shut and his hair standing on end like quills on the fretful porcupine' to break the tape in a world amateur record of 4:17.8.

In January 1894, Conneff announced that he had obtained the 'best job he had ever filled' working with the ex-mayor of NYC, Hugh J. Grant, and would therefore be retiring from athletics to concentrate on his work. The retirement was brief, and he was back in top form by June 1895 when he easily defeated his Canadian rival Orton over a mile at the New York Athletic Club (NYAC) Games winning in 4:25.4. Shortly afterwards Bacon broke Conneff's world record, taking it down to 4:17.0, when winning the AAA Championships at Stamford Bridge on 7 July 1895.

Conneff hit back almost immediately running 4:15.6 at a meeting in New York on 20 August. He followed that up eight days later at Travers Island with a world best for both 1.25 and 1.5 miles with marks of 5:38.8 and 6:45.2, respectively. This was all in preparation for the much-anticipated New York v London AC match the following month.

Held on what was the hottest day in New York for fifteen years, the contest proved one-sided with the Americans taking all eleven events. Conneff was in scintillating form for New York, winning both the one mile in 4:18.0 – he was said to have run 4:12 time trial for the distance as part of his preparations – and three miles in 15:36.2.

He came home to Ireland to recuperate from a bout of malaria in 1896 and was not back to full health when he ran an exhibition mile against the top Irish miler J.J. Mullen at the Celtic Sports in Glasgow. Conneff only ran two laps while Mullen stopped a lap later, but both were given a tumultuous reception by the fans. However, Conneff's decision about turning professional was made for him when both he and Mullen were suspended for taking part in the meeting which had not been sanctioned by the Scottish Amateur Athletics Association.

Around the same time that Fred Bacon was suspended from amateur competition by the AAA in England for taking money, he was said to be making £20 per week from running – a huge amount at the time. This set up a match between the Conneff and Bacon which was to be decided over three distances, a three-mile race in Dublin, a mile in Bolton and a two-mile at the Celtic stadium in Glasgow. Conneff, obviously still not fully recovered from the malaria, failed to finish the three miles but put up better displays at Burnden Park, Bolton and Celtic Park, Glasgow. Nevertheless, Bacon beat him on all three occasions which diminished Conneff's reputation, if not his legacy, and consequently his earning power.

He went home to Kildare to recover his strength and no doubt lick his wounds. After returning to the USA in August 1897 he lost a match in Franklin Falls, New Hampshire to Charles Bean, the ex-American three mile and five mile champion, by seven yards in what was described as the 'hottest finish sprint ever'. Conneff then challenged the Irish professional George Blennerhasset Tincler to a mile race. Nicknamed 'The Gander' for his awkward posture, Tincler defeated Conneff in a flying finish recording at Worcester, Massachusetts in a time of 4:15.2, faster than the Kildare man's amateur record.

When the Spanish-American war broke out in April 1898, Conneff enlisted in the US Army and saw service in Cuba, Puerto Rico, St Michael, Alaska, and the Philippines. When hostilities finished after only ten weeks, he was stationed in the Philippines working as a clerk. He was found drowned in the Pasig River on 10 October 1912.

Thomas Patrick Conneff is buried in the San Francisco National Cemetery, near the Golden Gate Bridge, a long way from his native Clane where the local GAA grounds are named in his honour.

NEIL CUSACK
Boston Winner in a Dunnes Stores Vest

In these days of big city marathons, it is almost impossible to picture some relatively unknown athlete arriving at the finish line well clear of a world class field, wearing an improvised vest that he had put together the previous evening. When the unknown is an Irish athlete still at college, it is *Boy's Own* stuff and would be rejected as implausible by even the most gullible of athletics followers. Yet that is exactly what happened at the Boston Marathon in 1974.

At a time when most television sets were still black and white, the images coming out of Ireland were even darker, as bombs in Dublin, Belfast, Guildford, and Birmingham were grabbing the headlines. The *Sunday Independent* reported on the growing problem of teenage violence in Dublin. Juvenile delinquency had grown by fifty per cent in ten years. Ireland appeared a very dark and sinister place.

Step onto the world athletics stage: a talented student-athlete. Young, gifted, and green, that was Neil Cusack, a twenty-two-year-old student at East Tennessee State University (ETSU) in Johnson City. The Limerick man was barely known in athletics circles despite having won the National Collegiate Athletics Association (NCAA) cross-country championships in 1972. He had only run the marathon distance once previously when in Atlanta's Peach Bowl he had recorded the fastest time ever by a teenager – 2 hrs 16 mins 17 secs.

In 1897, the first Boston Marathon took place inspired by the marathon race at the previous year's Olympics in Greece, attracting an entry of only fifteen men. These days up to 30,000 run and many of them are women, with the. course running from Hopkinton in Middlesex County to Copley Square in Boston. The race had run without interruption until the cancellation of the 2020 event. It is now one of the six World Marathon Majors.

Before Cusack, the only Ireland-born winners were John Lordan from Cork in 1903 and Jimmy Duffy from Sligo; Duffy had represented Canada at the 1912 Olympics in Stockholm and took the laurels in 1914.

Cusack entered on a whim in 1974 and had his way paid to the event by his university. Years later he would admit: 'I still don't know why I actually decided to run the race. It was a howl and I'm still above the ground and able to talk about it. I have a lifetime of memories to draw on, but Boston is right up there.'

Although ETSU had paid his way to Boston and he would get into bother for not wearing his university vest, he wanted to let everyone know where he came from. So, the night before the race, he took the crest from one of his Irish vests and sewed it onto a mesh vest he had bought in Dunnes Stores. The British runner Ron Hill had popularised the use of mesh vests to ventilate the body in long distance races and had a connection with the Boston Marathon having set a course record of 2:09.28 when winning the 1970 race.

Cusack had a clear plan: remain about a hundred metres off the front for the first six miles, then gradually move to the front, if possible. He executed the plan to perfection and at the halfway point was a minute ahead of his nearest pursuer, pre-race favourite Tom Fleming who had won the New York Marathon the previous year.

He attacked the notorious Heartbreak Hill at the 21-mile mark and flew over the top. Despite Fleming's best efforts, Cusack crossed the line forty-six seconds ahead of him in 2:13:39. Jerome Drayton of Canada, who would return to win the race three years later, took third in 2:15:40. Finishing well down the field was an up-and-coming Bill Rogers, whose name subsequently became synonymous with Boston and New York.

'I was on a 2:09 pace coming off Heartbreak Hill and feeling no strain, running on my own,' said Cusack. 'I didn't see another body from six miles to the finish. 'I started the race as an unknown and crossed the finish line into immediate international recognition. I didn't realise how big this event was until I crossed the line. It was bedlam.'

On crossing the finish line, Cusack was immediately crowned with an olive wreath and every newspaper in America rushed to interview him. Members of the massive Irish diaspora in Boston thrust $10 and $20 bills into his bag. It was only sometime after the race, when he had looked at all the photos, that he realised there had been so many cars and cameras following him. And it was only later too that he realised just how big a deal it was to win Boston.

After the race, legendary American broadcaster Walter Cronkite asked Cusack how he proposed to celebrate his victory: 'By drinking lashings of porter,' he said. The tabloids were quick to revert to stereotypes and ran the storyline: 'Irishman wins Boston, trains on beer' said the *New York Daily News*. Practically every newspaper in America the following day carried photos of the Irish winner replete in his mesh vest with the huge badge of shamrocks. Here was something to be proud of and it kept the more shocking news from Ireland off the front pages for twenty-four hours. It was a good day to be Irish.

Cusack was born in Limerick on 30 December 1951 and attended St. Munchin's College where his running ability was first spotted. This was in part attributed to his father Connie who smoked eighty cigarettes a day and would often send his son to the local shop to buy a packet. Neil would sprint there during the television adverts, trying to be back before the resumption of the programme he was watching. His father's habit would cost him his life at just fifty-three, but his son's dashes to the shop would help provide him with a ticket to a healthy life.

Aided by astute coaching at St. Munchin's and Limerick Athletics Club, Neil was offered and took up the offer of an athletics scholarship to ETSU in the late summer of 1969 aged just seventeen. He was soon on a plane for the first time and destined for JFK Airport in New York. Dressed in a new three-piece suit with a special pocket sown in his pants to accommodate his dollars, it was a far cry from the more casual dress he was to adopt on campus.

First, he had to get there. He spent his first night in the United States in a New York hotel barely able to sleep because of the noise, the heat and the humidity. Tennessee would be different again, as he discovered when coach Walker collected him at the Tri-Cities airport the following morning and drove him to Johnson City where the ETSU campus was located.

'At times it was like that movie *Deliverance*,' he recalled. 'We'd run up into the mountains (the Appalachians) which were right beside the university, and you'd come across guys shooting beer cans. One day this guy was swinging on a hammock, and I was running with my T-shirt off, tied around my neck, the sweat dripping off me. Next thing I hear: "Hey, boy, get your clothes back on or I'll shoot your ass!"'

Cusack found it difficult adjusting to twice-a-day training particularly since he was only on a half scholarship and had to work in a canteen cleaning dishes to survive. In his first NCAA national cross-country championships, he finished a lowly 186th. He came home at the end of his first year without any desire to return to the US but at home he could feel himself getting stronger as the summer progressed, and he went back with fresh motivation.

In Johnson City, he found that his work increasingly caused him to miss track sessions. On one such occasion, he cycled down to the track with his kitchen apron still on and told Walker that he needed to be training more and doing less dishwashing. The coach was suitably impressed by his frankness and ambition. Within a few weeks into his second year, he was on a full scholarship.

Cusack's fortunes prospered. In 1972, he competed in the Munich Olympics and set a new Irish 10,000m record, although it was not fast enough to qualify him out of the heats. He also represented Ireland four years later in the marathon at the Montreal Olympics, finishing fifty-fifth after apparently over-training for the event.

For all his undoubted talent, Cusack never fully realised his vast potential. Part of this can be put down to working full time on his return to Ireland. By his own admission, he trained too hard and never rested enough. After failing to make the team, one of his saddest days was attending the 1979 World Cross-Country in Limerick, where the Irish men's team finished second, as a spectator.

Cusack represented Ireland at two Olympics, competed thirteen times in the World Cross-Country, and won ten NCAA titles including the cross-country in 1972. He and his wife Imelda now live in County Clare, around the Cratloe-Bunratty area, a long way from downtown Boston where he sent out such a positive image of Ireland all those years ago.

JOHN JOSEPH DALY
The Tough of the Track

Born the son of a wealthy farmer at Dowriss, Kilmoylan, County Galway on 22 February 1880, John Joseph Daly was 'in a position to indulge his athletic bent unrestrained by the severer exigencies of existence,' *Celt* noted in a profile published in *An Camán*. In July 1900, Daly who was a big man, possibly more suited to the field events, had first attracted attention when winning the high jump and coming second in the long jump at the Mountbellew Sports. In October, he won the 440 yards event confined to members of the local football club at Corofin Sports.

Galway City Harriers provided John Daly with an opportunity to make an impression on the national stage after he joined the club in November 1900. On 30 March 1901, he won the All-Ireland senior cross-country title. A few months later, a second-place finish in the IAAA 4-mile championship secured him a place on the Ireland team for the annual international against Scotland in Glasgow on 29 June, where he was narrowly beaten despite losing a shoe six laps from the finish.

At this stage of his career John Daly was a multi-event athlete who hoovered up prizes at local meets. In Roscommon, for example, he won the 220 yds, 440 yds, and

880 yds as well as the long and high jumps. In 1902, Daly won both the mile and 4-mile IAAA titles on 21 June later wining both events in the match against Scotland. A week after his IAAA victories, he added the GAA 3-mile national title to his collection.

Daly began a busy 1903 season by winning the national cross-country title and captaining the Ireland team at the inaugural international cross-country championships between the Home Nations which were hosted by Scotland at Hamilton Park, near Glasgow. In a race won by England's Alfred Shrubb, Daly finished best of the Irish in fourth place, with the Irish team second behind England. Daly retained his IAAA mile title but was beaten on the line by Hugh Muldoon in the 4-mile final. A week later he competed at the Edinburgh Harriers Sports and then competed on six successive days in Mullingar, Callan, Nenagh, Ballsbridge, Ardagh in County Longford and Athenry, winning on nine occasions. Next up were victories in the mile at the Grocers' Sports at Jones's Road and in the 880 yards steeplechase at the DMP Sports at Ballsbridge before the international against Scotland on 18 July where he finished second to John McGough in the mile and retired towards the end of the four-mile race.

An equally hectic month of August began with Daly competing at the Rangers Sports in Ibrox Park, Glasgow on 1 August, at Queenstown in Cork the following day and at the RIC Sports in Ballsbridge on 3 August. On 16 August in Tipperary, he won the 2-mile GAA title before racing in Killarney the following day. On 30 August, he was back in Jones's Road for the GAA's national championships where he was narrowly beaten in the 440 yards and finished third in the mile. Just to confirm his fitness and versatility he rounded off his season by winning a 'go as you please' 22-mile race from Athlone to Moate and back. His time was two hours four minutes and three seconds and he finished over two miles ahead of his nearest rival.

Normal order continued for Daly in 1904 when he won his third national cross-country title and again represented Ireland in the international cross-country championships. On 23 May, he won the IAAA 4-mile national title, and he represented Ireland against Scotland in Belfast on 16 July. Earlier in the month, he travelled to Rochdale and finished second in the AAA steeplechase championships, falling at the final obstacle 'when he seemed all over a winner'. Undaunted, Daly made the overnight journey to Dublin and won the scratch mile at the Trades' Sports in Jones's Road.

On 31 July he departed from Queenstown aboard the SS *Campania* for New York, en route to St Louis to compete in the Olympic Games where the steeplechase over a 2,590m distance was held on 29 August 1904. Daly, the only non-American in the field of seven, dominated the race from the start but faded on the final lap when he was overtaken by James Lightbody, with Daly crossing the line a second later. He did not participate in the mile race, which seems strange since he won a mile handicap race at a meeting held in conjunction with the Olympics, coming off a twenty-yard mark to win in 4:27.4.

Daly remained in New York until December 1904 and, as a member of the Greater New York Irish American Athletic Association, won the AAU steeplechase title and was first across the line in a 5-mile championship staged at Celtic Park. There, patrons 'never saw such a race' the *New York Daily News* reported, as John Joyce and Daly engaged in 'a very unsportsmanlike exhibition of jostling' which ended with Joyce on the ground. Daly defeated Joyce in a rematch and again when he won the Metropolitan cross-country title before returning to Galway.

Restricted by injury in 1905, in 1906 Daly won both the GAA and IAAA senior cross-country titles and again represented Ireland in the international cross-country championships, finishing fourth. Athens was the venue for the Intercalated Olympic Games in 1906 but despite his long-distance successes, and unlike Peter O'Connor and Con Leahy, Daly was not funded by W. C. Firth of the *Irish Field* for the trip. Undaunted, Daly travelled to Athens at his own expense. He explained the circumstances in the *Tuam Herald* : 'I being winner of the longest championships held in the country naturally thought that I was entitled to run for Ireland in the distance races and marathon race. I signified my intention but was told that none but those who were rated as sure winners could have their expenses out of the fund collected.'

In Athens, Daly had great difficulty adjusting to the olive oil and goat-based Athenian food. 'We got goat's milk, goat's butter and meat in every form from roast to devilled. It was always goat, all but horns and whiskers. I could not drink the tea served nor use any of the food, and gradually became weak.'

Clearly, it was not what dieticians would recommend before a marathon race. John J. Daly competed in the 5-mile race and the marathon in Athens and suffered for the cause. In the former event, Daly and Edward Dahl of Sweden were involved in a head-to-head struggle down the finishing straight for third place. Daly weaved in and out several times, blocking Dahl from passing him and holding on to third place. He was relegated to fourth the following day when he was judged to have impeded Dahl.

On 30 April 1906, the eve of the marathon, a party of English-speaking athletes were driven to Marathon 'in the carriage of Mr Bossequet of the English School in Athens' who sent 'his cook with beds and food for us to Marathon'. The athletes stayed with a friendly villager and after a sleepless and insect-bitten night took their places at the start the following day. Daly 'wore good leather' shoes with 'the soles covered with strips of rubber'. After fifteen miles, his feet began to blister badly, and a recurrence of an old football injury reduced him to walking pace before he retired with hardly any skin left on his feet.

Daly's association with Irish athletics virtually ended when he moved permanently to the USA becoming a star attraction in races at Celtic Park and other New York venues. His significant victories in 1907 included the AAU 5- and 10-mile titles and the Canadian 3-mile title. The *New York Daily News* believed that the USA now had an athlete with 'enough speed, stamina and vitality to compete against the best runners that Great Britain can produce' and that 'America for the first time in some years would have a representative who can really give the Britishers a close battle in a long distance race'.

He was entered for four events in the 1908 Olympics but for some unknown reason failed to compete. On holiday in Galway in 1911, Daly won the national 880 yard steeplechase title in Mullingar on 9 July. By now, John J. Daly and his brother M. J. were operating the Daly Brothers Tavern at 488 6th Avenue in Manhattan, with their property and business empire soon expanding to include several other taverns in New York all decorated with cups and trophies Daly had won during his athletics career. He remained closely involved with athletics in New York, and for many years was a judge at the US Indoor Championships at Madison Square Gardens. Tragedy visited Daly's family following his marriage to Marie Hogan on 17 July 1912. On 17 October 1913, the couple's first daughter died at just five months of age. Then on 22 April 1920, Marie died soon after giving birth to John Junior. John senior died in New York on 11 March 1969.

MAURICE DAVIN
Father of Irish Athletics

Although Maurice Davin from Carrick-on-Suir in County Tipperary, is widely considered the 'Father of Irish Athletics', he began his sporting career not as an athlete but as a bare-knuckle boxer later switching to rowing, racing in boats he had built himself. Only in 1869 did Davin, born on 29 June 1842, compete at his first athletics meet.

Davin was the eldest son of John and Bridget Davin who farmed at Deerpark on the northern bank of the river Suir, a short distance outside the town. The family controlled the river haulage trade between Carrick-on-Suir and Clonmel, with goods from Waterford shipped up-river to Carrick-on-Suir where they were transferred to barges and were pulled by teams of Davin-owned horses to Clonmel. Maurice would take over the family farm and river haulage business, in association with his mother Bridget after the death of his father in 1859.

Athletics as a participant and spectator sport would grow in popularity during the 1870s with athletics meetings taking place during the summer months in the towns and villages of Ireland. In 1869, Davin had become part of the phenomenon. Not only did he compete in Gurteen and Tramore, and at athletics meetings organised by Queen's

College Cork and the Civil Service Club in Dublin, he was appointed 'perpetual chairman' of the newly-formed Carrick-on-Suir Amateur Athletics, Cricket and Football Club.

In 1871, now twenty-nine years of age, Davin decided to specialise in the weight throwing events. In the words of Paul Rouse, 'he was no idealised amateur, content merely to turn up, take off his coat and compete.' He designed his own hammer and weights and adopted a new training regime to develop the muscles essential for his new challenge. He constructed a mini-gymnasium and used dumb-bells and assorted weighted clubs to develop muscular power. He was meticulous in his diet, drinking pints of fresh water every morning. Breakfast consisted of a bowl of porridge, a little bread and some beef or mutton. The mid-day meal was usually beef or mutton and vegetables. In the evening he ate toast and porridge. Fresh fish was consumed but salty bacon and butter were avoided. He abstained from tea, coffee, and alcohol, and smoking was out of the question.

Nationally, the first attempt to provide a management structure for Irish athletics was made in 1872 when the Irish Champion Athletic Club (ICAC) open 'to all gentlemen Irish amateurs' was established. On Monday 7 July 1873, the ICAC organised its first national championships. Davin had entered and finished second in the hammer, shot put, putting the 42lb weight and throwing the 56lb weight.

A year later, at the 1874 Civil Service Sports, Davin sensationally won these four events although he bypassed the ICAC championships. In 1875 he won both the hammer and shot put ICAC titles and in 1876, retained the hammer title and finished runner-up in the shot put. At the time, the hammer was thrown using a wooden handle 3' 6" long. Only Davin and Patrick Hickey entered for the weight events in 1877 with Davin finishing first in the shot put, hammer and throwing the 56lb weight and in second place in the 42lb throw. In 1878 and 1879, Maurice completed the shot put and hammer double and completed his collection of ten Irish titles won under the jurisdiction of the ICAC.

On Monday, 5 June 1876, at Lansdowne Road, Davin was part of athletics history when Ireland faced England in the first international athletics match ever staged. First on the schedule was the hammer throw, which Davin duly won from fellow Irishman J.C. Daly with a throw of 40.08m; two English competitors opted not to compete. He went on to win the shot put with a 12.24m effort, beating the English champion, Thomas Stone by two inches.

According to legend, Maurice Davin's most spectacular feat of strength took place on the infield during a break in the competition. When members of the English team performed feats of strength to entertain the spectators, Davin proposed carrying three of the heaviest members of the English team across the field single-handedly. The challenge was accepted and three men with a combined weight of forty-six stone stepped forward. Davin threw one on his back and the other two on each shoulder and set off in front of the main stand with the Irish crowd roaring its approval. His brother, Pat Davin, noted in his 1938 memoir that Maurice 'appeared to be no way overloaded'. A year later, Maurice travelled to Stamford Bridge for the return international staged on 26 May where he was one of only two Irish successes, winning the hammer event with a 38.20m throw, but losing out to John Stone in the shot.

Although Davin had retired from athletics in 1879, he made a sensational comeback in 1881 when he competed in the Amateur Athletic Association Championships (AAA) staged at the Aston Lower Grounds, Birmingham on 16 June. His brother Pat also made the journey. Apparently, he was inspired to make a comeback by suggestions in *The Field*, an English sporting newspaper, about the poor quality of athletics in Ireland. After just a few weeks' training and having to adapt to the restrictions of throwing from a 7-foot circle, Maurice won the hammer and shotput titles while Pat completed a long and high-jump double. In addition, Maurice Davin's winning throws of 30.12m in the hammer and 12.05m in the shot were recognised as world best efforts for throws from a 7-foot circle.

In the 1880s, the Irish athletics world was in chaos. The ICAC had collapsed, and the AAA's rules were used to organise Irish athletic meets. On 11 October 1884, Michael Cusack's seminal article, '*A Word About Irish Athletics*', which called on the 'Irish people to take the management of their games into their own hands' was published in the *United Ireland* newspaper. Maurice Davin responded and expressed his concern at the absence of jumping and weight throwing events at leading meetings. It was his experience 'for one bystander who takes off his coat to run a foot race, forty strip to throw weights or try a jump of some kind'. He agreed to 'gladly lend a hand if I can be of any use.' His response was measured: 'The code of the AAA was a good one and in the management of Irish athletics and games they could not do better than adopt rules similar …'

The eventual outcome of this Cusack-Davin choreography was a meeting in Hayes' Commercial Hotel in Thurles on 1 November 1884 when the Gaelic Athletic Association for the Preservation of National Pastimes was established. Maurice Davin chaired the meeting and spoke of the need to establish an organisation that would organise Irish sport using Irish rules for ordinary Irish people who were born 'into no other inheritance than an everlasting round of labour'.

Maurice Davin was elected first president of the GAA and by the time of the next meeting of the association on 27 December 1884 in the Victoria Hotel in Cork, had drafted the rules for athletics and hurling and had effectively invented the game of Gaelic football by adapting the rules of soccer and rugby to create a distinctive Irish football code. He was also the architect of the constitution adopted at the GAA's annual convention in November 1886. The new association concentrated on athletics initially, staging its first athletics championships 'under the experienced supervision of Mr Maurice Davin' in Tramore on 6 October 1885. These championships continued unbroken until 9 July 1922.

Davin resigned as GAA president after members of the Irish Republican Brotherhood gained control of the association's executive and in February 1887 introduced amendments that clearly breached the association's constitution. In the months that followed, he played a leading role in brokering the agreement that achieved a reconciliation and at the reconstruction convention held in Thurles on 4 January 1888, he was again unanimously elected president. Buoyed by his return, he organised and led the 'American invasion' of September 1888, when a party of fifty hurlers, athletes, and officials travelled to give hurling and athletics exhibitions in New York and Boston. Although it drew favourable comment in the press, the trip was a financial disaster and only a grant of £450 from Michael Davitt enabled them to travel home. This loss, on top of the financial problems already facing the GAA, brought Davin under renewed fire from the IRB element and led to his resignation January 1889.

Davin's involvement in GAA administration at national level ended at this stage, although his love of sport remained. He developed a hurling and football pitch and an athletics arena in one of the fields of his Deerpark farm, with a pavilion for athletes and teams to dress before events and a timber stand with seating for officials and spectators. Maurice Davin, who never married, died on 26 January 1927 after a brief illness.

PAT DAVIN
Record-breaking All-Rounder

Like his brother Maurice, Patrick Davin, born on 4 June 1857 at Deerpark, Carrick-on-Suir, County Tipperary became an outstanding athlete. He was fifteen years younger than his weight-throwing brother, while another brother, Tom, excelled in the jumps and from the age of seventeen, Pat was competing alongside his brothers at athletics meets all over the country.

At the age of sixteen, Pat Davin had begun training for athletics and was soon credited with marks of 6.40m in long jump and 1.73m in high jump. He would outshine his brothers by winning sixteen Irish championship titles (five high jumps, five 120 yards hurdles, four long jumps, one shot put and one 100 yards) also winning AAA championships titles in long and high jump in 1881. He set world records of 1.90m in high jump and 7.06m in the long jump but he was much more than a jumper.

Pat Davin's senior Irish championships debut took place on 27 May 1876, when he placed second to his brother Tom in both the high jump and long jump with 1.67m and 6.27m efforts. He also competed in the 100 yards, and although he won his heat from John T. Belcher in 10.8 secs, he was disqualified for running 'out of his course'.

Pat Davin was selected with both of his brothers to represent Ireland against England in the world's first dual international meeting at Lansdowne Road, Dublin on 5 June that year, placing equal first with Tom in the high jump on 1.73m and second in the long jump with 6.36m. The following day he won the long jump and competed in the high jump in the Civil Service Sports at Lansdowne Road. On 14 September at the Limerick County Cricket Club Sports, he won the 100 yards, 120 yards hurdles and long jump.

In 1877, Pat only competed twice. At the Limerick CCC Sports on 21 June, he won the 120 yards hurdles), long jump and high jump and placed third in the 100 yards. A month later at the Dublin Amateur Athletic Club Sports, he won the high jump and long jump and placed second in the 100 yards and 120 yards hurdles handicap.

On 10 June 1878 he became a triple Irish champion in the 120 yards hurdles, high jump and long jump. He also placed equal first in the 100 yards and but declined to contest a run-off, conceding victory to James H. Stewart. At the inaugural Limerick Amateur Athletic Club Sports on 3 July, he won the high jump, 120 yards hurdles and 100 yards. At the Kilkenny Athletic Sports on 19 August, he won four events – the long jump, the 42lb, and 16lb shot puts, and in the high jump leaped over the bar at 1.81m, setting his first Irish record. At the Kilsheelan Sports, County Tipperary, he won the high jump and long jump but strained his thigh in the 120 yards hurdles when on the verge of winning.

At the ICAC championships on 2 June 1879, Davin retained his 120 yards hurdles, long jump and high jump titles and placed third in the 100 yards. At the Thurles

Athletic Sports on 26 June, he improved his national high jump record to 1.84m on very soft ground, achieving a 6ft mark for the first time. He also won the 120 yards hurdles and finished second in the long jump and the 100 yards. At the Callan Sports, County Kilkenny, he won the high jump and 28lb shot and at the Kilkenny Athletic Sports he further improved his Irish high jump record to 1.86m.

At the 1880 ICAC Championships at Lansdowne Road Pat Davin was the outstanding athlete of the meeting, winning five titles – 100 yards, 120 yards hurdles, high jump, long jump and shot put. On 5 July at the Carrick Amateur Athletic Club Sports, Davin won the high jump with a mighty leap of 1.90m, a world record which would stand for seven years. He also won the 120 yards hurdles.

The Davins became the first trio of brothers to establish world records – as well as Maurice's shot put and hammer records of 1881, Thomas Davin would set a world high jump record of 1.78m on 7 July 1883. Two weeks later at the Kilkenny AC Sports of 1880, Pat won the long jump with 6.93m. At the inaugural Monasterevin Sports held at Moore Abbey Demesne on 21 September he demonstrated his exceptional versatility by winning seven events – 16lb shot put (11.28m), slinging 56lb weight (7.92m), long jump (6.58m), high jump (1.83m), 100 yards (10.4s), 120 yards hurdles (18.0s) and the 220 yards hurdles for the Monasterevin Challenge Cup.

On 18 June 1881, Pat Davin competed in his first athletics meet in England – the Northern Counties Athletic Association Championships held at Farnworth-on-Widnes, Cheshire. Although unwell and not fit to compete, he won the high jump with a 1.73m effort and, in stormy conditions, placed second in the long jump with a mediocre 6.11m. He also finished second in both the shot and 120 yards hurdles. These performances generated some scepticism within the English sporting community about his Irish performances.

A month later at the AAA championships in Birmingham on 16 July, Davin silenced English critics with a 1.84 high jump and a 6.98m long jump; enough to win him both competitions. His high jump mark was a championship record which would stand until 1893. In his 120 yards hurdles heat, Davin fell after he had cleared the final flight and was unplaced. Despite that, one newspaper correspondent commented: 'a better all-round athlete than Patrick Davin I have never seen'.

Davin won the high jump at the Kilkenny Sports on 4 August with 1.88m and, at the Dublin Athletic Club Sports at Lansdowne Road on 29 May 1882, took victories in the high jump), the 120 yards hurdles and throwing a cricket ball (92.96m). He placed second in the 16lb and 42lb shot puts but was unplaced in the long jump. He was described in the *Belfast Newsletter* as 'a modern Hercules…a splendidly formed athlete …built to order all round'. At the Irish Championship meeting on 19 August, he only competed in two events, winning the 120 yards hurdles and high jump titles. At the Monasterevin Sports five days later, he won the 120 yards hurdles and the Challenge Cup for the 220 yard hurdles. His last appearance that year was at the Clonmel Sports where he took the 120 yards hurdles title and won the high jump with 1.82m off soft ground after heavy rain.

At the Irish Championships on 16 June 1883, Davin won the three events he contested – 120 yards hurdles, high jump and the long jump into a strong wind. At the Clonmel Sports on 6 August, he won the 120 yards hurdles, had a best of 6.60m in the long jump although not competing for a prize, and was second in the high jump handicap with 1.79m, losing out by half an inch on handicap. On the 30 August at Hybla, Monasterevin, he set a long jump world record of 7.06m, emulating his eldest brother Maurice in setting world records in two athletic disciplines. He also won the 16lb shot put, 120 yards hurdles and the 220 yards hurdles winning the Challenge Cup for a third time and so entitled to bring it home. Two weeks later at the Portarlington Sports, he replicated his long jump world record and won the high jump with a leap of 1.84m.

With the death of his mother in early 1884, Pat stepped back from athletics to run the family farm. In October 1884, he contracted rheumatic fever, which effectively ended his competitive career. However, in July 1888 the first Irish All-Round Championship was due to take place in Ballsbridge, Dublin. Despite a five-year break from the sport and with only three weeks to prepare, Davin returned to training. It paid off when, on 9 July, in front of 8,000 spectators, he became the inaugural Irish All-Round champion.

Later that year, on 16 September, he sailed from Cobh to the USA with the GAA's ill-fated 'American Invasion Tour' which hoped to raise funds for a planned revival of the ancient Tailteann Games. Davin kept diary of that tour and noted that the first of the hurling exhibition matches took place in New York on Saturday 30 September: 'First exhibition of hurling on the Manhattan Grounds – about 2,000 people present. Exhibition very good. Wicked match – about 12 hurleys broken'.

When the party boarded the SS *City of Rome* at New York harbour for the return journey five weeks later on 31 October, Davin noted that it 'sailed away at 2.30 today bearing home the sad remnant of the 53 hurlers and athletes who landed on American soil just five weeks yesterday. Only 24 men returned.'

Pat Davin died on 20 September 1949 at Deerpark, Carrick-on-Suir, aged 92. His coffin was carried into the church by fellow Irish athletes Tom Kiely, Peter O'Connor, Percy Kirwan and Dr Pat O'Callaghan.

RONNIE DELANY
Mining for Gold in Melbourne

At 4:19 pm on the evening of 1 December 1956, Ronnie Delany was exactly where he planned to be – about 150 metres from the finish line in the Olympic 1,500m final and ready to unleash the powerful finishing sprint that he hoped would propel him to the Olympic title.

Delany's selection for the Games had caused some controversy, with members of the Olympic Council of Ireland believing that his acceptance of a US college scholarship was contrary to Baron de Coubertin's understanding of the amateur ethos which prevailed at the Olympic Games. That ethos and the council's lack of money encouraged a conservative approach to selection. Delany was selected by a single vote and only had his selection confirmed in October – less than two months before the Games.

It had been quite a journey for the twenty-one year-old Ronald Michael Delany who was born on 6 March 1935 in Arklow, County Wicklow. Shortly after the outbreak of the Second World War, the Delany family moved to Sandymount, Dublin, where the teenage Delany sampled 'a kaleidoscope of different sports' among them cricket, hockey, tennis, lawn bowls and rugby. Later he would recall running a relay race as a twelve-year old, and running to and from school, racing his brother Joe, who became a champion long jumper and sprinter. At the Catholic University School where he was a student, maths teacher Jack Sweeney, who was one of Ireland's outstanding athletics coaches, was the first to identify Delany's potential. In 1952 and 1953, he won All-Ireland Colleges 880 yard title as well as some AAUE youths' titles.

After joining Crusaders AC, Delany worked with Sweeney on tactical awareness and fine-tuned his 'kicking' technique. On 22 August 1953, he ran 1 min 58.7 secs for the 880 yards becoming the first Irish schoolboy to break two minutes for distance. At that point, Delany was training as an officer at the Irish Army's Cadet School. Deciding to concentrate his energies on athletics, Delany applied for an honourable discharge and early in 1954 began working as a door-to-door salesman of domestic appliances in Carlow and Kilkenny, a position that allowed him to train almost full-time.

In the spring of 1954, he began training at a school cinder track, where he was able to carry out speed-work sessions, and in the summer of 1954, competed with a new sense of purpose. On 11 June, he won his first AAU 880 yards title in a new national record of 1:54.7, using the 'kick' that would become his trademark. A week later, he reduced his Irish record to 1:53.7 in another 880 yard race, again using his kick, and later went faster again with a time of 1:53.2. Qualifying for the European Championships in Berne, Switzerland, he set a national record of 1:50.2 in the 800m semi-finals to qualify for the final. That proved a race too far and he finished last in 2:03.5.

Just a few weeks later, Delany was off to the USA after accepting an athletics scholarship from Villanova University where his coach was Jumbo Elliott. Indoor racing on a board track was added to the Delany athletics portfolio when he ran a 1,000 yard race in Boston coming off bruised and battered. Elliott soon taught him how to protect himself, and he would win four of his six races that season.

In September 1955 Delany was advised by Elliott 'to eat, drink and sleep the mile' with the Melbourne Olympic 1,500m title as the objective. 'If you want glory, if you want to go down in history, you must win,' he would say. As it turned out, Delany's preparation for the Games was far from ideal. An injury picked up in America troubled him and he lost two races at Lansdowne Road to Britain's Brian Hewson who he saw as one of his great rivals for the Olympic title. Earlier in the season, he had also lost in two races to Australia's John Landy, the world mile record holder.

With the Olympics taking place in November and December, outsiders thought he might have peaked too early when in June he won the prestigious Compton Mile in California with a time of 3:59, a 5.9 second improvement on his previous best. He was the seventh athlete overall and the then youngest ever to break the four minute barrier. The next day he ran a personal best 1:49.5 for the 880 yards and his winning ways continued at the NCAA Championships where he won the 1,500m in 3:47.3.

By now, he had both 800m and 1500m qualifying times for Melbourne in his pocket, but he still had no idea whether he'd been selected for the Games. A spiking injury in Paris put him out of action for July and yet, after only six days of training, he ran a 4:06.4 mile in London to prove his fitness to the selectors. That was followed by a poor run in Dublin. Delany returned to Villanova for the autumn term still not knowing whether he was going to Melbourne, although he never gave up hope. Only in October did he find out from a newspaper that he had made it.

In Melbourne, the thirty-seven athletes who entered the 1,500m formed the strongest ever field assembled. Eighteen had run faster than the 1,500m Olympic record and nine were faster than the world record as it stood prior to the Helsinki Games. Five of the six athletes who had lowered the world 1500m record since Roger Bannister's sub-4 mile, and six of the world's ten sub 4-minute milers competed, including Landy.

Delany always raced to win with time of secondary significance. In the most important day of his career, he executed the perfect tactical race implementing one of Jack Sweeney's beliefs: that an athlete should 'make one dynamic move in a race'. When Delany Ronnie switched to overdrive and sprinted for the line in Melbourne, he destroyed the field, establishing a lead that increased with every stride. He would win the 1,500m Olympic title with about five metres to spare in the new Olympic record time of 3:41.2. With the first eight finishers breaking the Olympic record of 3:45.1 and Ken Wood, in ninth place, also unofficially inside the mark, the race could be described as the greatest 1500m race of all time.

Ronnie Delany's victory provided the inspiration for a new generation of Irish middle-distance runners. In *Sports Illustrated*, he acknowledged his debt to Villanova:

'There is no doubt in my mind that I would not have won an Olympic title if I had remained in Ireland. I benefited and developed under the expert tuition of Jumbo Elliott. I learned tactical sense from my many skirmishes on the board tracks. And above all I competed against the best competition available week after week, year after year, throughout the USA …'

While Delany's athletics career was defined by his Olympic victory, it was not his only significant achievement. He would break the four minute barrier for the mile again in July 1957, finishing second in 3:58.58 when British athlete Derek Ibbotson set a new world record of 3:57.2. Then on 6 August 1958 at Dublin's Santry Stadium, when Australia's Herb Elliott broke the world record with a stunning time of 3:54.5, Delany finished fifth in 3:57.5. Later that month, at the European Championship in Stockholm, Delany finished third in the 1500m.

Only a small number of Irish athletes have won American collegiate titles. Delany won four NCAA outdoor titles, a record for an Irish athlete: the 1,500m title in 1956 and 1957 and a 'Delany Double' in the mile and 880 yards within 45 minutes of each other in Berkeley, California in 1958. A year earlier, he had finished second in the 880 yards in a new Irish record of 1:47.8.

If Eamonn Coghlan was the 'Chairman of the Boards' then Ronnie Delany was the 'Master of the Indoor Mile' with a winning streak of thirty-six successive mile wins from Madison Square Gardens on 25 March 1955 to Chicago on 28 March 1959 where he was winning his forty-third successive race in what was his last indoor race as an individual. Only twice was Delany beaten twice indoors and that was early in his career. Along the way, he established three world best times for the mile the last of them a 4:02.5 time on 7 March 1959 at Madison Square Garden.

Delany's indoor race in Chicago on 28 March 1959 was his last at peak fitness. An Achilles tendon ankle injury was troubling him, although he did qualify for the 800m at the Rome Olympics of 1960, going out in the semi-finals.

Still aged only twenty-six, Delany returned to the track in 1961 and, at the World University Games in Sofia on 1 September 1961, he won the 800m in a time of 1:51.1, becoming the first Irish winner at these games. It was also his last race as an individual. In early 1962, Delany was part of an Irish relay squad that toured the north-eastern USA. His athletics career ended on 2 March 1962 at Madison Square Gardens when he was part of an Irish 4 x 880 yds relay team that included Basil Clifford, Noel Carroll and Derek McCleane. A recurrence of the tendon injury put a final stop to a brilliant and pioneering career.

In November 2023, Delany was named by the Olympic Federation of Ireland as the IOA President Emeritus, a title to reflect his exceptional contribution to the Irish Olympic movement and association over the years. This followed his stepping down as President of the IOA, during which time he led and was directly involved in many initiatives, including the Torch Relay through Ireland ahead of the London 2012 Olympics, a fundraiser in the USA ahead of Atlanta 1996, and a celebration lunch for the 1948 Olympians ahead of London 2012.

JOHN FLANAGAN
Putting Hammer Throwing on the Map

At the prize-giving ceremony for the St Louis Olympic Games, held in 1904, John Flanagan, from the Kilmallock area of County Limerick, became one of the first athletes to receive a solid gold Olympic medal for his victory in the hammer. The practice was quickly discontinued, with gold plate replacing pure gold after 1912.

In St. Louis, Flanagan was winning his second Olympic hammer title. Although not included in the programme of the first 'Olympian' games of 1896 in Athens, hammer throwing had become part of the schedule for the second such games held in Paris in 1900.

Hammer throwing has a long history; it was mentioned in the romances of the Middle Ages and legend has it that no less than Henry VIII excelled at throwing the 'sledgehammer'. Around 1550, a young woman called Betty Welch regularly beat all the men in sledge-hammer throwing. In Ireland, hammer throwing in various forms can be traced back to the Tailteann Games of 1829 BC.

By the late nineteenth century, Irish throwers were setting the pace for the discipline as the rules evolved rapidly. Rather than taking off at a run before releasing the implement, the accepted – and less hair-raising – means of launching the hammer became rotating in a circle nine foot in diameter; this was later reduced to seven foot. For slinging the 16lb or 7.2kg hammer, the wooden shaft was replaced by piano wire.

With competition becoming more regularised, the first of many Irish throwing giants to impress was William Barry, followed soon after by James Mitchel. Next was Flanagan, who is widely considered the father of modern hammer throwing because of his life-long commitment to improving technique. Only in his thirties would he perfect the three-spin pivoting style he had first seen executed by the American Alfred Plaw.

His first 'world record' came in Clonmel on 9 September 1895, when he threw 44.46m, breaking Mitchel's best effort of 44.19m set in 1892. It is worth noting that since implements and throwing circles varied greatly, world records in the hammer were not recognised by the international athletics body until 1913.

Some forty-two years later in 1937, at Fermoy, Flanagan would witness his protégée Pat O'Callaghan unofficially breaking the world record with a throw of 59.54m – well over a metre further than the first official world record of 57.77m set by his old friend Paddy Ryan in 1913. Because of the complicated politics of Irish athletics, this record was not ratified.

John Joseph Flanagan was born on 28 January 1868 and grew up in the town-land of Kilbreedy East, near Kilmallock in County Limerick, Ireland. He was one of seven sons and a daughter. His father Michael, a champion weight thrower in his time, was a farmer. His mother Ellen Kinkead had strong connections with the USA.

A short but powerfully built man, Flanagan, who had played hurling for Munster, began his athletics career as a sprinter and jumper. At the age of twenty, he jumped 6.70m in the long jump and 14.04m for the triple jump. In 1893, he won a Munster title in the 56lbs weight throw, which was his first notable throws win. At that time, he was in the great Irish tradition of all-rounders; a tradition encouraged by the system of handicapping, which meant athletes tended to avoid their best events where they would have had no chance of winning a prize.

Not until 1895, at the age of twenty-seven, did Flanagan decide to concentrate on the throws, studying the hammer technique of Maurice Davin and Tom Kiely and evolving his own two-spin technique. A year later, in 1896, just a week before Athens 'Olympian' Games opened, Flanagan was competing in a GAA-organised festival of Irish sport at Stamford Bridge in London. At the meet, Flanagan broke not only his own hammer world record but also set a world record for throwing the hammer from an old-style nine foot circle. Both Flanagan and Kiely played for a Munster hurling team that beat Leinster at the festival. On 4 July Flanagan also won the British AAA title using the old-fashioned hammer with cane handle. He threw the hammer 40.22m.

Later that year, he was persuaded by his uncle Eugene Kinkead, a former US congressman, to emigrate to the USA. After joining the New York Athletic Club, he began setting records in a range of throwing events. He would switch to the Irish-American Athletic Club in 1905.

Technically, the hammer had progressed since a wire handle and the seven-foot circle had become standard. Ever the innovator, Flanagan was responsible for introducing ball-bearing swivels and a double grip to the implement.

Flanagan's first US competition was at a Knickerbocker club match in Bayonne, New Jersey on 31 May 1897 where his 45.94m effort saw him become the first man to throw a hammer more than 150 feet (45.72m). Soon after, he won the first of his seven American hammer titles and the first of six 56lb titles.

He was thought without rival until news filtered through in 1899 that Tom Kiely had thrown 49.38m. Six weeks later, on 22 July 1899 in Boston, Flanagan responded with a mighty throw of 50.01m, making him the first man to throw further than fifty metres.

From 1898 to 1908, Flanagan was the biggest draw in North American athletics, topping the bill at meets all over the USA and Canada. Adding to the spice were his many battles with Matt McGrath and later Con Walsh. Like many other Irish emigrants, in December 1902 Flanagan had joined the New York police force, taking five years off his age to ensure his acceptance. A few months later, he married Mary Lillis, from Kilmihill, in County Clare, with the couple settling in the Bronx. They had one child, a boy, who died in infancy.

Flanagan's peak years were 1904 and 1905 when he collected titles for the hammer and the 56lb at championships in the USA and Canada as well as at a Tailteann Games organised in New York. In 1905, Flanagan competed in the Police Athletic Association Games at Celtic Park in New York. A local newspaper reported: 'Not only did he win four weight-throwing events, but, as if to show that he could do a little sprinting as readily as he can outclass his competitors with the 16 and 56 pound weights, he not only had the temerity to enter the fat men's race, but actually won it.'

His first of three Olympic titles came in Paris 1900. With the American team, Flanagan warmed up for Paris by competing at the AAA Championships at Stamford Bridge on 7 July, which at that time, was the world's most prestigious athletics meeting. Flanagan duly won the hammer, stretching his own championship record to 49.78m.

In Paris, Flanagan was trailing Truxton Hare, an ex-American footballer, who threw 49.13m in the early rounds. He pulled out a final 51.02m effort for victory. Four years later, in St Louis, Flanagan won by less than a metre with an Olympic record throw of 51.23m. He also finished second ahead of James Mitchel in a closely fought 56lb weight throw, with a best of 10.16m. In the discus, won by Martin Sheridan, he finished fourth.

Four years later, in London, Matt McGrath was favourite to win the event following a 52.91m throw a year earlier. Despite an injured leg, McGrath threw 51.18m and, as in 1900, it came down to the final round. Flanagan put everything into his sixth and final throw, hurling the hammer out to 51.93m. 'When it all came down to my last throw, I knew I had to put everything into it and as it turned out I did. If I have any regret at all now, it is that I was not competing for Ireland on that day,' he would say afterwards.

Following those games, Flanagan travelled to Ireland setting a new world record of 52.98m in the DMP Games at Ballsbridge. Flanagan's final record came on 24 July 1909 at New Haven, Connecticut when, at the age of forty-one years and 196 days, he threw 56.19m. It made him the oldest world record breaker in the history of track and field.

Flanagan returned home to Limerick in 1911 taking over the family farm following the death of his father in February 1912. He continued to compete in Ireland winning hammer titles in both 1911 and 1912. His final international appearance was at the annual match against Scotland of 1911, held in Ballsbridge, where he won the hammer with a throw of 51.94m.

Following his retirement, John Flanagan coached a number of athletes, including Patrick O'Callaghan, who took Olympic gold in the hammer at the 1928 and 1932 Games. He died at home in Limerick, aged seventy, on 3 June 1938. Matt McGrath paid tribute in the *Amateur Athlete*:

'His skill and form was (sic) cultivated from early youth, and while I had an advantage of height and weight over him, still his form was more to perfection than mine.'

RAY FLYNN
Mighty Miler and Meet Director

On 7 July 1982, Longford man Ray Flynn finished third in the Dream Mile at the Bislett Games in Oslo, Norway. Although disappointed to have lost to Steve Scott and John Walker after a lung-busting final lap, exhaustion quickly gave away to euphoria when Flynn realised that he run a time of 3 mins 49.77 secs not only breaking the Irish record but becoming the first Irishman to break 3 mins 50 secs for the classic mile distance.

Today, even with the arrival of hi-tech tracks and footwear, the record still stands, with only Flynn and Eamonn Coghlan having broken 3 mins 50 secs for the mile, either outdoors or indoors.

In that epic race, Flynn had also set an Irish 1500m record of 3:33.5. That record survived for over forty years until 25 February 2023 when Andrew Coscoran ran 3.33.49 indoors in Birmingham; later Coscoran would go even faster running 3:32.68 outdoors in Nice, France on 17 June 2023. The first to congratulate the young Balbriggan athlete was Ray Treacy.

Ray Flynn, born on 22 January 1957 and the eldest of nine children, loved to move fast from an early age, running home from school each day at lunchtime. He would win his first race, the St Mel's College annual cross-country, as a second year pupil.

Flynn's potential was recognised at St Mel's with training advice provided by Fr Peter Brady, P.J. Quinn and Michael Wall as well as from Ray's father Paddy, a founder member and first chairman of the Longford Athletics Club when it was established in 1969. More importantly, links were established with experienced national coaches, in particular Brother John Dooley who would become a key figure in coaching Ray Flynn to national and international success.

'I grew up with a love of running and its history. I wanted to be a great runner following in the footsteps of the legendary milers, especially Ron Delany who won the metric mile at the 1956 Olympic Games,' he would later say.

In 1974 Flynn, then aged seventeen, won both British and Irish schools' mile titles, alerting USA colleges to his potential. By the 1970s, Villanova was no longer the college of choice for talented Irish athletes and, in 1975, after leaving school, Flynn accepted an athletics scholarship from East Tennessee State University (ETSU) where Dave Walker was coach. In his first year at the college, Flynn was a member of the ETSU team that won the US Track and Field Federation (USTAFF) CrossCountry Championship title.

Flynn was an early member of the 'Irish Brigade', a group of runners brought to Johnson City by Walker. 'Big Dave was like a second dad to me. He was tough but principled and instilled a strong work ethic into all his runners. He was loyal to those around him, and he had the belief that we could beat anyone anywhere. He was larger than life and was my greatest mentor besides my dad.'

His times over 1500m quickly improved. In August 1975, Flynn had run 3:50.1 for 1500m in Athens Greece. Nine months later, he ran a time of 3:42.66 in Knoxville, Tennessee. A year later again, he broke four minutes for the mile, with a time of 3:59.4 at the Penn Relays on 30 April 1977. 'Running sub four minutes for the mile at the Penn Relays in 1977 gave me the validation that I was on my way in that journey. I had been sick the night before but good old Dave got me some Epsom salts to help my stomach settle and convinced me that I had done the work to break four minutes. There was nothing like it.'

Arguably his finest moment as a student athlete came in the 1500m final at the 1978 NCAA Championships in Eugene Oregon when he finished less than a second behind Steve Scott in 3:37.66. Internationally, Flynn represented Ireland at the European Indoor Championships in 1979 in Vienna where a fall in the final ended his prospects of taking a medal; he finished seventh. There was some compensation at the next European Indoors held at Sindelfingen, West Germany in 1980, where he chased the German athlete Thomas Wessinghage all the way to the line in the 1,500m final finishing second in personal best time of 3:38.50.

It would prove to be his only major championship medal. Flynn had chosen to travel to the European championships because of the uncertainty surrounding the Olympic Games. 'If one had a guarantee that Moscow would go ahead then perhaps, I would have concentrated on building up for it, but it's so much up in the air at present,' he said at the time.

Flynn's concerns about the 1980 Games proved unfounded, despite a boycott by the USA and allies over the 1979 Soviet invasion of Afghanistan. He duly travelled to Moscow for his Olympic debut but failed to make it out of the 1500m heats. In 1982, he made the Irish team for the European Championships, held in Athens, Greece in September of that year. Competing in the 1500m, he finished third in his heat in 3:38.62 and, in the final, led the race for the first 800m before fading to finish eighth in 3:40.44.

After that first sub-four minute mile in 1977, Flynn would notch up forty-four sub-4 minute miles between 1981 and 1984 making him an undoubted star in a golden era for Irish middle distance running. He raced often and over varied distances all over the globe. In August 1981 he ran 2:18.96 for 1,000m in Nice, and in January 1983 clocked 2:20.85 for the same distance in Wellington, New Zealand. When Eamonn Coghlan ran his sub-3:50 world indoor record at East Rutherford, New Jersey in February 1983, he was chased home by Flynn in a time of 3:51.20. At the time, Flynn's was the third fastest indoor mile in the history of the sport.

In 1983, he was involved in the fastest mile in athletics history, held in Auckland, New Zealand. The Molenberg Mile was staged over a super-fast downhill course and Flynn finished third in a time of 3:29.66. Race winner was the Kenyan Mike Boit in 3:28.36, with Steve Scott second in 3:29.44. This remains the fastest-ever recorded mile but does not count as an official record because it was run on a downhill course.

After duelling with some of the greatest milers in athletic history, in 1984, Flynn moved up to the 5000m. In his first major race over the distance on 24 June at Crystal Palace in London, he was an impressive winner of the AAA title, sprinting away from England's Nick Rose in a personal best time of 13:19.52.

At the Los Angeles Olympics a few weeks later, Flynn qualified for the 5000m final after finishing fourth in both his heat and semi-final. In the final packed with some of the greatest middle distance runners ever, he had to settle for eleventh place in 13:34.50. The great Moroccan athlete Saïd Aouita took the title in a new Olympic record time of 13:05.59, with four of the top six finishers improving on their personal best times by at least five seconds.

On a 17 August 1985, Flynn was one of the quartet of Irish milers setting a world 4 x 1 mile relay record at the GOAL meet staged at the UCD Belfield track in Dublin. Flynn had the responsibility of anchoring the team and brought the baton home in 3:56.98 for a cumulative time of 15:49.08 to smash the existing record of 15:59.57 previously held by New Zealand. Four days later, Flynn clocked 3:52.79 for the mile at the Weltklasse, in Zurich and on August 30 ran a time of 3:34.65 for 1500m in Brussels – his second fastest time ever.

On 6 August 1986 in Dublin, Flynn ran 28:44.29 for 10,000m. Indoors, he ran the unusual distance of two miles in Cosford in March 1987 recording a time of 8:27.06. He would reject criticism for over-racing. 'One of the main reasons I ran so fast was from racing so much at that level. And that's what it's all about. The more races you get at that level the faster you can go.'

'We were just machines. Just running. It was all we knew how to do', Flynn told John Greene of the *Irish Independent*.

Injury ended Flynn's career at the age of thirty-two in 1989, a career that by then included eighty-nine sub-4-minute miles.

Remaining in the USA and based in Tennessee, Flynn established the Flynn Sports Management Agency, becoming a highly respected athletes' agent with over sixty athletes on his books. In 2012, the year the meet moved to the Armory track in the Bronx after almost a century at Madison Square Garden, he became director of the Millrose Games. The 115th meeting in 2023 was reportedly one of the best with countless records across the board. More importantly, Flynn has turned what was a loss-making though still popular meet into a sound financial success. It took a cute Longford man to do that.

DAVID GILLICK
Masterchef of the 400m

While Ireland can boast numerous top-rated middle-distance, long-distance and cross-country runners, the country has produced far fewer winners over the shorter distances.

David Gillick, a 400m specialist, is one of the few exceptions to that rule, winning the European Indoor 400m title in 2005 and retaining that title in 2007.

A major goal for Gillick was to qualify for a global 400m final, a feat never achieved by an Irish athlete. This he achieved in August 2009 at the Berlin World Championships. Gillick, who retired in 2016, still holds both the indoor and outdoor Irish 400m records.

Like many of Ireland's best known athletes, Gillick, born in Dublin on 9 July 1983, began his competitive career while at school, and as a student at St Benildus College in Kilmacud, competed successfully in All-Ireland Schools' and national juvenile athletics championships. After winning the National U20 400m title in 2002, he was selected for the 4x400m relay squad for the at the World Junior Championships in Kingston, Jamaica. The quartet of Gillick, Daniel Tobin, Liam McDermid and David McCarthy placed seventh in their heat. This experience ignited his desire to achieve at the highest international levels.

In 2002, Gillick began four years of study at the Dublin Institute of Technology (DIT) for a BSc in Logistics, Materials and Supply Chain Management. In the colours of DIT, he finished second in both 200m and 400m at the Irish Universities' Championships of 2003 also taking a National U23 bronze medal at 200m. Selected for the 400m at the European Athletics U23 Championships in Bydgoszcz, Poland, he placed eighth in his heat.

In 2004 at the National Indoor Championships in Belfast, Gillick clocked the third-fastest time ever by an Irish athlete of 47.75 seconds. His performance gained him selection for the 4×400m relay squad at the World Indoor Championships in Budapest. To qualify for the final, the quartet of Robert Daly, Gary Ryan, Gillick and David McCarthy set a national record of 3:08.83. When the USA dropped the baton and the Bahamian athlete tripped over it, it left the way open for Ireland to take the bronze medal behind Jamaica and Russia. That same year, Gillick finished third in the 400m at the National Championships in Santry in a personal best 46.27.

Gillick's 2005 season got off to a promising start when he won the Scottish Indoor 400m title in 47.28. He followed this up with a 47.14 at the Birmingham Games and then won the AAA Indoor 400m title at Sheffield, clocking 46.43 when winning his semi-final. At the European Indoor Championships in Madrid, Gillick won his heat in a personal best 46.17, which was the fastest qualifying time. In the final, he powered past David Canal of Spain on the final back straight to take gold in 46.30 so becoming become Ireland's first European indoor sprint champion and first international sprint gold medal winner since 1932 when Bob Tisdall won in the 400m hurdles at the Los Angeles Olympic Games.

In April he began his outdoor season at the Irish Universities Championships, retaining his Irish Universities 200m title with a PB of 21.21 in his semi-final. He then clocked 45.96 in the 400m when part of the Irish team at the European Cup in Leiria, Portugal in early June, and 46.72 at the Bangor North Down International Games. At the European U23 Championships at Erfurt, Germany in mid-July, a lower-back injury forced his withdrawal from the 400m final and effectively ended his season.

The year 2006 saw Gillick back in action and at the AAA Indoors in Sheffield in February 2006, he took silver in the 200m with a time of 21.47. A week later, he won the 200m at the National Indoors Belfast in an even faster time of 21.45. In July, at the National Track and Field Championships in Santry, Gillick won his first Irish 400m title with a time of 45.67, earning him selection for the European Championships in Göteborg, Sweden in August. There he qualified easily for the semi-finals, where he was eliminated when placing seventh. Now finished with DIT, and encouraged by his mother, Gillick moved to Loughborough University in October 2006, where Nick Dakin became his coach; he would combine full time-training with part-time studying for an MSc in sports management.

Dramatic improvements were already visible by February 2007 when he set an Irish indoor record of 45.91 when winning a 400m in Düsseldorf, Germany. A month later, he successfully defended his European indoors title in Birmingham, snatching victory from the German athlete Bastian Swillims with a time of 45.52, which remains the Irish indoor record. It made him the first Irish athlete to retain a European Indoor title since Noel Carroll at 800m in the 1960s.

More was to come in June when he broke the Irish 400m outdoor record with a time of 45.23 in Geneva, Switzerland. By now one of the biggest names in Irish athletics, Gillick retained his national 400m title in July, qualifying him for the World Athletics Championships in Osaka, Japan, where he went out in the semi-finals with a time of 45.37.

For 2008, Gillick's main target was the Beijing Olympics and he showed he was in top form at Villeneuve d'Ascq, France, in June, when he lowered his Irish record to 45.12, which was well inside the Olympics 'A' standard. In Beijing, he was unlucky not to progress, finishing fourth in his heat in a time of 45.83 with only the top three guaranteed a place in the semi-finals.

Gillick's principal target in 2009 was the World Athletics Championships in Berlin in August, where he hoped to become the first Irish sprinter to make a final. His season started with four straight international 400m wins from April through June – Walnut, Geneva, Thessaloniki and Milan, with 45.16 in Thessaloniki his fastest time. In Madrid on 4 July, he ran a world class time of 44.77, a national 400m record that was still standing in 2023. A week later he proved that this performance was no fluke when he placed second in 44.82 at the Rome Golden Gala. At the

World Championships in Berlin, he achieved his ambition of making the final, placing second in his heat in 45.45 and a fighting fourth in his semi-final in 44.88. In the final, his time of 45.53 was enough for sixth place. After also finishing sixth in the 400m at the IAAF World Athletics Final in Thessaloniki, Gillick finished fourth in the 2009 Golden League 400m series.

His good form carried forward into 2010, when at the Birmingham Indoor Grand Prix in February, Gillick equalled his Irish indoors 400m record of 45.52 when winning the 400m. He made the final at the World Indoors held in Doha, Qatar in March, but disaster struck when he was disqualified after tangling with an American sprinter mid-race. Key event for the year was the European Championships in Barcelona, Spain at the end of July, and in the build-up, he scored two sub-45 wins. In Barcelona, he finished fifth in the final in 45.28, with only 0.05 sec covering second to fifth places in a blanket dip at the finish line.

While winter training in Orlando, Florida, early in 2011, Gillick sustained a calf injury, which forced him out of the European Indoors. Poor performances by his own standard, where he was barely breaking 47 seconds at meetings in June and early July persuaded him to call a halt to his season and to concentrate his efforts on qualifying for the 2012 London Olympic Games.

His injury woes continued in 2012 with a repeat calf injury, followed two months later by a gastrocnemius tear. He failed to break 48 seconds at international meetings in June in Turin and Moscow, well off the 45.30 Olympic qualifying standard. He did however make the Irish 4 x 400 team which competed at the European Championships in Helsinki at the end of June but was disqualified.

In May 2013, Gillick injured his Achilles tendon forcing an end to his career. Although he formally retired in 2014, he made a low-key return in 2016 with a season's best of 46.44. It was enough to find him selected for the Irish 4×400m relay team competing at the European Championships in Amsterdam. They finished fifth in 3:04.32, just 0.07 outside the qualifying standard for the Rio Olympics.

Gillick is now a regular media commentator. He won the first Celebrity MasterChef Ireland in August 2013 and has since written two books – *David Gillick's Kitchen* (2015) and *Back on Track* (2018). In August 2014, he married Charlotte Wickham whom he had met while at Loughborough University. They have three children – Oscar, Olivia and Louis. In recent years, Gillick has openly discussed the mental health issues he faced after 2012 and how this reached a crisis point in late 2015 when he sought help and counselling. He completed a Certificate in Sport Psychology course at IADT, Dún Laoghaire in 2018.

MARY HEATH
Pioneering Athlete Flying High

Lady Mary Heath, as she is best known, was born Sophie Peirce-Evans in Knockaderry, Co Limerick, on 17 November 1896. When only a year old, the infant destined to become a pioneer both of women's athletics and of aviation was taken to live with her grandfather and two maiden aunts in the nearby town of Newcastle West after her father bludgeoned her mother to death. Quite how much she knew of her tragic background is open to question.

While at boarding schools in Cork, Belfast and Dublin, the teenaged Sophie was introduced to sport, playing hockey and tennis. She continued playing hockey after she enrolled at the Royal College of Science for Ireland and, tall at 1.82m, became a mainstay of her team's defence. Following an early marriage in late 1916, the newly-minted 'Mrs Eliott-Lynn' signed up as a motor dispatch rider with the War Office, only returning to Dublin in mid-1919 when World War 1 was over. With her husband granted a farm in Africa, Sophie stayed on in Dublin, resuming her studies and continuing her involvement in sport, attempting among other things to set up a ladies' cricket team in Rathmines.

At the time, women's athletics was something of a novelty, as indeed were women's sports generally. In May

1921, with women's athletics not included in the Olympic programme, the French woman Alice Milliat organised the first *Olympiades Feminines* held in the glamorous surroundings of Monte Carlo. A dominant English team captured the imagination of adventurous young women, among them Sophie, who began her competitive career in the summer of 1921. Later she was to remember her first attempt at the high jump: 'The first time I ever jumped in 1921, I could not clear 3 feet 10 inches (1.16m).'

In early July 1921, she did a lot better, jumping 4ft 1ins in a women's high jump 'exhibition' at the Moate Sports in Co Westmeath. Two days later, she was in Birr, Co Offaly, jumping even higher, although these results are impossible to confirm, and the format of the competition is unknown. In those pioneering days, athletes jumped scissors-style either over a rope attached to two upright poles, or a piece of stick balanced between the poles, landing in a pit of soft sand.

Sophie's Dublin debut came at the Dublin Tramway Sports in Lansdowne Road, where she won the high jump with a modest height of 4ft. 'Not a bad effort for the sex in these days of general male mediocrity,' says the report in *Sport*. A considerably better jump of 4ft 6ins (1.371m) at the Clonliffe Harriers Sports in Lansdowne Road was enough to rank her second in Britain and Ireland for the year 1921.

Even better was a leap of 4ft 9ins (1.447m) in Ballygar, County Galway on 21 August that equalled the best known performance in the world at that time. Quite how seriously we can take this mark is open to question, with no official record of any women's high jump taking place in Ballygar that year.

During the academic year of 1921/22, Sophie attended Aberdeen University in Scotland as a post-graduate student and 'zoology demonstrator'. There she played hockey and received her first coaching as an athlete. Meanwhile, women's athletics continued to progress, with Alice Milliatt organising a first ever international match between England and France in Paris on 30 October 1921. England won, and a day later, the *Fédération Sportive Féminine Internationale* (FSFI) was formed. Affiliating to the FSFI in 1922 was the newly formed British Women's Amateur Athletic Association in England of which Sophie, now based in London, was elected vice-president.

She competed for the first time in 1922 at a sports day organised by the King's College in May, winning the high jump and 220 yards and finishing third in the long jump. Later that year, she organised the first of several trips to Torquay for competition, while in early August, at a meet in Paddington, she made her first appearance in a two-handed javelin competition, where the best of three throws with each arm were added together and the spear held with both hands. She finished second. At the time, women threw the same 800g implement as men.

The highlight of the season was the first Women's Modern Olympic Games in Paris, organised to coincide with the second FSFI conference on 20 August and attracting 20,000 spectators. Britain finished top of the medals table, ahead of the Americans and France. In the two-handed shot, Sophie finished ninth.

Back in London, Kensington Ladies, with Sophie in the line-up, won a women's inter-club match held at the

Croydon Sports Club. This, the first competition of its kind to be held in Britain, included the first English Women's Championships for the 120-yard hurdles and the 220 yard sprint.

After she arrived in Africa that autumn, Sophie trained every day and at the third Monte Carlo meet in early April 1923, finished third in both the high jump and javelin. These were her first international medals. On 18 August 1923, the inaugural English Women's Athletics Championships took place at the Oxo Sports Ground, Bromley with Sophie winning the javelin with a throw of 35.76m.

In a letter to her aunt Cis in Ireland, she mentions that she broke the world's high jump record on 6 August by jumping 4ft 11ins (1.495m) and that on 18 August, she had won the British javelin throwing championships. No evidence for this high jump record has ever been uncovered; apart from the doubts surrounding Sophie's mark, there was some evidence of a German jump of 1.50m set in 1921 over a proper, modern-style bar. A week after the championships, Sophie finished second in both the hurdles and javelin at the annual match between Britain and France in Paris.

After another winter in east Africa, Sophie returned to England in early 1924, joining the newly formed Middlesex Ladies Athletic Club. Her finest moment as an athlete came at the second annual English Women's Championships in the Woolwich Stadium, London, on 28 June 1924. In the two-handed javelin, she added over 17 metres to her throw of a year earlier with a magnificent aggregate total of 52.78m which obliterated the world record although a slight wind meant her performance was never officially ratified. She also won the high jump.

A highlight of the 1924 season was the United Kingdom's first international women's athletic meet at Stamford Bridge on Bank Holiday Monday 4 August. Thanks to widespread publicity, the meet attracted 25,000 spectators and the spectators watched the Swiss athlete Louise Groslimond set an unofficial world record for the two-handed javelin of 47.55m, far below Sophie's total of two months earlier. Sophie, then busy divorcing her husband, wasn't competing although she was back in action at the end of the month when she threw 38.93m in the javelin.

Her life was to change forever after she had attended the Olympic Congress in Prague from 29 May to 4 June as part of the FSFI delegation, travelling by aeroplane for the first time in her life. Sophie presented two papers on 'Women's Participation in Sport', later expanded into a book called *Athletics for Women and Girls*. On the flight home, a pilot told her about the national air club scheme and the newly founded London Aero Club.

In early June, she competed in the first *Daily Mirror* Trophy at Stamford Bridge, and a month later, at the WAAA Championships again at Stamford Bridge, where she finished third in the high jump and second in the javelin. After her well-publicised first flight at the opening of the London Aero Club at Stag Lane on 19 August, Sophie had decided to take flying lessons. Over the next year, she would juggle her two interests, practising her javelin at Stag Lane when she could not fly.

Her 1925 season culminated with a trip to Sweden, where local enthusiasts hoped a visit from the glamorous British squad might help promote athletics for women. At the first meet in Göteborg on 20 September, Sophie finished third in the high jump and won the javelin. Two days later at Falkenberg, she was second in the javelin and third in both the shot and discus.

On 18 October 1925, Sophie flew solo for the first time, later describing it as 'the most thrilling adventure of my life'. A year later, just shy of her twenty-ninth birthday, she became the first woman in Britain to be awarded a private pilot's license. Her final appearance as an athlete came in May 1927 when she competed in a pentathlon in London.

In 1928, now remarried and officially known as Mary Lady Heath, she would become the first person, man or woman, to fly a small plane single-handed from Cape Town to London. She travelled to the USA in late 1928, where a tragic accident on 29 August 1929 effectively ended her career. Aged just forty-two, she would die alone and unknown in London on 9 May 1939 following a fall in a double-decker tram car.

ROB HEFFERNAN
Walking with the Elite

Born on 28 February 1978 in Cork, Robert Heffernan attended Coláiste Chríost Rí. Deemed to be too small for his school's Gaelic football team at the age of fourteen, he took up race walking on a whim. It was an upward progression and, by the end of the 1990s, Heffernan was competing on the international stage.

From then, he consistently placed in the top eight finishers at championship walks until that purple patch starting in 2010 when he won European bronze over 20km and Olympic bronze over 50km in 2012. In 2013 came that 50km walk at the World Championships in Moscow when Heffernan attained the highest pinnacle of the sport, taking gold and becoming world champion.

Heffernan's time when walking to gold in Moscow in 2013 of 3 hours, 37 minutes 56 seconds was his second-best time over the 50km. His best 50km time of 3:37:54 was returned a year earlier when claiming bronze at the 2012 Olympic Games in London.

Heffernan had announced himself on the national scene in 1999 when taking the national 35km title in 2:35:58. Further successes over this rarely contested distance came the following year, in 2008, and 2009 and in 2011 when he established the championship record of 2:07:44. The event was cancelled in 2010 due to snow. His international debut came at the 1999 World Race Walking Cup in Mézidon-Canon, France. The somewhat inauspicious 70th placing in 1 hr 32 mins 14 secs in the 20km was no indication of his latent talent. The European Under 23 Championships in Göteborg, Sweden later that summer proved altogether more reflective of his ability when he finished 13th over the 20km course in 1:36:26.

The following year, 2000, Heffernan won his first 20km national title in a new course record of 1:23:49 succeeding Pierce O'Callaghan (author of this chapter) as 20km champion. This was the first of a triple sequence with his 2002 winning time 1:21:32 remaining the championship record. His inaugural Olympic appearance at Sydney 2000, saw him placed 28th over 20km in 1:26:04; ahead of him. Polish walking legend Robert Korzeniowski was striding to gold.

In 2001, Heffernan won the first of his nine national 10km track titles in a championships record time of 38 mins 58.83 secs. He knocked ten seconds off that time when taking the title, the following year and a further twenty seconds off that again in 2008 when returning a time of 38:27.57 which remains the championships record. Back to 2001, his 17th placing at the European Race-Walking Cup and 14th at his first World Championships in Edmonton, both over 20km, showed huge improvement and potential at international level.

That great dread of all race walkers – the 'red card' – befell Heffernan at both the Athens Olympic Games in 2004 and the Helsinki World Championships the following year. Concentration and focus over a 20km course and the effort involved in maintaining your own standard, never mind chasing the leaders, invariably will lead to pushing yourself to the limit and beyond.

At the 2007 World Championships in Osaka, Heffernan placed sixth over 20km in 1:23.42. It was a turning point in his career as he now rarely placed out of the top eight at any major walk he contested. The following year he was ninth at the World Race-Walking Cup in Cheboksary, Russia, setting a best of 1:19.22. Despite finishing a minute slower than that over 20km at the Beijing Olympics, he raced to eighth place.

The year 2009 proved auspicious with Heffernan placing fourth over 20km at the European Race-Walking Cup in Metz, France, even if the 15th placing, again over 20km, at the World Championships in Berlin was somewhat disappointing. The other highlight of the year was Heffernan's marriage to Marian Andrews. An established sprinter at 400m in her own right, Marian would compete at the 2011 World Championship and the 2012 Olympic Games as a member of the women's 4x400m relay team.

Marriage suited Heffernan. At the 2010 European Championships in Barcelona, he strode to the bronze medal position in the 20km and placed an unbelievable fourth over 50km – unbelievable as there were a mere three days between both events. His 3:45:30 was a national record. The bronze medal came after the original winner was disqualified (retrospectively in 2014, after Russian Stanislav Emelyanov was found to have committed an anti-doping violation), but a mere twenty-two seconds separated first from third with Heffernan – in third place – a minute and a quarter clear of fourth.

At the 2012 Olympics in London, Heffernan finished ninth in the 20km race and fourth in the 50km, finishing seven minutes faster than the previous national record – 3:37:54. That time remains his best over the distance. His achievements in London were the top two performances for the Irish athletics team at the 2012 Olympics.

Heffernan's major victory in 2013 surely ranks as among the greatest ever achievements by an Irish athlete. On 14 August, he finished first in the 2013 World Championships in Athletics 50km event in Moscow, finishing over a minute clear of the silver medal position with a winning time of 3:37.56, the fastest time in the world that year by more than three minutes.

'It's surreal, it's just a great feeling,' Heffernan said. 'When I came into the stadium it just felt like an out of body experience. It's hard to take it all in at the moment. I'm delighted.'

In early 2015, it was revealed that several Russian male and female champion race walkers were under investigation for doping violations, including the winner of the 50km walk in London, Sergey Kirdyapkin. The athlete was retrospectively suspended during specific periods between 2009 and 2012 by his federation (RUSADA) and had most of his results annulled, including world titles, but not his Olympic title. The IAAF was unhappy with the verdict made by the Russian athletics federation and made it clear that they would be taking the case to the Court of Arbitration for Sport (CAS), believing that the ban should include his participation in the London Olympics. In a statement, the IAAF disagreed with the selective disqualification of results applied by RUSADA. On 24 March 2016, the Court of Arbitration for Sport backed up the IAAF and Heffernan was upgraded to Olympic bronze. He received his medal in November 2016.

Heffernan continued his walking career until 2016, placing fifth in the 50km at the World Championships in Beijing in 2015 and sixth over the same distance at the Rio Olympics of 2016. His autobiography *Walking Tall* was published the same year. In a no-holds-barred account of his life, Heffernan describes his battles with injury, depression and abject poverty on his way to the top. Even when at his best, he often found himself cheated out of medals by those who crossed the dark line into doping.

Heffernan gave up race walking in 2018 after admitting he just did not have the love for it anymore, and that the final two years felt like a 'drag'. Reflecting on his lengthy career, he has noted that: 'Years of dedication, self-sacrifice and hard work might get you qualification for the Games, but even after that you still have to time everything right to be in the best form of your life on that one day that counts, the day of your race.'

As for the Heffernan family: with two sporting parents, the talent follows on, although not in athletics but in football. In June 2022, Cathal, who had captained the Irish

Under 17 national squad, joined the AC Milan Under-18 team from Cork City for a year and in 2023, signed for Newcastle United. His sister Meghan too has represented Ireland in football at Under-19 age level and plays her club football with Cork City. Perhaps the younger two daughters – Regan and Tara – will follow this trend. In 2019, Rob, Marian, Meghan and Cathal were crowned champions in *Ireland's Fittest Family: Celebrity Special*, nabbing €10,000 for autism charity Cork Rainbow Club.

JIM HOGAN
The Irishman who Ran for Great Britain

James Joseph Cregan was born in Croom Hospital, County Limerick on 28 May 1933. He did not start running until early 1952 when his training consisted of running repetitions of 440 yards and 880 yards, timed by his sister Betty on an old wind-up clock in a field on the family farm at Athlacca.

He tasted almost instant success in cross-country, finishing fourth in the novice and second in both the junior and senior Limerick County cross-country championships. Such was his progress in the sport that by the end of the year he had even won an Irish NACA (National Athletic and Cycling Association) five-mile title in Tralee.

What he considered 'one of his best days in Ireland' came at the same venue two years later when barefoot, which would become his trademark, he won both the Irish 5-mile and Munster 3-mile titles in the one afternoon. Some years further on, one of his proudest moments came when he went to Santry, accompanied by his father and mother. By then he had switched associations to the Amateur Athletic Union (of Eire), and he lapped the entire field in the Irish (AAUE/NIAAA) 6-mile championship.

'We wasted a lot of time in Ireland under the NACA,' he wrote in his book. 'The officials were no help because you couldn't run outside the country. But one good thing about the NACA was that you had athletics every Sunday from May to September. You could go somewhere almost every Sunday and race, whereas under the AAU, you didn't get as much competition except in Dublin.'

Jim's big life change came in February 1960 when he moved to London to get work. He had quit running in August the year before and did not start again until April, two months after his arrival. Thinking he would not be able to compete in Britain on account of being a former NACA athlete, he changed his name by deed poll to Hogan.

As a member of Polytechnic Harriers, he quickly became known nationally in running circles for his bold front-running tactics – *Geronimo Jim* he was dubbed – and of course for competing barefoot in his cross-country and track races.

A confessed anglophile, it did not cause Jim any regret when he changed nationality to British. And it was in a British vest that he enjoyed by far the greatest success of his running career. After finishing second in the trial earlier in the year, Hogan lined up for his Great Britain debut running the marathon at the 1966 European Championships in Budapest.

'Britain ended these disappointing European Athletics championships today with a flourish – winning a second gold medal – and it took a lean 33-year-old marathon runner from Limerick, in Southern Ireland, to do it. Jim Hogan, who became qualified to run for Britain only in July after being nationalised two years ago, won by 500 yards, and was never out of the leading group, finishing in 2 hr, 20 min. 4.6

sec for the 26 miles 385 yards course from the Nep Stadium to and from one of Budapest's many beautiful parks,' wrote Gron Williams in the *Birmingham Post*.

'I had been eating a lot all week trying to get as strong as I could. I was also very well hydrated,' Hogan explained in his autobiography. 'I warmed up for about twenty-five minutes before the marathon and got a stitch! I didn't panic, though, and after doing some exercises and stretches I got rid of it. Once the race started, I had no worries at all. At the turn my breathing was easy while the other five or six around at that stage were all running hard, and some were labouring…

'At 30 kilometres there were five of us jostling for position as we approached a drinks table. I grabbed one and it fell out of my hand or something and I just carried on running. I got about twenty-five yards on them didn't increase my pace at all. I expected them to see them coming up on my shoulder, but I was away… After about three-quarters of a mile, I realised they weren't closing in. This is it now, I thought, and put the boot down. I ran the next 5000 metres faster than any of the previous and the gap lengthened. The race was effectively over at this point, but I kept the pressure on.'

It had been a different story two years earlier when sixty-eight runners assembled for the start of the Olympic marathon in Tokyo. It was thought that the home runners and the British trio of Basil Heatley, Ron Hill and Brian Kilby would offer a challenge to the defending champion, Abebe Bikila. Bikila, the Ethiopian bodyguard to Emperor Haile Selassie, had undergone an appendectomy just five weeks earlier and his form was uncertain.

One thing for sure was that nobody expected an Irishman to be battling it out with the reigning Olympic champion for most of the distance. Jim Hogan, distinctive in his green vest, was already clear of the field in the company of Bikila and multi-world record holder Ron Clarke of Australia at the 5km mark. The Limerick native was still within a stride or two of Bekele at the turn, but his challenge slowly petered out after 30km.

Finally, after being overtaken by a string of runners, Hogan took a seat by the side of the road with just five kilometres remaining, while Bekele successfully defended his crown and Heatley grabbed the silver medal on the final lap of the stadium. Kilby was fourth while Ron Hill finished down the field. Hogan had met regularly and on occasions beaten Heatley in the years leading up to Tokyo.

Hogan was treated in hospital after the race for dehydration and it had been noticeable that while Bikila and others paused for drinks, the Limerick man had forged on regardless. His failure to finish the race followed him dropping out of the 10,000m earlier in the Games when well down the field, despite being fifth ranked in the world at the distance the previous year.

Nonetheless, Hogan was pleased with his performance: 'I knew I had to redeem myself after the 10,000m and I gave this race everything I had,' he told journalist Dave Guiney in Tokyo. 'I was within a few miles of a silver medal, or perhaps a bronze one, and I kept going until I collapsed… It came on me suddenly, I was a little tired but felt I could keep going. Then I collapsed and that was that. I feel that I have redeemed myself. I was not interested in finishing far down the field just to earn a few sympathetic claps when I arrived at the stadium. It had to be all or nothing and I'm quite happy I tried my best.'

Relations with the officials of the Amateur Athletics Union (AAU) were never particularly amicable and the AAUE were aware too that Hogan had also dropped out of both the 5,000m and 10,000m when selected for the European Athletics Championships in Belgrade in 1962. But it all came to a head in 1965 at the International Cross-Country Championships to be held in Ostend, Belgium.

The Irish officials wanted Hogan to travel by boat on the Thursday before the event while Hogan wanted to fly over on the Saturday morning. In that way he would not lose two days' work. They refused his request but stubbornly he flew over with his wife Mary on the Saturday morning and both sat in the stand and watched the race to cock a snook at the AAUE officials. He had crossed the Rubicon and would never pull on the green singlet of his native country again:

'I decided then that this was the end of the road for Ireland as I never got any international races or recognition. I was never sent to any international event, even in Europe - they always seem to pick fellows who were living in Ireland… It was as if I was an alien because I worked and ran in London. By this time, I had been living in London for so many years that I had no problem changing nationality. I got a British passport in order to run for Britain. I've never had an Irish passport since then although I had one before that. I'd have loved to win the European Championship for Ireland if I had been allowed to do it.'

Hogan also ran the 10,000m, finishing 26th, at the 1968 Olympics, again as part of the British team. His claims to fame also include setting a world record for 30km on the track, running 1 hr 32 mins 25 secs, and a European indoor three-mile record of 13:37.2.

In 1995, Hogan and his wife Mary returned to Ireland after living in England for over thirty years, settling in Knocklong. After the death of Mary, Hogan spent much of his time in the horse-racing world, breaking and training horses until well into his seventies. He died peacefully at home on 10 January 2015. He is buried in the grounds of St. John the Baptist Church, Athlacca, County Limerick.

If not one of Ireland's most successful distance runners, Hogan was certainly one of our most enigmatic. He is still the only Irish man to win a European Championship gold medal. His book *The Irishman Who Ran for England*, was published in 2008.

THELMA HOPKINS
Jumping for Joy

At the London Olympic Games of 1948, Fanny Blankers Koen from the Netherlands won a brilliant four gold medals. For the first time, women's athletics was front page news all over the world.

Visits to both Dublin and Belfast by the 'Flying Dutchwoman' after the Olympics were received rapturously. At the same time, a team of West Indian women sprinters, on their way home from London, stopped off in Belfast. A local team was hastily put together to compete against them and from this grew the women's section of Short and Harland – one of the first Irish athletics clubs to accept women.

Two years later, in 1950, the North had its first women's championships. Then, in an inspired move, the Northern Irish Athletics Board hired Franz Stampfl to promote athletics in the province. Stampfl, who would later coach Roger Bannister to the world's first sub-four-minute mile, remained in Belfast for four years as resident coach at Queen's University. Stampfl encouraged Northern Irish women to try athletics and from this sprung three outstanding Olympians, with Thelma Hopkins the first great talent to emerge, followed by Mary Peters and Maeve Kyle.

Like Mary Peters a few years later, Hopkins, born 16 March 1936, had arrived in Belfast almost by accident. Her father John was a Wicklow man, and after the Shell Oil company transferred him to Hull, he married and fathered two daughters, Moira and Thelma. He was then moved again, this time to Belfast. With their mother Mildred heavily involved in hockey the sisters' involvement in sport began early.

'We got our first hockey sticks when we were about three years old, playing out on the lawn, and we used to sit and watch our mum, who used to play. You can absorb a lot by watching before you even think about learning,' Hopkins said later.

By their early teens, both sisters were showing exceptional sporting talent, and their proud dad built a high jump area in the back yard so they could practise. Stampfl had spotted Hopkin's potential from the start, predicting that she would be a world beater in due course. In 1951, at the age of fifteen, she won the first two of thirty-three Northern Ireland titles, most of them for the high jump and long jump. That year, despite her youth, she was also awarded her first international vest for the annual match against Scotland, setting her first Irish record of 1.55m.

High jumping then was not for the faint-hearted with the athletes jumping straddle-style over the bar and landing in a sand pit. 'I jumped on to dirt all my career; you used to get quite a lot of shoulder injuries landing. But you learned to fall.' The following year, still only sixteen, she won the British women's high jump title – the first of thirty-three British titles – and was selected for the Olympic Games in

Helsinki, where she came a respectable fourth in the high jump. 'I was very disappointed. I thought it was terrible really only to get fourth place,' said the teenager at the time. In a five year period, she would set multiple Irish high jump and long jump records several times.

In the winter, she returned to hockey and won the first of some forty-five international caps. Over the next couple of years, she continued to improve as an athlete, and in August 1954, at the Commonwealth Games in Toronto, Canada, took gold in the high jump at 1.67m and silver in the long jump as well as competing in the 80m hurdles. She again cleared 1.67m to take gold at the European Championships in Berne, Switzerland, three weeks later, where she attempted to jump 1.74m – one centimetre higher than Russian athlete Aleksandra Chudina's world record.

On a late season tour of the Soviet Union, Czechoslovakia and other Eastern Bloc countries the following year, Hopkins proved the star of the team. She improved her own Irish high jump record to 1.70m in Moscow, where she also competed in the long jump and hurdles and was voted woman athlete of the meet. Three days later in Prague, after clearing 1.71m in the high jump, she again failed at the world record height of 1.74m.

On 5 May 1956, at the Queen's University grounds in Cherryvale Park, Belfast, it all finally came good at her second competition of the season – an open high jump in an intervarsity match organised by the college. Hopkins' sights were set firmly on breaking the record and her father had made sure the legal niceties were in order for any record to be ratified. After going higher and higher, the bar was set at

1.74m. With the watching crowd holding its collective breath, Hopkins soared over it with ease on her second attempt. She then attempted 1.75m but knocked the bar with her knee.

That same day, Hopkins clocked a wind-assisted time of 11.2 seconds in the 80m hurdles to beat British champion Margaret Francis. She also won the long jump with a best of 6.11m, and the javelin with a throw of 30.78m.

She was clearly in top form, but unfortunately, the Olympics were not until December that year. After taking a term off from her dental studies, she travelled to Australia in October, staying with Stampfl and a group of British athletes in Melbourne for two months of acclimatisation and training: 'It was good to get the coaching, but maybe a month would have been enough because you get homesick, especially when you're working hard in training.'

Coinciding with the marathon on the last day of competition, the woman's high jump proved one of the most dramatic competitions of the Games. In the stadium, every one of the 103,000 seats had been sold well in advance. By now, Hopkins had lost the world record to the long-legged Yolanda Balas of Romania, who was the pre-event favourite. An unheralded American, Mildred McDaniel upstaged them both, straddling 1.70m and then 1.76m for a new world best before failing at 1.80m. Behind the American, the next six jumpers, including Hopkins had all failed at 1.70m and were tied on 1.67m. When this happens, the procedure is to lower the bar and have everyone left in the competition jump again. When Hopkins and the Russian Maria Pisareva remained equal, both were awarded silver medals. Balas, who was to win 140 consecutive competitions over the next decade, finished fifth.

After Melbourne, Hopkins took a long holiday and in 1957, set a new record of 4,148 points when regaining her Northern Ireland pentathlon title. Pentathlon in those days consisted of the 80m hurdles, shot put, high jump, long jump and 200m.

The following year, with Maeve Kyle, Mary Peters, and javelin thrower Bridget Robinson, Hopkins was selected for the Commonwealth Games in Cardiff, Wales, and, for the first time, she found herself running the opening leg in a 4x110 yard relay. The inexperienced quartet made the final by default and finished in sixth place, a full five seconds behind a rampant England quartet winning in a world record of 45.37 secs.

Individually Hopkins came eighth in the high jump, clearing 1.57m. At the annual match against Scotland in 1960, she won not only her favoured high jump, but also the discus with a respectable throw of 35.88m. A year later in 1961, she jumped 1.65m for a bronze medal in the high jump at the World University Games in Sofia, also coming fifth in both 80m hurdles and long jump.

The 1962 European Championships in Belgrade and the Commonwealth Games in Perth were her two final outings. For Belgrade, she had qualified for the pentathlon and despite a poor shot put, always her weakest event, all was going well until the long jump when she injured her ankle, forcing her pull out of the 200m, then the final event. At the Commonwealth Games later in the year, she was sixth in the long jump and ninth in the high jump.

Her career was not quite over. In 1963, Hopkins was part of the first ever North/South team which took on Belgium at a Billy Morton-organised promotion in Dublin's Santry Stadium. Her wins in the high jump and 80m hurdles helped the Irish team to a memorable victory.

A couple of Northern Irish titles the following year at long and high jump and that was it, although her hockey career continued for one year more when she was part of a combined Great Britain and Ireland team that toured the USA in 1965. Hopkins later married and emigrated to Edmonton, Canada, where she had three children, worked with special needs children and attempted to start a hockey team.

In June 2006, Hopkins returned to Cherryvale Park, Belfast where a plaque was unveiled to mark the fiftieth anniversary of her world record.

DENIS HORGAN
Shot-Putting Pocket Dynamo

William Dooley, the noted athletics scribe, once wrote of Denis Horgan: 'He was usually so superior to his fellow competitors that he seldom trained in any sort of systematic way, yet he showed a marked consistency of performance, in all conditions, over a period of twenty years.' Few athletes have dominated an event like Denis did with the shot. For a fifteen-year period in the closing years of the 19th century and into the first decade of the 20th he was the supreme exponent of the event in the world.

'From his teens he displayed great strength and at 16 his huge proportions and vigorous health – resulting from hard manual farm work – gave him the proportions of a full-grown man,' added Dooley. He had 'two arms the size of the pillars of a gate', ideally suited to the shot, from 16lbs through to the 56lbs weight, though his unwieldy bulk made hammer throwing and similar throwing events altogether more difficult for him to perfect. Dependent on speed due to his relatively short stature, his wide stance at the front of the circle allowed for maximum push. His speed of delivery was frequently commented on as was his follow through and drive when propelling the shot away from the circle. Like so many of his throwing contemporaries he was a capable high jumper with a best of 1.74m.

Born on 18 May 1871 in Banteer, County Cork, Horgan's early career as a shot putter was limited to the local circuit in Cork and Munster. By 1892, his 12.72m in Tralee placed him sixth on the world list; he improved to 13.26m the following year which was good enough for number two in the world and took his first National Championship titles in the shot – winning both GAA and IAAA national titles.

Horgan retained the 1894 IAAA title with an Irish record of 13.82m, beating the record held by James O'Brien (13.79m). One of the more remarkable achievements in the long annals of Irish athletics occurred on the afternoon of 15 August that year when Horgan announced his arrival as a thrower to be reckoned with. At the Dublin Metropolitan Police (DMP) meeting at Ballsbridge, Dublin he would eclipse that mark and his initial put of 13.87m was greeted with a standing ovation from the crowd. However, the crowd must have been as exhausted as Denis by the end of the competition as the national record continually fell and Horgan proceeded to put ever further – 14.00m, 14.02m, 14.15m and finally 14.16m. That latter mark was not alone the best in the world that year but also a world record.

Making his international debut against Scotland in 1895 in Glasgow, Horgan set new Scottish best figures of 13.59m. He bettered this mark at the Celtic FC Sports in 1899 with a 14.71m effort.

Horgan's career exploded from there. In all, he would win twenty-three national titles and another twenty placed medal positions. He was at his peak at a time when many regarded the AAA Championships as the equivalent of a world championships. At the AAA Championships he took his first shot title in 1893 beginning a sequence that lasted until 1899. Further titles came in 1904, 1905, 1908, 1909, 1910 and 1912. There were a further seven runners-up medals, mostly in the hammer where Tom Kiely was supreme. Horgan ranked number one in the world in the shot every year from 1894 to the end of the century, except in 1898. In 1899, he had the top seven marks in the world, going one better with eight the following year.

After setting a world record of 14.68m with the 16lbs shot at Queenstown, County Cork in 1897, Horgan's name became well known beyond Ireland, in particular in the USA. At the 1900 AAA Championships, Horgan had lost to the American Richard Sheldon, partly because he had been seasick when travelling overnight to Britain for the championships. Peeved at losing to an athlete he perceived as an inferior, he duly set off for America working his passage on a cattle-boat to Boston and then getting an overnight train to New York. The *New York Times* glowed with the anticipation of the arrival of Horgan that August: '[The] last foreign mail brought news that Denis Horgan, the Irish shot putter and holder of the world's record... for the sixteen-pound shot, will leave for America on the 15th.

That summer, Horgan joined the Greater New York Irish Athletic Association, the predecessor of the Irish-American Athletic Club, for a brief period. At the Columbia Manhattan Field, he won the US championships title, beating both Wesley Coe and Sheldon into the minor placings, with a winning put of 14.06m. In an exhibition at the Pastime

AC Games in New York the following month, he returned 14.69m in the shot and exceeded the best on record with the 12lbs with 17m. Horgan lost his amateur status on return to these islands after participating in the professional Highland Games and two years in the wilderness followed. His return to competition in 1903 was very much business as usual. His best shot mark after his return was a world record 14.88m set in Mallow in September 1904.

In 1905, Horgan left for America again and joined the New York Athletic Club. In 1906, he was runner-up in the American Championships in the shot but set a world record for the 28lbs shot, with a distance of 11.05m a fortnight later at the Ancient Order of Hibernians games held at Celtic Park, in Queen's, New York. While working as a police officer, Horgan was assaulted in a fracas with a crazed shopkeeper named Clement Lug in New York and was left with a fractured skull. He subsequently recovered but his injuries were enough to see him pensioned from the police force. He returned to Ireland and would bear the scars and the metal plate inserted in his skull for the rest of his life.

Horgan's sole Olympic appearance was in 1908. Although he was the dominant force in shot-putting throughout this era, he had not competed in the first three Olympics for a variety of reasons, largely financial, and gold medals were won in every staging of the event from 1900 to 1906 with throws far below his standard. In addition to his ban from amateur competition for two years, he was in the USA when the 1906 'Intercalated' Games were held in Athens.

At the 1908 Games in London, he won a silver medal but was battling against the odds – his age (he was 37), the serious injury he had received when a policeman in New York, the attitude of the American competitors and the inclement weather, with the heavens opening just in time for the shot competition. His best effort of 13.82m was not enough to beat the 6 ft 6 ins of American Ralph Rose who took gold with a 14.21m heave.

The first 50-foot shot put mark was credited to Ralph Rose on 26 September 1908. Yet at Kanturk earlier that month – on the 6th – Horgan was credited with a world record mark of 15.37m according to both the *Cork Examiner* and the *Independent* although the distance never received international ratification.

The quality of the field in Kanturk that day tells us a lot about the state of Irish athletics, with the meet attended by a number of the Irish-born Olympic medal winners from London, some of them visiting relatives at home before heading back across the Atlantic. Con Walsh was runner-up to Horgan in the shot with 12.29m. Walsh enjoyed a double that day in Kanturk with further phenomenal marks. His 51.92m in the hammer (Horgan was second with 43.94m) was a mere metre and a half behind John Flanagan's world record (53.38m) and his 4.65m in the 56lbs for height is astonishing. Tim Ahearne, the 1908 Olympic triple jump champion, also enjoyed a double – 1.81m in the high jump and an amazing 7.57m in the long jump at a time when Peter O'Connor's world record stood at 7.61m.

One noteworthy feature of Denis Horgan's throwing career was his interest in all throwing events. He could throw 42m-plus with the hammer, over 4m in the 56lbs-for-height throw, and 8m with the 56lbs for distance as well as being a useful discus thrower and holding the world record for the 28lbs put. It was said at the time that if he had focused purely on the shot, he would have taken his best beyond 15m. A larger than life character, he prepared for major competitions by consuming a dozen eggs helped on their way by a pint of sherry.

On his final return to Ireland in 1908, Denis married and settled in Crookstown. He died at a relatively young age of fifty-one on 2 June 1922.

ROBERT (BOBBY) KERR
The Shamrock and the Maple

When Andre de Grasse crossed the finish line to take 200 metres gold at Tokyo 2020, he was probably aware that he was continuing the great tradition of Canadian sprinters at the Olympics. It is very unlikely however that he would have known that it was a man from County Fermanagh in Ireland who started that tradition with a victory in the 200m at the London Games over a century earlier.

Robert Kerr was born on 9 June 1882 near Enniskillen, County Fermanagh. His father was George Kerr and his mother Rebecca's maiden name was McCourt. The family emigrated to Canada when he was four, eventually settling in Hamilton, Ontario.

When Robert ('Bobby') was a teenager, he joined the International Harvester Fire Brigade and enjoyed running in his spare time. While working as a fireman, he won the 100 yard, 440 yard and 880 yard titles at the 1902 Hamilton Coronation Games. Now established as the best sprinter in Canada, he used his savings to travel to St. Louis for 1904 Summer Olympics. Although he was eliminated in the heats of all three events he entered (60m, 100m and 200m), he gained valuable experience.

He missed Athens 1906 due to a lack of finance but came to international notice the following year when he set a world record for the 220 yards. Running in the Penman Games in Hamilton, Kerr whizzed to a time of 21.4 seconds on a circular track. That was within four-tenths of a second off the straight course record. For good measure he also ran 9.8 seconds for 100 yards at the same meeting although put back a yard behind the start line for a false start.

He did make it to London in 1908 where he warmed up for the Olympic Games by competing in the AAA Championships at Stamford Bridge. Showing that he had been unaffected by the transatlantic journey, he claimed both the 100 yard and 220 yard titles and was awarded the Harvey Gold Cup as the meeting's outstanding athlete.

Buoyed by this AAA success, he would have entered the Olympic arena full of confidence. The 100m and 200m were held in parallel, meaning that Kerr was some days running heats both in the morning and the afternoon. Only the winner progressed during each round of the preliminaries for both distances meaning there was no such thing as an easy qualification.

He opened with a 100m heat on 20 July, winning the tenth heat in eleven seconds even. In the quarter finals of the 200m the following morning, he moved through to the semis in 22.2 secs – the fastest time of the day – after a tough race with the American Will May. The afternoon saw him lined up in the 100m semi-final where he won again with the same time as his first-round heat, seeing off the challenge of another US representative Nate Sherman.

On a busy 22 July, the Irish-Canadian claimed victory in the morning's 200m semi-final in 22.6 secs with yet another American, William ('Red') Hamilton who had an easy passage in the first round, being the victim. He was back on track in the afternoon in the 100m with Walker of South Africa and the top American James Rector, who had already equalled the Olympic record, the hot favourites for the gold medal.

Walker got off to a quick lead, but Kerr and Rector caught him about midway through the race and passed him. Walker responded with a great effort, pulling ahead to win by half a yard. Rector finished six inches ahead of Kerr to claim the silver medal. Walker again equalled the Olympic record of 10.8 secs, with Rector just a tenth of a second in arrears and the same margin back to Kerr in third.

Disappointingly, Kerr had beaten Walker at the AAA Championships, and his fatigue was obvious in the final of the 200m. He was fast away and led around the bend, but with his lead dissipating down the home straight, just held on to win by the narrowest of margins as he and the runner-up, the Irish-American Bobbie Cloughen, shared the same 22.6 second time.

Cloughen had also contested the 100m, winning his opening round heat but withdrawing from the semi-final of the event to concentrate on the longer distance, giving him an edge over the Fermanagh native.

'In the 100 metres dash I was first away,' Kerr later told the *Mail and Empire* newspaper of Toronto. 'Rector and I ran a dead heat for the first 60 metres then Walker suddenly caught us and passed us both as though we were standing still. I had done too much work before the 100 metres and was a trifle stale. I had a hard man in every heat of the 200 metres.'

During his stay, Kerr firmly established himself not only as the darling of the athletics-following public but also the sporting press. It was not surprising then that he should be fulsome in his praise the way the London Games had been hosted, rejecting complaints of the Americans that the seeding had been unfair to them.

'The officials throughout were all that could be desired, and the Americans certainly have no cause to protest. The draws were unfavourable to them in some cases, but it could not be otherwise when they had by far the greatest numerical representation.'

He returned to Europe in June of the following year, along with his coach George Anderson, and his sister. On arrival he declared himself stronger than ever before but that was not borne out at the AAA Championships when he was beaten by Walker and Cartmell in the 100 yard and by the latter again in the 220 yard races.

However, while he failed to retain either of his AAA titles, he did fulfil a life-long ambition when representing Ireland in the annual international against Scotland. In front of a crowd of 4,500 at the Royal Dublin Society's enclosure in Ballsbridge, he won both sprints comfortably setting an Irish record of 22.2 secs in the 220 yard. He had not been the original selection for the events but was included when the Irish champion Paddy Roche withdrew from the team.

'I hope it will not be my last,' said Kerr at a reception in his hometown after the international. 'I was very much pleased with the reception I got both from spectators and competitors alike.'

Unfortunately, it would be his last appearance on an international stage and on his return to Canada, he was very frank in his analysis of the season. Speaking to the *Hamilton Spectator*, he responded to the question, 'Bob, what was the matter?'

'Can't say what was the matter,' he said. 'In the first place I was not in the shape that I should have been, and I think that I did not do as much work as I should have done, owing to the fact that I was under the impression that I was in better condition than I really was, and that too much work would tend to make me stale, when, to tell the truth about the matter, I could have spent several harder week's work in training before I was right.'

He was again selected for the Canadian Olympic team in 1912, but he declined because he believed that he was past his prime and ready for retirement. During the First World War, Kerr became an officer with the 205th (Tiger) Battalion in the Canadian army, also known as the 'sportsmen's battalion', because many of its members were prominent local athletes.

After the War, Kerr returned to athletics as an administrator. He was Canadian team captain at Amsterdam in 1928 where he witnessed Percy Williams succeeding him as Canadian winner of the 200m. Four years later he was back again in the Olympic arena as manager of the Canadian track and field team in Los Angeles.

He served as an official with various local and national sport organisations, including the Hamilton Olympic Club, the Highlanders' Athletic Association, the Amateur Athletic

Union of Canada, and the Canadian Olympic Association. He was also a driving force behind Canada hosting the first British Empire Games in Hamilton in 1930 in which Ireland competed uniquely as a thirty-two county state.

Kerr was the Canadian champion in the 100 yard in 1907 and 220 yard in 1906-08 and set Canadian records for all distances between 40 yards and 220 yards. He was inducted into the Canadian Olympic Hall of Fame in 1949 and Canada's Sports Hall of Fame in 1955. He died in Hamilton at the age of eighty and was posthumously inducted into the Hamilton Sports Hall of Fame in 2012, where his Olympic medals were brought out of storage for the first time in decades. A park in his hometown is named in his honour.

Andre de Grasse will do well to match that *curriculum vitae*.

TOM KIELY
The Champion

Tom Kiely from Ballyneale, near Carrick-on-Suir in south Tipperary can be regarded either as the last of the great 'old style' Irish athletes, or the first of the great modern ones and was certainly one of the great all-rounders of his day.

His sporting career included 53 national wins, two world titles and an Olympic gold medal in the 'all-around' event (forerunner of the decathlon), and numerous world records. In addition, he captained the Grangemockler Gaelic football team and represented Munster in hurling.

Born on 5 August 1869, the oldest son of ten children, he grew up working on the farm, building the strength and stamina he would later draw on for his sport. His career spanned a period which saw athletics become a sport with consistent rules, international governing bodies and regulated competitions, although his career pre-dated a time when the shape and size of hammers and throwing circles was consistent and record-keeping could be trusted. He was also perhaps too good at too many athletic events. He never liked specialising in one or two but preferred to compete in many. Indeed, at one Gaelic Sports tournament in Stamford Bridge, London in 1896, Kiely not only competed in hammer throwing contests, but he also played in the interprovincial hurling and football matches for Munster.

Kiely's father, William, wanted his sons concentrating on the family cattle business, not on sport. The Kielys, however, lived just a few short miles away from Deerpark, home of Maurice, Pat and Tom Davin and the Davins nurtured the potential of the strapping youngster; the 6 foot 2 inch Kiely was incredibly strong but also agile. Aged just twenty, Kiely took four second places at the GAA All-Ireland championships of 1889 in putting the 28lb (12.7kg) and 56lb (25.4kg) and throwing the 16lb (7.25) hammer and 7lb (3.2kg) weight. He was also third in the standing long jump, the 120 yard hurdles and in the Irish event of three standing jumps, with weights held in the hands.

Two days in 1892 cemented Kiely's reputation. Competing at the national all-round championships in Ballsbridge, a one-day event organised by the Irish Amateur Athletic Association, a less nationalist body than the GAA, Kiely won the high jump, long jump, shot put, hammer, 120 yard hurdles and 440 yards. He had the competition won without even running the final mile event – Kiely was not fond of running!

A few weeks later, he won seven individual national titles at the GAA championships, held in Croke Park. Here he was not competing against other all-rounders and each victory was won against the best specialist athletes in the events, which included four weights events, two jumping and the 120 yard hurdles. The columnist 'Cuchulinn' noted in *Sport*, 17 September 1892:

'Rarely in the history of athletics has such splendid performances as those of Keily [sic] been seen. Perhaps Keily's victory in the 120 yards hurdles was the most meritorious of all. In this event, he left such "clinkers" Pedlow and Ryan behind him and finished the last three hurdles as fast as any man did.'

In 1893 and 1894, Kiely completed a hat-trick of national all-round titles, with performances that caught the eye in American and British athletics circles. He was allowed keep the all-round championship belt in honour of his third title. Several newspapers had begun to refer to him at 'The Champion'. Years later, he still received letters addressed simply to 'The Champion Kiely.'

A lovely insight into Kiely's own character comes from the scrapbook he kept, with cuttings from all his exploits. His name was frequently misspelt, often as 'Keily', and the young man regularly corrected this error in black pen when he inserted his cuttings. He also kept a meticulous record of every sports meeting and every victory in these early years, including one for Irish dancing.

While Irish commentators could claim that Kiely was the best athlete in the world, it was difficult to prove it. In the murky days when record setting was arbitrarily based on national or local traditions, it was often impossible to compare an Irish-based record to one set in England, USA or elsewhere. If you took Irish newspaper accounts as definitive, Tom Kiely had broken over twenty national or world records, in hammer or 56lb throwing between 1893 and 1895. Although scrupulously recorded by reputable sports organisers, some of these were ratified and others were not. While rumours of efforts to entice Kiely to America abounded from 1895, he found other means of achieving international recognition and was the central figure on the Irish athletics team at the annual match against Scotland from its first year in 1895 until 1903. In 1895 when the event was held in Glasgow, Kiely had already finished his four chosen events and was dressing in the changing rooms when Irish officials asked him to take part in the long jump as a substitute. His win in a Scottish all-comers record would nail down victory for Ireland.

A year later, the revived Olympic Games were scheduled for Athens, Greece. Kiely and other top athletes of the time preferred to compete in British and American contests, such as the Amateur Athletics Association of England Championships, known as 'the AAA', where Kiely won five hammer titles between 1897 and 1902. Had the AAA held an all-round or decathlon championship then, Kiely would have won many more titles.

It can be argued that it was athletes like Kiely who kept the GAA going especially during some lean years in the 1890s at events such as a ten-event athletics contest at Dungarvan in 1900 when Tipperary took on Cork before a crowd of at least 8,000 spectators. Kiely won five events: long jump, 16lb hammer, 120 yard hurdles, 56lb unlimited run up and hop-step and jump. With each win worth four points, Kiely alone scored twenty points. The entire Cork team, with two athletes scoring in each event, only recorded a total of 27.5 points against Tipperary's 63.5 points.

Throughout his career, Tom Kiely competed at both the GAA and the IAAA national championships, winning the only four all-round events he entered, the fourth of these in 1898. He also won more Irish titles than any other athlete, with his total of fifty-three titles spanning ten different athletic disciplines and including thirty-eight GAA and fifteen IAAA titles. Counting GAA titles alone, Kiely held more Irish titles than any other athlete in history at a time when Irish athletics was in its golden age.

When he was semi-retired and aged almost thirty-five came the crowning achievement of Tom Kiely's career. He paid his own way to St. Louis in 1904 and, reputedly representing 'Tipperary and Ireland', won the All-Round Championship of the World at the Olympic Games. The ten-event competition included events like the pole vault, a half-mile walk, and a one-mile run of which Kiely had little experience. Yet on 4 July, he beat a field of Americans, and spent several months afterwards in the USA, lauded wherever he went. The *Washington Times* wrote on 7 August 1904:

'Kiely is undoubtedly the brightest star that athletic firmament has ever known… Never in the history of athletics has anyone achieved the enviable reputation that Thomas Kiely retires with… in all branches of athletics: running, jumping and weight throwing…'

Irish America presented Kiely with a silver cup, valued in 1904 at $1,000, at a magnificent reception in Harlem, New York the evening before he left for Ireland. Kiely's achievement did much to enhance the position of Irish people in American society. When the morning came for Tom Kiely to leave for home, the *New York Daily News* of 22 October 1904 gushed:

'He who was accompanied to the dock by scores of friends, and was given a parting ovation seldom recalled, was Thomas F. Kiely, world's champion athlete, who returns to his native land, the Emerald Isle.'

The expectation that Kiely would retire after the Olympics was premature. He returned to the USA in 1906 and won the AAU All-Round championship, effectively another world championship, in Boston.

In later life, Tom Kiely was given the honour of carrying the national flag into Croke Park at the Tailteann Games in 1924, accompanied that day by other legends of Irish athletics like Peter O'Connor and John Flanagan. Kiely lived a long and prosperous life. He was a farmer and cattle dealer and dabbled in stocks and shares. He retained an interest in athletics all his life, but also enjoyed horse racing and greyhounds. He had bought a farm at Fruithill, near Dungarvan, County Waterford around 1906 and married soon after. He and his wife, Mary, had three sons and five daughters. He died aged eighty-two in Dublin on 6 November 1951.

Kiely has been described by commentators as 'the greatest athlete of Ireland's greatest athletic period'. The American decathlon expert, Frank Zarnowski, summed him up neatly: 'He was, in his day, the world's best athlete. Everyone knew it. Period.'

No argument here.

MAEVE KYLE
Suffragette of Irish Athletics

Many words have been used over the years to describe Maeve Kyle's place in the pantheon of Irish athletics – trailblazer, pioneer, front-runner, ground breaker, modernist vanguard. Her legacy was secured in 1956 when she became the first woman to represent Ireland in athletics at the Olympic Games, in Melbourne, and was further cemented when she became Ireland's first triple Olympian – Melbourne 1956, Rome 1960 and Tokyo 1964. She was also the first Irish female representative at the European Championships in Belgrade, Serbia, in 1962, and in 1966 at the inaugural European Indoor Games at Dortmund in Germany where she became the first Irishwoman to win a medal at a major international athletics championship.

In the late 1940s and early 1950s, athletics for women in Ireland was virtually non-existent. Attempts to foster athletics for women by the National Athletic and Cycling Association of Ireland in the mid-1930s had met with ecclesiastical disapproval. Against this background, Kyle's determination and courage proved pivotal, paving the way for future generations of Irish women to follow their athletics dreams. She herself has likened her role to that of a suffragette in the cause of Irish athletics.

Maeve Esther Enid Shankey was born on 6 October 1928 in Kilkenny, daughter of Carrodus Gilbert Shankey, headmaster of Kilkenny College, and Enid Kathleen, second daughter of William Edward Thrift, Professor of Natural and Experimental Philosophy (Physics) in Trinity College Dublin, who would become Provost of the University of Dublin from 1937 to 1942. She was eldest of five children.

In her early years, Maeve was educated by her mother and father at Kilkenny College. In 1938, aged nine, she travelled to Dublin to further her education at Alexandra College, at that time based in Earlsfort Terrace. She stayed with her grandparents in the Provost's House at No.1 Grafton Street. After the death of Provost Thrift in 1942, she became a boarder at Alexandra College.

While at school, she played hockey, helping her team win the Schools' Cup in 1946. In October 1946, Kyle entered Trinity College and continued to play hockey. In 1948, she was selected for the Irish senior team, making her debut against Wales on 6 March in Belfast, a match won 5-1 by Ireland. In 1950, Maeve captained Dublin University to an 8-6 victory over Queen's University in the Chilean Cup scoring three goals. She was part of the Irish team which won an historic first Triple Crown, defeating Wales 4-0 England 5-3 and Scotland 3-0 with Kyle featuring in all three home matches and playing 'a blinder' in the final match against Scotland in Glasgow. Kyle, with fifty-eight caps for Ireland, was named in the World All-Star team in 1953 and 1959 and in June 2006, was one of ten players inducted into the inaugural Irish Hockey Hall of Fame.

In 1950, Kyle graduated with a BA in natural science and began teaching in Alexandra College while studying for her Higher Diploma in Education at Trinity College which she gained 1951. On Saturday 7 March 1953, she met Sean Kyle at a dance in Hall's Hotel, Antrim on a blind date. A whirlwind romance ensued, and they married less than a year later on 24 February 1954, with the newly-wed Mrs Kyle then taking up a teaching position at Cambridge House School, Ballymena. Sean encouraged his new bride to take up competitive running – something she had always wished to do – and arranged for her to compete at the prestigious RUC Coronation Sports in Belfast, where she won the 80 yards sprint, and also at the Short and Harland Sports where she won the 100 yard sprint and the long jump. Their marriage and partnership in athletics endured for over sixty-one years until Sean's death on 10 November 2015, aged eighty-eight.

Kyle's first competitive outing had been a low-key Irish Ladies Select Team v London Hospitals meet held in July 1949 at Lansdowne Road where she won the high jump and placed second in the 100 yards. Despite the high profile of women's athletics after the thrilling performances of Fanny Blankers-Koen from the Netherlands at the 1948 Olympics, few Irish athletics meetings offered events for women and an attempt to start a women's section in Crusaders Athletics Club foundered largely because of the hostile pulpit oratory of the Catholic Archbishop of Dublin, John Charles McQuaid. A few Crusaders AC women had taken part in the Clonliffe International at Lansdowne Road of 8 and 9 June 8 in 1949, where Blankers-Koen was the star, but were not heard from again. In 1950, the Northern Ireland Women's Athletic Association was formed.

After her 1954 races in Belfast, Kyle took a break to give birth to her daughter Shauna. She was back in action in 1955 when the Kyles founded Ballymena AC as a club for women and girls to promote female participation in athletics. After returning to training under the supervision of her husband, Kyle won the Northern Ireland 100 yard and 220 yard titles that year. She retained those titles in 1956, also winning the pentathlon title from a young Mary Peters.

At the Olympic Games of 1948, 1952 and 1956, the only track events for women were the 100m, 200m, 80m hurdles and 4×100m relay. The 800m, one of the three women's events in 1928, was not restored until 1960 while the 400m was added for Tokyo in 1964.

Kyle was selected for the 100m and 200m in Melbourne based on her consistent performances and times during the summer months of 1956. The concept of a married women 'deserting' her husband and young child for over a month was too audacious for some critics. Kyle had to raise £200 (equivalent to €6,000 today) towards the individual cost of £625 to send each team member to Australia. She was eliminated in the heats in Melbourne, but the experience proved invaluable.

In July 1958 Kyle was selected to represent Northern Ireland at the Commonwealth Games in Cardiff. Although she did not progress from the heats of the 100 and 220 yards, the quartet of Thelma Hopkins, Bridget Robinson, Mary Peters and Kyle qualified for the 4 x 110 yard relay by default and finished sixth in a final won by the English quartet in a world record time.

At the Rome Olympics of 1960, Kyle failed to qualify from her 100m heat by 0.01 sec and placed fifth in her 200m heat in a personal best time of 25.06 seconds. Now aged thirty-three, she was moving up the distances to 400m and 800m. In 1959, she had won the inaugural women's Northern Ireland 440 yard championship, and she would retain this title for twelve consecutive years. Kyle regarded the 400m, with its mental as well as physical challenges, as her favourite event. She won the AAA 440 yds title in 1961, placed third in 1962, second in 1963 and third in 1964. At the European Championships in Belgrade in September 1962 she finished sixth in the 400m final but did not progress from the 800m heats. In October 1964 at the Olympic Games in Tokyo aged thirty-six, she made the semi-finals of both the 400m and 800m.

Her commitment to the 400m was finally awarded with a bronze medal at the inaugural European Indoor Games held in Dortmund, Germany in March 1966. After winning her heat in 56.4 seconds to make the final, she lost out on the silver medal to Libuše Macounová of Czechoslovakia, who was eight years younger than her, by only 0.1 sec. The only other Irish competitor was the late Noel Carroll who won the men's 800m – two representatives, two medals. In August that year, Kyle could not reproduce her indoor form at the European Championships in Budapest where she went out in the heats of both the 400m and 800m.

At the Commonwealth Games of July 1970 in Edinburgh, Kyle, aged forty-one, placed eighth in the 400m in 55.78 seconds and ran the third leg of the 4 x 100m relay helping the Northern Ireland team to seventh place. It proved to be her swan-song as a senior international.

Kyle however was not finished and went on to set numerous age group records as a masters asters athlete. She played club hockey until 1982 when a motor accident in which she broke her back forced her to stop. As well as competing, she officiated at club, school and national level, coached athletes of all standards, and held office with the governing bodies of sport in both the Republic and Northern Ireland. Maeve Kyle's contribution to athletics has been recognised by numerous awards including an OBE in 2008 and an International Olympic Committee 'Women and Sport Achievement Diploma in 2016. In 2020, her face appeared on an Irish postage stamp.

It truly does not get better than that!

CON LEAHY
The All-Round Jumper

Con Leahy from Cregane, just inside the Limerick border near Charleville, winner of medals at both the 1906 Intercalated Games in Athens and the 1908 Olympics in London, was a late starter in senior athletics.

After two or three years of mainly local competition, Leahy, born 27 April 1876, was already twenty-six when he competed in his first Irish championships, and his career was almost a mirror image of his brother Pat's. When Con began to compete seriously in his mid-twenties, Pat, though a year younger, was close to retirement.

The brothers were the eldest of nine and from an early age were required to help on the family farm, which could be one reason for their careers barely coinciding. When they did compete against each other, they generally split the spoils, with Pat considered a more talented but less consistent athlete. A third brother, Timothy, also won Irish high-jump titles in 1909, 1911, 1913, and 1914.

Con Leahy's domestic championship record in jumping events was phenomenal; no other athlete has ever won as many Irish jumps titles. He benefited from competing in two different Irish championships for most of his career, winning seven IAAA high jump titles (every year from 1902 to 1908) and four in the long jump. In the GAA Championships, he won four high jump titles, and one each in the long jump, triple jump, standing long jump and the 'two hops and a jump'. That makes a total of nineteen Irish jumps titles, all between the years 1902 and 1908.

Had a triple jump championships been contested annually he might have won more. After regulations prohibiting IAAA athletes from competing at GAA championships were tightened up, Leahy won no more GAA titles.

Despite his many titles and honours, Con Leahy was probably best known in Charleville as the boy who could jump over the 'Mannix Gate', over six feet high, on his way to and from school every day.

Con Leahy also performed superbly in Britain. In the annual Ireland v Scotland match, he had the best win ratio of any athlete in the years he competed, with nine wins and three second places in the seven years from 1902 to 1908. Seven of the wins came in the high jump. In 1902, he tied with his brother Pat in the high jump and only once in 1906, when he finished third in the long jump, did he finish outside the top two in an event. Leahy won the English AAA high jump championship four times in a row between 1905 and 1908, although his best jump at the AAAs had come in 1902 when he cleared 1.854 metres but only managed to finish third. He tied for second place in the AAA long jump behind Peter O'Connor that same year. Again, the lack of a regular triple jump competition in England denied Leahy more AAA medals. Not until well after he retired did the AAA standardise the triple jump (hop, step and jump in that order).

Con Leahy and Peter O'Connor were funded by subscribers to an *Irish Field* appeal to represent the IAAA at the tenth anniversary so-called 'Intercalated' Olympic Games in Athens, 1906. Despite their protests, they were registered as part of the Great Britain team since Ireland at the time did not have an Olympic committee. Technically the team should have been called 'Great Britain and Ireland'. Leahy was favourite in the high jump, the most poorly organised and certainly longest such competition in Olympic history, with officials deciding that the bar would start at a ridiculously low height of 1.375 metres and could only be raised by one centimetre after each round. All eight athletes duly cleared every height up to 1.675 metres and after almost six hours of competition only two had been eliminated. With darkness falling, the contest was adjourned reconvening at 6am the following morning.

Although the Americans were highly competitive and anxious not to be beaten by any British team representative, the story goes that they made an exception for Con Leahy, possibly because he was liked by some of the US officials, or maybe because he celebrated his thirtieth birthday just before the competition. Peter O'Connor's biographer records that some Americans brought an exhausted and footsore Con Leahy back to their hotel that first evening, where they gave him a warm bath, an olive-oil infused rub down and a bottle of stout. Where they located a bottle of stout in Athens in 1906 may well be the biggest mystery of all in that story.

When competition resumed the next day, the heights were increased by 2.5 centimetres after every round, which suited Leahy. With the remaining jumpers quickly eliminated, Leahy was the only jumper to clear 1.775 centimetres. He then failed twice at 1.83m. It was the lowest winning height in Olympic high jump history and the world record at the time was 1.97m but that should take nothing from Leahy's win. In those days, jumpers were landing on a bare sand pit with nothing to break their fall and techniques had not evolved. Olympic historian Bill Mallon declared that in the years around 1906, although he held no world records, 'the top high jumper in the world was certainly Ireland's Cornelius 'Con' Leahy.'

With the Olympic title of 1906, Con Leahy achieved a remarkable quadruple of being Irish, English, American and Olympic high jump champion at the same time.

During the 1906 Olympic triple jump, Leahy had difficulty with his run-up, possibly because for part of the evening he was also competing simultaneously in both the triple jump and the high jump. While he was better known as a high jumper, his performance in the triple jump was superb. After five rounds, not only was he in the lead but he had registered the best four jumps in the competition. Only Peter O'Connor was within a foot of Leahy's lead jump as the final round began. With Leahy fouling his last jump, O'Connor put in one huge leap clearing 14 metres and snatching victory from the Limerick man. Despite that, Leahy guarded O'Connor when he climbed a flagpole to wave an Irish flag to celebrate Irish – and not British – domination of the event.

In 1907, Leahy travelled back to the USA where he won the American high jump title at the unusual venue of Jamestown, Virginia. An international exposition was held at Jamestown that year to commemorate the 300th anniversary of the colony; an event forever associated with the story of Pocahontas.

Although Leahy was in his early thirties by the time of the London Olympics, 1908 London Olympics came around, he was still favourite for high jump gold. This time, Irish athletes were very definitely designated as representing 'Great Britain and Ireland'. Leahy qualified for the high jump final with an impressive 1.88 metres, or 6 feet 2 inches in 'old money'. In the final he was pipped by American jumper Harry Porter who cleared 1.90 metres and ended up in a tie for second place with two others who had cleared 1.88m. His brother Pat finished ninth in the same event. If today's scoring system had been used in 1908, Con Leahy could have been second on his own, since he had cleared 1.88m at his first attempt, unlike the other two athletes.

Late in 1908, Con Leahy left Creggane for good, paying for a one-way passage to New York on board the SS *Campania*. The records from Ellis Island show that he arrived on 28 November, with $50 in his pocket. His initial address in New York was 2016 Jerome Avenue, the Bronx, home of John Flanagan the triple Olympic hammer champion and, of course, originally from Kilbreedy, County Limerick. Con was soon joined in the USA by his brother Pat, leaving younger members of the Leahy family to help their mother Mary run the family farm.

In December 1921, Leahy died at the age of just forty-five in Manhattan. In 2006, to mark the 100th anniversary of his Olympic medal win, a memorial was unveiled in Thomas Street, Limerick.

Eamonn Coghlan - King of the Boards on his way to another victory

Robert Heffernan - World champion walker and Olympic medallist

Derval O'Rourke - World Indoor champion and European medallist

Jason Smyth - Unbeaten in Paralympic sprinting throughout his long career

Neil Cusack was the unexpected winner of the 1974 Boston Marathon

Sonia O'Sullivan - Ireland's most successful female athlete

Ronny Delany's unforgettable victory in Melbourne

Bob Tisdall Olympic 400m Hurdles champion and superb all-rounder

Tommy Conneff was one the leading amateur milers of the 19th century in the world

Dr. Pat O'Callaghan two-time Olympic champion was prevented from completing a hat-trick by politics

John J. Daly from Galway was the "Tough of the Track"

Lady Mary Heath was a pioneer both on the ground and in the air

PAT LEAHY
Jumping with Style

Some existing biographies of Pat Leahy mention that he was one of six brothers in a great athletics family. Although certainly true, this fact neglects to mention the three Leahy sisters with at least one of them, Ellie Mary, every bit as good a high jumper as most of her brothers.

The 1901 Census returns suggest that the Leahy family, all ten of them, lived in a thatched stone house of just two rooms, with Pat and his siblings ranging in age from seven to twenty-four. Pat (often known as Paddy) was the second son, aged twenty-three in 1901. Though only 5 foot 9 inches in height, Pat Leahy emerged at the age of seventeen as a talented high jumper well able to jump his own height at that stage in his development. According to Tom Aherne:

'He was universally acknowledged as the most stylish jumper that ever crossed a lath. Beautifully built, he ran like all the Leahys, straight at his leap, rose almost perpendicularly, picked his knees up to his chin, in a most natural fashion, swung around on top with no apparent effort and landed facing his take off as lightly as a thistle down.'

Pat Leahy made his international debut in 1897 at the annual match against Scotland at Powderhall, Edinburgh, when he was aged just twenty. He finished second in the high jump and third in the long jump that first year. A year later, at the RDS, he won the high jump but had to settle for third in the long jump, where Walter Newburn became the first long jumper to clear 24 feet (7.32m). Leahy also won the high jump in this international match in 1899 and 1900 but had to settle for minor placings in the long jump in 1900 and 1901.

It was hard luck for Leahy that there was no hop, step and jump in the Ireland v Scotland match. He was also unlucky to be long jumping at a time when both Walter Newburn and Peter O'Connor were breaking world long jump records. O'Connor would not only win the long jump against Scotland in 1900 and 1901 but break the world record four times in those years. In O'Connor's absence, Pat Leahy won the long jump against Scotland in 1902 and 1903, beating his elder brother Con on both of those occasions. Pat and Con also tied for the high jump victory in the 1902 international match.

Judging any athlete by Irish championships victories is challenging and this is particularly true of Pat Leahy's career, since it ignores the incredible array of prizes he won at major athletics meetings, often against some of the best athletes in the world, who just happened to be Irish as well. In 1888 alone, for instance, Pat Leahy won forty-one jumping prizes at sports meetings in Ireland. His brothers were often among the competition, as were the likes of Newburn, O'Connor and the Ryans of Tipperary.

Another complicating factor was the existence of two annual Irish championships organised by the GAA and the IAAA. Pat Leahy competed at both championships between

1897 and 1903 and in all won eight Irish titles, five in the high jump, two in the long jump and one in the hop, step and jump. In a telling indication of his athletic quality, he also had eleven second placings and two thirds across those three events and the three other 'standing' jumps then contested (long, high and three jumps with weights). He won seven consecutive high-jump titles under GAA rules (1897–1905), four consecutive high-jump titles under IAAA rules (1897–1900, tying with Peter O'Connor in 1900) and long-jump titles under both rules in 1903.

Since Pat Leahy was competing in a period that pre-dated the establishment of the International Amateur Athletic Federation, ratifying records was often a challenge, especially when such records were set at meetings organised by of the GAA, which was not recognised by the AAA in England. For instance, while Leahy jumped 1.97m at a meet in Limerick in July 1898, the height was not ratified as an Irish, British or European record, while the 1.95m he cleared two months later in Millstreet was ratified and considered a European record for many years. Leahy was reported to have cleared 1.96m three times the following year but none of the heights were ratified as a new record.

Pat Leahy won two AAA high jump titles in succession in 1898 and 1899 and was third in the AAA long jump in 1900. Just a week after that latter event, he would become the first Irish-born track and field athlete to win an Olympic medal. This he did on 15 July 1900 in Paris, when on one afternoon, he took second place in the high jump and third place in the long jump. What these results do not show is the single-minded commitment of Pat Leahy in getting to Paris at all.

On the weekend before the Olympic jumping events, the AAA championships had taken place at Stamford Bridge in London. Bizarrely, the top Irish competitors were under the illusion that the Olympic contests in Paris were not to be held until September. While competing in London, they found out that the Paris competitions were only a week away. Alone of the Irish athletes competing in the AAA championships, Pat Leahy decided he would head for Paris. Although he suffered horrendously from sea sickness when making his way to France the following Friday night, he managed to qualify for the long jump final the following morning of 14 July. In winning his medals a day later, he found himself juggling between events because the high jump which had started at 3.45pm was still in progress by the time the long jump final began an hour and a half later.

In Ireland, Leahy had come up against two of the world's top four long jumpers, and in Paris he came up against the other two, Alvin Kraenzlein and Meyer Prinstein, finishing third with a jump of 6.95m, with Prinstein's winning leap of 7.186m; an Olympic record. Had it not been for the seasickness and fixtures mix-up, many have argued that the Irishman would at least have won the high jump in Paris. His second-place height of 1.78m, which was four inches (or twelve centimetres) below the winner, Irving Baxter of USA, was over six inches below what Leahy had cleared several times in Ireland.

One way or another, what cannot be taken from Pat Leahy is that on 15 July 1900, he became the first Irish-born athlete to win Olympic medals. His friend John Flanagan, from further east in County Limerick, won the Olympic hammer title when competing for the USA the following day. On that day, 16 July, Leahy was lining out in the triple jump, in which he finished fourth for 'GB/IRL' although some records omit him, on the basis that he had not entered the event on time!

Pat Leahy's athletic career was relatively short. Though his best long jump of 7.29m came in 1902, from 1903 he no longer participated at Irish championships or at the AAAs, although he was only twenty-six in 1904. More surprisingly still, he came out of what appears to have been five years of semi-retirement in 1908 and was placed ninth in the Olympic high jump at the London Olympics, with only the top eight qualifying for the final jump off. His height that day, 1.778m, was one he had beaten on dozens of previous occasions.

In August 1909, Pat Leahy emigrated to America with his brother Con and in September 1916, it is claimed that he set a new Irish record for three standing jumps at the GAA Games in Chicago. Pat Leahy was just fifty when he died in the USA on 29 December 1927.

OLIVE LOUGHNANE
World Champion Walker

Few Irish athletes can lay claim to have competed in four Olympic Games; walker Olive Loughnane from County Galway is on that select list. After she retired, Loughnane could look back at an athletics career that included six world and two European championships as well as a host of European and World Cup competitions. Of those, one race stands out.

At the 2009 World Championships in Berlin, Germany, the women's 20 km walk could not have hoped for a better backdrop, beginning and ending as it did at the Brandenburg Gate. Olympic and world champion Olga Kaniskina was the clear favourite for gold, while fellow Russian Vera Sokolova was a possible threat, as were the German walker Sabine Krantz and Kjersti Platzer from Norway who had both performed well in competitions prior to the Championships. Italy's Olympic medal winner Elisa Rigaudo and Masumi Fuchise from Japan, World Universities' runner-up from just a month earlier, were other possible for a medal. No one mentioned Ireland's Olive Loughnane.

When Krantz, who had taken an early lead, dropped out halfway into the race and Platzer was disqualified with five kilometres to go, Kaniskina was left as the clear leader and forged on to seal the victory and the distinction of becoming the first woman to win the race walking gold in consecutive World Championships. Finishing forty-nine seconds behind her came the unheralded Irish woman who had walked the perfect race and would take the silver medal.

'I had the ability to really hurt myself – I don't know if there's a nicer way to put it – in order to get the most out of myself,' she told the *Irish Examiner*. 'That was a good talent to have when it mattered: I remember in 2009 feeling I couldn't do another step at 14 km but carrying on.'

Quite rightly Olive was fêted the length and breadth of the country, but the story did not end there. Almost six years later, in January 2015, Kaniskina was disqualified for three years and two months starting from 15 October 2012, with all her results between 15 July 2009 and 16 September 2009, as well as between 30 July 2011 and 8 November 2011 annulled. Anomalies in her biological passport had caught the eyes of the doping authorities.

A year later, Loughnane, by then forty years old, received her gold medal in a ceremony at the 2016 European Athletics Championships in the Netherlands. She was presented with the medal by the IAAF president Sebastian Coe before the Irish national anthem rang out over the Amsterdam stadium, which had been the venue of the 1928 Olympics.

'There's value in sentiment and it was great to share the moment with all the Irish fans here,' said an emotional Olive at the time. Justice was said to be done. But was it? She had been denied that magic moment every athlete dreams of – that of crossing the line in first place, followed by standing at the top of the medal dais, hearing your national anthem ringing out and enjoying the acclaim reserved only for winners. While the medal ceremony seven years later was surely much appreciated, it must have been a saccharin substitute instead of the authentic Demerara sugar.

Svein Arne Hansen, the then European Athletics president was aware of the significance and not shy with his criticism: 'It's a very important signal. I have no sympathy for the athletes who have been cheating. All athletes will also wear bibs saying, "I Run Clean." If they are doing that, it will be very shameful if they are caught afterwards.'

Fired up by the World Championships silver medal, Loughnane continued in the sport. The following year, she failed to finish at the European Championships in Barcelona where the winner was again Kaniskina who would again be deleted from the results because of the subsequent ban. Her Russian teammate Anisya Kirdyapkina was later declared winner and later also banned for doping irregularities, as indeed was Vera Sokolova who finished third that day.

Early in the 2011 season, Loughnane found herself disqualified in the European Cup. It was her first disqualification since the World Championships of 2005. Later that year, her form improved at the World Championships in Daegu, South Korea, a race where three of the leading finishers were subsequently disqualified for doping violations.

One of these was Kaniskina who crossed the line in the gold medal position. She was joined on the banned list by compatriot Anisya Kirdyapkina who finished third, and Ukraine's Olena Shumkina. It meant Loughnane moved up three places to thirteenth. Her focus now switched to the

London Olympics the following year – her fourth Olympics. After sixteen years in the sport and approaching her thirty-sixth birthday, she was determined to go out on a high.

The Olympic year started promisingly for Loughnane with a ninth place in the prestigious Lugano Cup in March, but she failed to finish at the IAAF Challenge in Portugal the following month. A sixth place in the World Cup in May gave confidence for a good performance in London later that summer. Even better in June was a fine second place at the IAAF Challenge in Italy, setting Olive up nicely for the Olympics.

Venue for the 20 km walk was the Mall with Buckingham Palace the perfect backdrop to what would be Loughnane's penultimate competition. Again, Russian athletes dominated with Russians Elena Lashmanova and Kaniskina first and second and again the Russians were later disqualified, as was their Russian teammate Kirdyapkina who finished fifth.

After the medals had been reallocated, the Chinese took all three top places with the gold medal going to Shenjie Qieyang and Loughnane elevated to tenth in the final placings. She was to have one final outing on the international stage, travelling to China in September for an IAAF Challenge over the shorter 10km distance. A ninth place behind China's Wang, who would go on to become Olympic champion in Rio, ended a long and illustrious career.

'For me, the hardest thing in sport is having to perform on the day when it's needed most,' she said in the interview with *The Irish Examiner* in which she reviewed her career. 'It's the physical side more than the mental side because you'd always be up for the race. In training you're trying get it right so that your best day is the day of the race, and that didn't always happen for me.'

'It did in 2008 when I did well in the Olympics and when I won in 2009, but there were other times when I had a good race – but just not at the right time of the year. In 2011, I was going in as a silver medallist, but it just didn't go right for me. We all have a job to do, but you must perform when it matters, and when it doesn't go right for you, and you're in the eye of the public...'

It had been a long career at the highest level for Olive who was born in County Cork on 14 January 1976, the eldest of seven siblings. The family moved to Galway when she was a child. She started training in athletics when she was thirteen but did not move to competitive race walking until six years later.

A career-long member of the Loughrea Athletic Club she has paid tribute to the 'inspirational' support she received from the club. Although she loved running with relay and cross-country teams Loughnane was attracted to race walking because, among other reasons, it combined a technical side with endurance.

From the outset she had wanted to compete at the highest level and was encouraged to do so after seeing Jimmy McDonald finish sixth in the 50 km walk at the 1992 Olympics in Barcelona. Getting fit again for competition after the birth of her first child in 2006 was the greatest challenge of her career while her world title in 2009 was the highlight – even if she only received the medal, she was due long after the event. Because it was her first Olympics, the Sydney Games of 2000 retained a special place in her memory since it was such a big deal to qualify. In 2016, Loughnane was appointed to the board of Sport Ireland and continues to serve the sport of athletics away from the roads and tracks.

Olive Loughnane has etched her name indelibly in the annals of Irish athletics, not just because of her longevity but also for her consistency, competing with distinction in four Olympic Games, six consecutive World Championships and representing Ireland at the European Athletics Championships twice.

KEN MCARTHUR
'I Came Here to Win or to Die'

When the sixty-eight runners lined up for the 1:45pm start of the marathon at 1912 Olympics in Stockholm, the heat was oppressive, with most of the runners wearing linen caps or handkerchiefs to protect their heads from the sun. A Swedish athlete, running on home turf, was strongly expected to do well, while the Finnish team, as always, was strong. Although Great Britain had sent twelve runners, four did not start, and the main British hopes centred on Fred Lord and Septimus Francom. Leitrim-born James Duffy, who would go on to win the Boston Marathon two years later, carried Canadian hopes.

With the memory of Dorando Pietri's disqualification in London four years earlier still fresh, the Swedish organisers tried to frame rules to prevent it happening again. In London, the Italian had entered the White City Stadium well clear of the field and then collapsed. After he was assisted rubber-legged to the finish line, USA officials lodged an objection. Pietri was disqualified and their man Johnny Hayes was awarded the gold medal. Both of Hayes's parents were natives of Ireland with a statue erected to his memory in Nenagh, County Tipperary.

To stop a reoccurrence of the incident, the Swedish organising committee decided that no-one should accompany the runners and the entire route was strictly monitored to ensure that no-one interfered with or hindered any of the competitors. A runner could only receive such assistance on the direction of a member of the International Olympic Committee. Places of refreshment, attended by appointed officials, were set up along the route. At one of these occurred an incident that would prove crucial in deciding the winner of the race and remains contentious right down to the present day.

With admirable Scandinavian thoroughness, the Swedes literally and metaphorically left no stone unturned in preparing a 40.2km course – 1.8 km shorter than the now standard distance of 42km. When the initial plan for a circular course proved impossible, they opted for an out and back journey with a turn at the village church in the village of Sollentuna. Distance markers were posted at five kilometre intervals and medical points were set up at five and fifteen kilometres to administer assistance if required. Gangs of workmen walked the course in the days before the race to remove any large stones and watered the dust which became thick and choking during the summer months.

All was ready when the field was dispatched from in front of the royal box with Alexis Ahlgren of Sweden leading the runners out of the stadium and Finland's Tatu Kolehmainen on his shoulder. At the five kilometre mark, Kolehmainen, whose brother Hannes would later write his name in athletics history as a four times Olympic winner, was fractionally ahead of Ahlgren and the Italian Carlo

Speroni while the South Africans were back in the main pack. By fifteen kilometres, Kolehmainen had dropped Ahlgren with the Springbok representatives Ken McArthur and Chris Gitsham in the minor medal positions. Britain's Lord held down fourth place ahead of Ahlgren with another Swede Sigfrid Jacobsson just behind him.

At the turn, the three leaders refused to take any refreshment despite the heat and humidity. Behind them, the conditions were taking their toll with a third of the field already having retired. Gitsham moved to the front but despite his best efforts could not shake off Kolehmainen, nor for that matter his South African compatriot McArthur. Coming through the field were the USA runners led by the native American Lewis Tewanima in seventh place with Gaston Strobino and Joseph Forshaw, bronze medal winner three years earlier, not far behind him.

With about 8km to go, Kolehmainen, realising that victory was beyond him, walked off the course, leaving the two South Africans well clear at the front of the field. By now the American Strobino was challenging Jacobsson for third place. At Stocksund, the last control station before the stadium, Gitsham and McArthur were still running strongly with Strobino straining every sinew to close the minute advantage held by the leaders. For Canada, Jimmy Duffy had now passed Speroni and was in fifth place.

When the leaders paused for refreshment in the final stages, Gitsham stopped for a drink while McArthur declined, stealing a crucial few metres on his teammate that was to increase to almost a minute by the time he entered the stadium. Despite looking visibly wilted, he was reinvigorated by a shout from the stands of 'Hurrah for County Antrim' and crossed the line in a time of 2 hours, 36 minutes 54.8 seconds for 40.2km course. Gitsham came in slightly less than a minute later with Strobino fifty seconds back in third place and fellow American Andrew Sockalexis fourth. Duffy in fifth place was only three and half minutes off a medal spot.

Tragedy stuck when Portugal's Francisco Lázaro collapsed at the thirty kilometre mark with a body temperature of 41° C. Initially severe dehydration was suspected due to the high temperatures, but it was later discovered that he had covered large portions of his body with suet to prevent sunburn, which interfered with his body's natural ability to sweat; it killed him. A street was named after him in Lisbon.

Only thirty-four of the sixty-eight starters had completed the course although that number would increase to thirty-five in unusual circumstances. Shizo Kanakuri, weakened by the long journey from Japan, and having problems with the local food, fainted during the race and, embarrassed from his 'failure' returned to Japan without notifying race officials. Swedish authorities considered him missing for fifty years before discovering that he was alive and well in Japan and had competed in subsequent Olympic marathons. In 1967, he was invited back by Swedish television to complete the marathon which he did, giving him the unbeaten record of taking 54 years 8 months 6 days, 5 hours 32 minutes and 20.3 seconds to complete the distance!

It had been a long road for Kennedy Kane (Ken) McArthur born 10 February 1881 near the small village Dervock in County Antrim. He seems to have caught the running 'bug' while working as a postman around his native area and covering a considerable distance by foot each day. Although he frequently raced the train six miles (10 kilometres) to the town of Ballymoney along the narrow gauge railway, there is no record of him competing in a race. Instead, he played for Ballymoney Football Club against teams from Ballymena and was said to be popular with all he met.

Around 1900, he emigrated to South Africa to serve in the South African Constabulary set up by Robert Baden-Powell to look after law and order in some areas of the country during what was to be the last two years of the Boer War. Baden-Powell would later found the Boy Scouts movement. While most of the Irish volunteers returned to their native country after the war, McArthur stayed on after falling in love with a young woman called Joey Louw who he had met in Potchefstroom.

As a police officer in Johannesburg, he rarely rode his patrol on horseback, preferring to walk his rounds and eventually, starting to take athletics seriously and winning the Transvaal half mile, one mile and five mile track championships. At 1.88m (6'3") tall and weighing 77kg (170lbs), McArthur cut an imposing figure in athletics competitions and yet despite his height, was said to run with a relatively short and low stride that covered the ground with deceptive ease.

In April 1908, McArthur first raced a near-marathon distance of twenty miles in Johannesburg winning in 2 hrs 30 mins 30 secs. A year earlier, when back in Ireland on holiday, he had finished third in a seventeen-mile *Go As You*

Please. From then on until 1910, he ran five marathons in South Africa, winning them all and defeating 1908 Olympic marathon silver medal winner Charles Hefferon along the way. His Olympic marathon win in 1912 was his sixth victory at the distance and he would retire undefeated after suffering a career-ending foot injury in 1914 although he had indicated that he would not race again competitively after Stockholm.

He finally married Joey Louw on 4 May 1921, almost two decades after their initial meeting. After he retired from the police, he and his wife came to live in Dervock but never settled, returning to South Africa after five years. There McArthur died suddenly on 13 June 1960, aged seventy-nine years. Today, the stadium in Potchefstroom is called after him and his name still appears frequently in the South African sporting press.

PAT MCDONALD
All-Round Weight Thrower

Standing 6' 4" (1.93m) and weighing about 300lbs (136kg) in his prime, Pat McDonald, from Doonbeg in County Clare was the epitome of a larger-than-life character. One of the celebrated Irish-American weight throwers known as the 'Irish Whales', his huge bulk may have disguised his abilities as a superb weight thrower and technician. Born on 29 July 1878, he had not really competed seriously in Ireland as a young man before emigrating to the USA when in his early twenties.

There is a more curious reason why you will not find McDonald's name in Irish historical documents. When he and his siblings arrived in Ellis Island, the immigration officials allocated them a name badge with the name McDonald, not their true name of McDonnell. Fearing immediate deportation if they made a fuss, they accepted the name McDonald.

McDonald's huge frame meant that he had little trouble finding work in New York as a warehouseman, working sixty-six hours a week for a twelve-dollar wage before he decided to follow in the footsteps of many Irishmen before him joining the New York Police Department in 1905. In those early years of the motor car, a traffic policeman of

McDonald's height could prove useful, so he was assigned one of the most famous and busiest junctions in the city at Times Square, in downtown Manhattan. Because McDonald was three inches taller than a 1912 Model T Ford, a reporter wrote that he was like a 'living Statue of Liberty' at Times Square. 'Never in the record of swirling traffic of autos did any chauffeur ever venture to ignore McDonald's great bulk,' he added.

Discovering the world of athletics and subsequently joining the Irish-American Athletic Club in Long Island City, McDonald took a particular interest in throwing the 56lb weight, an event which had long been popular back at home in Munster. He also learnt his trade as a shot putter though generally he found the shot a little 'light' for him. When asked in 1915 to write an article on putting the shot for the book *How to Become a Weight Thrower*, McDonald explained that he trained with an 18lb shot, so that the normal 16lb one would feel lighter still when in competition.

In 1907, McDonald, at twenty-eight years old, won his first AAU junior 56lbs shot title. After placing second to the great Californian Olympic champion, Ralph Rose at the AAU championships in 1909 and 1910, he took the title in Rose's absence in 1911 and defeated him at the 1912 championships. By the end of his career, McDonald would amass a total of six AAU shot put titles and an incredible ten titles for throwing the 56lb weight. He is also the oldest AAU champion ever winning the last of his titles in the 56lb weight throw in 1933 at fifty-five years of age.

Much of McDonald's early career pre-dated the standardisation of athletics weights that the International

Amateur Athletics Federation would put in place. Accordingly, he managed to set several 'world records' in events which no longer exist. For instance, you will find him setting a world 24lb shot record at Celtic Park in 1911 of 118.61m. The following year, he set a 12lb shot 'record' at the Eccentric Firemen's Games in Celtic Park which was disallowed because it was not measured with a steel tape. In 1914, at a Laurel Hill benefit in aid of Patrick Pearse's St. Enda's school in Dublin, McDonald broke the 18lb shot put outdoor record with 14.90m. The *New York Times* wrote on 27 July 1914: 'The accomplishment of the task came as a great surprise to the followers of McDonald for during the last month he has done little in the way of preparation.' In 1918, when almost 40 years old, he set a world record in the 35lb weight with 19.33m.

In McDonald's time, New York and specifically Madison Square Garden, hosted popular indoor athletics meetings, some of them run by the Irish-American A.C. (I-AAC). McDonald's specialist events were tailor-made for indoors meets, where running races were restricted and events like the hammer and discus impossible. New Yorkers could watch McDonald stroll the eight blocks or so from his Times Square beat to 'the Garden' for evening meetings, having a word with every newsboy at every street corner. At that venue alone, he broke the world indoor 56lb throwing record and set non-IAAF records for both an 18lb and a 24lb shot put.

It was at the Olympic Games that Pat McDonald made probably his greatest impact on world athletics. In the Stockholm Games of 1912, McDonald won the shot put, defeating his great friend and rival Ralph Rose and breaking the Olympic record with a put of 15.34m. He also took part in a two-handed shot event the following day, where athletes threw with each hand and their combined total of left and right hands was calculated; the only time this event was included in the Olympic programme. Given that McDonald had little or no experience whatsoever of putting with his left hand, he did remarkably well to finish second to Rose, the world record holder in that event. Indeed, McDonald had led the competition until Rose's very last throw.

During First World War years, the I-AAC was in serious decline although its most consistent performer was the evergreen McDonald. Had the proposed Berlin Games of 1916 gone ahead, there is little doubt that McDonald would have been a champion once more at least. At Antwerp in 1920, McDonald hit the news away from track and field even before the athletics had started. A heavily publicised 'mutiny' by America's athletes, unhappy with their living quarters on board the US army transport ship *Princess Matoika*, saw Athea-born athlete Dan Ahearne as one of the prime rebels. While American Olympic Council members, US army athletes and female team members were given first-class cabins, the remaining male athletes were relegated to troop quarters on lower decks. Training conditions were less than ideal, with rough seas adding to the athletes' misery.

Although the distance runners could train by making multiple circuits of the ship, the sprinters and hurdlers had only a 64 metre cork track to work with, while the javelin throwers resorted to throwing out to sea, tethering their implements to the ship by rope. Many members of the team either fell ill or picked up injuries. Pat McDonald, who had himself sprained a thumb while tossing a medicine ball on the ship's rolling deck, helped resolve the dispute and secured better accommodation for the team after it arrived in Antwerp and for the trip home. Underlining the esteem in which McDonald was held, he was chosen as the US team flag bearer, an honour repeated in 1924 at the Paris Games

When the programme for the Antwerp Olympics was announced, McDonald had been delighted to discover that his favourite 56lb event was on the programme and he had concentrated his training heavily for that event. As a result, he only finished fourth in the men's shot put. In the 56lb, he was a clear winner beating Limerick man Paddy Ryan into second place and becoming the oldest Olympic athletic champion, less than a month short of his forty-second birthday. To this day, he remains the oldest athletics champion at any Games. Since the 56lb weight event was never held after 1920, Pat McDonald has already spent over a century as a 'reigning' Olympic champion, and his 1920 distance of 11.26.5m is technically still an Olympic record.

McDonald rose to the rank of captain in the NYPD and concluded a career of forty-one years before retiring in 1946. When he died in 1954 at the age of seventy-five, he was interred at Gate of Heaven Cemetery in New York. Arthur Daley, a *New York Times* journalist, wrote on McDonald's death: 'Pat is dead now, that gargantuan laughter forever stilled and that lilting brogue no longer delighting the ear… when he laughed everything shook. It started as a low rumble down deep, like lava stirring in the pit of a volcano. Then came the eruption, and it engulfed everything before it in irresistible surge. He had the snow-white hair, the red cheeks, and the twinkling blue eyes of Santa Claus. He was twice as big, of course, but also left happiness behind him wherever he went'.

In 2012, on the centenary of his first Olympic success, McDonald was inducted into the US athletics Hall of Fame. He is commemorated by a large stone memorial near Doonbeg, County Clare.

JOHN MCGOUGH
'The Runner' McGough

Early on Easter Saturday 1906, 14 April, John McGough and his friend and training partner William Anderson left Glasgow by train for London and after an overnight stay in London, met up with the rest of the British Olympic team at Victoria train station on Monday morning.

After a short 50 mile train journey to Newhaven, they took the ferry to the French port of Dieppe before starting a gruelling journey in an overcrowded train to Turin, Italy. Next was another train trip, this time to Bari and then the seaport of Brindisi on the Adriatic Sea.

By this time, it was Wednesday, and all the travellers were weary, thanks to the lack of sleep and little food and water. In Brindisi, they boarded the *Baron Call* for Greece but because of unseasonal sea storms, made an unscheduled stop in the Albanian town of Santa Quarante, then part of the Ottoman Empire. When they finally arrived at Corfu, they were welcomed by a band and enjoyed an evening of entertainment which was a welcome relief after the rigours of the journey. Next morning, they were back on board the *Baron Call* for the journey to Patras, arriving the following day. Because the boat could not enter the shallow harbour, the party was taken ashore by small craft to catch the train for Athens at the local station.

After a full seven days of travel, McGough and Anderson finally set foot in the Greek capital and were taken to the Zappeion building where athletes taking part in the Games – over 900 of them – were housed and fed. They had just a day to recover before the opening ceremony on 21 April. Fortunately, the athletics competitions did not start until the following day and McGough had until Wednesday before he competed in the first of the three events he had entered. Drawn in the fourth and final heat of the 800m, he failed to follow the early pace of Paul Pilgrim from the United States, the eventual gold medal winner and defending Olympic champion, and stepped off the track before the finish to concentrate on the 5-mile track race later that day; an event held only in 1906 and in the London Olympics of 1908.

Twenty-five athletes turned up for the longer race, which consisted of almost twenty laps of the stadium track. After four miles, McGough was fifth but although he completed the distance, he is not listed in the top eight. No doubt he was disappointed, but he had at least acclimatised himself to the eccentricities of the elongated horseshoe shaped four hundred metre circuit with long straights and bends so tight they were virtually turn-arounds. Worse still was the surface made of loose sand and ashes which, without an underlying layer of clay, made the going soft and heavy.

McGough was determined to make amends in the 1500m which he regarded as his best distance and was scheduled for two days later the Friday. Again, a good entry of twenty runners checked in to take their tilt at the gold medal. Given the size of the entry, it was decided to hold two heats with the final to be decided on Monday. McGough was drawn in the second race and, after sitting back in fifth place for most of the distance, came through in the home straight to take what seemed a comfortable victory. In the opening heat, the defending champion James Lightbody, who had also won the 800m and steeplechase at the St. Louis Games two years earlier, easily qualified in first place, which McGough can hardly have failed to notice.

In the final two days later, New York police officer George Bonhag set the early pace, with Greg Wheatley from Australia second and another American Harvey Cohn third. Lightbody, cruising just behind the leading trio, waited until the final bend to unleash his kick which caught McGough, sitting at the back in the pack, totally unawares. Despite a devastating turn of speed down the home straight which saw him close the gap on Lightbody to eight-tenths of a second by the finish line, McGough had to settle for the silver medal in a time of 4:12.8. Little did he realise it would be another 115 years before a Scot won a medal in an Olympic 1500m.

Although he represented Scotland throughout his athletics career, John McGough (McGeough) was born in Armagh City on 20 January 1881. His father Thomas and mother Bridget had moved there from their native Castleblayney in County Monaghan shortly after their marriage a little over a year earlier. They would not remain long in Armagh taking the boat to Glasgow when baby John was only six months old.

A shoemaker by trade Thomas, a stranger in town, had not managed to earn a living in Armagh and like so many before, he and his wife felt there may be a better life for them among their own kind in Glasgow. That dream was to be dashed quickly with the family only finding accommodation at 100 Rottenrow in one of the city's notorious Gorbals tenements. In the years ahead, the family was to increase to seven with the birth of six more children although one of these was to succumb to an unspecified illness.

The McGoughs, as they were now known, fell on even tougher times when Thomas turned to alcohol and was admitted to the Barnhill Poor House. Although later released, he had become delusional and would die on 28 January 1900 at just 42 years of age, leaving John, at nineteen, the family's principal bread winner. By this time, John had been working for six years, first as a messenger for the Post Office and later as a fully-fledged postal worker, a secure job in uncertain times.

As a mail carrier, McGough had a lot of walking to do, covering at least ten miles a day and sometimes even double that, carrying a heavy mailbag slung over his shoulder or pushing a cart laden with parcels. It was no surprise that in 1900 he should join an athletics club, specifically Bellahouston Harriers, a body long associated with postal workers. Although still a novice, McGough won his first open race in July of the following year at the Clydesdale Harriers sports off a 40 yard handicap. The *Glasgow Herald* reported that 'a comparatively unknown man in J. McGough, Bellahouston Harriers, 40 yards, won the half mile.' The following month, he was once again placed at the Celtic FC sports, where he finished second in the mile handicap off 60 yards. Even at this early stage, it was obvious that he was destined for bigger and better things.

In 1902, he had quickly announced his arrival as the leading Scottish middle-distance runner when he won the Scottish one mile and four miles titles. He went one better the following year at Ibrox Stadium winning the 880 yard, one mile and four miles, the only time that anyone had won all three of those distances at the Scottish championships. In total, he would win a total of twelve Scottish titles, three Irish championships and, of course, his Olympic silver medal. At one time he held every Scottish record from 1,000 yards to four miles.

His career didn't end after Athens, with McGough continuing to race prolifically all over the UK. Between 1901 and 1911, he averaged more than twenty wins a year, many of them handicap races where he was the scratch man. He also competed in Ireland occasionally and at the Irish Championships of 1905, won both the two and three mile titles. He also won the mile in 1907.

At the London Olympics of 1908, McGough, with a damaged ankle well strapped up, could only place third in the 1500m semi-finals and did not advance to the final.

After his retirement, McGough continued to work as a postman until he was appointed to the position of assistant trainer to his old coach Bob Davies at Celtic FC. His time at Celtic ended in 1914 when he went to Manchester to assist Davies with the training of the Manchester United players. When league football was suspended due to the outbreak of the First World War, he returned to his native Ireland and became a farmer in Annagleve, near Castleblayney, where he became known simply as the 'Runner' McGough.

McGough became involved with the Gaelic Athletic Association, helping found the Blackhill Emeralds Club, and elected to the Monaghan County board. Later he would train the Cavan football team which won the All-Ireland final in the New York Polo Grounds in 1947. He continued his work as masseur to many teams until well into his eighties. He died the 23 April 1967 and is buried in the family plot at St. Mary's Cemetery, Castleblayney.

A special programme of events held to mark the centenary of Blackhill Emeralds in 2016 included a John McGough's Sports Day featuring the inaugural running of the John McGough Mile.

MATT MCGRATH
Prince of Whales

As a small child sitting by the fireside at his home in Curraghmore, Boher, near the town of Nenagh in County Tipperary, Matt McGrath would hear tales of great Irish athletes such as Tom Kiely, who was a special favourite, Jim Mitchell and the Davin brothers.

According to his own stories, the foundation for his great strength was established in his early years when he took up the pastime of putting the stone from the shoulder, and the Irish games of hurling and football. Helping develop his stamina were the four mile walks – or runs – to and from Boher National School each day and his habit of hunting hares and rabbits on the mountains of Tipperary. He frequently walked over twenty-five miles in a day, jumping fences and farm boundaries along the way.

As a youth in Tipperary McGrath had allegedly walked ten miles to see hammer thrower John Flanagan in action at a sports meeting. After he returned home, he repaired to a field with an old-fashioned hammer in an attempt to turn with it in the Flanagan-style.

McGrath, born 20 December 1875, had a lifelong fascination with physical culture and the male form. Physical strength, McGrath believed, was a 'God-sent gift that brought with it a duty to develop it, as would a musician, a sculptor, a poet or a painter …a man's body was the temple of his soul, and to have that temple as it should be, its possessor should strive for its perfection physically as well as spiritually.'

When McGrath emigrated to New York as a teenager in the 1890s, he had yet to become seriously involved in competitive athletics, although he appears to have won a half-mile race in the parish athletic meeting in Killaloe and the 100 yards and long jump at another meet in Portroe; a leap of 6.55m was his most noteworthy achievement.

In the USA, McGrath worked as a blacksmith, bartender and salesman until joining the New York police force on the advice of his police captain father-in-law in 1902. At this time, he lived in East 90th Street, close to the Pastime Athletic Club's grounds and it was there that he became reacquainted with John Flanagan. Hammer throwing in his view required 'insistent intelligent' practice 'to acquire speed in restricted space, the control, poise and equilibrium of the body, and [to] learn how to make the sublime effort without losing balance or breaking the rules.' Over the next few years, Flanagan, McGrath and Con Walsh would trade records and titles at closely-fought competitions held all over the USA and Canada.

In 1906, McGrath competed in the Metropolitan Junior Championship at the Pastime Athletic Club's grounds winning his first hammer title with a throw of 46.73m. In 1907, he moved to south Brooklyn and 'purchased a set of weights, and began to train on a self-outlined routine, making the mistakes peculiar to novices.' He attracted the attention of James Mitchell who was 'generous with his advice and suggestions' and was the only one 'who made known to me the finer points of the game and how to take proper care of myself'.

Influenced by Mitchell, he joined the New York Athletic Club and in 1907, won the USA hammer with 49.12m at the AAU Junior Championships at Norfolk, Virginia. He followed this up by winning the Canadian title with a world best throw of 52.91m. In July 1907, he had already thrown the hammer 53.54m at the Tipperary Games in New York's Celtic Park, which because no AAU officials were in attendance, could not be ratified as a world best.

McGrath would twice surpass this distance in the next couple of years, when again technical issues prevented their recognition. A throw of 54.56m in 1908 was ruled out because the officials did not have a steel measuring tape, while one of 54.05m at Celtic Park on 16 May 1909 was deemed ineligible because the throwing circle lacked a surrounding steel rim.

McGrath won the first of his seven AAU hammer titles in 1908 and followed this with wins in 1910, 1912, 1918, 1922, 1925 and 1926. He also added seven 56lb weight throwing titles to the collection winning in 1913, 1916, 1918 and four-in-a-row from 1922-25, and four 56lb weight for height indoor titles in 1907, 1909, 1911 and 1915.

McGrath was little more than a novice and carrying an injury when he travelled to London for the 1908 Olympics, finishing second behind John Flanagan in the hammer final. After travelling to Ireland after the Olympics, he refused to compete with the USA team in the international against Ireland because it was organised by the IAAA. He did compete in his native Nenagh on 9 August in a GAA-organised meet where he established three world best marks in non-standard events. He threw the hammer from a 9-foot (2.74m) circle a distance of 53.64m; the 56lb weight from a 9-foot circle to 11.96m and the 56lb weight for height to a new world best of 4.82m.

The year 1909 proved pivotal for hammer throwing. On 21 June, John Flanagan threw 180 feet (54.86 m) in American League Park, become the first thrower to reach this mark. McGrath answered with an exhibition throw of 183' 8" at the Tipperarymen's Games, Ulmer Park, New York, although as an exhibition it would not be entertained as a record. Then on 24 July, Flanagan amazed the athletic world when, after close on two decades in competition, he threw a phenomenal 184' 4" at the Clan-na-Gael Games, in New Haven, Connecticut. McGrath was beaten by 13 feet and Con Walsh by 20 feet.

More than two years then passed before new ground was broken when on 29 October 1911, McGrath obliterated Flanagan's world best with a throw of 187' 4" (57.10m) at the Games of the Galwaymen's Association in Celtic Park. Fearing that the wire handle might stretch and exceed the stipulated length of 4" if he attempted to throw it again, he handed his hammer to a member of the AAU committee and took no further throws.

In 1912, at the Stockholm Olympics, McGrath overwhelmed the opposition with one of the all-time great Olympic field event performances. He set a new Olympic best with his opening effort and all six of his throws exceeded

John Flanagan's 1908 record. His final and winning throw of 54.74m was 6.02m better than the 48.39m of second placed Duncan Gillis from Canada. It remains the greatest winning margin in Olympic hammer throwing history and would have been good enough to win silver thirty-six years later at the London Olympics of 1948.

As a 44-year-old, McGrath was still a major force in hammer throwing and was narrowly defeated by Paddy Ryan for the AAU title (50.68m to 51.61m). The two Irish-born throwers were expected to battle for the gold medal at the 1920 Antwerp Olympics, but McGrath suffered a knee injury in the qualifying round and was forced to withdraw after two throws. His best throw of 46.67m was still good enough for fifth place. McGrath again qualified for the USA team in 1924 and won his third Olympic medal when he finished second with a 50.84m effort. At the age of 48 years and 203 days, he became and remains the oldest medal winner and finalist in Olympic track and field history and the oldest ever competitor in Olympic hammer throwing.

After the 1924 Games, he again visited Nenagh and competed in the first Tailteann Games winning the hammer title with a throw of 49.96m. Incredibly, in 1928, aged fifty-two, he came within an ace of becoming the only American track and field athlete to compete in five Olympic Games.

Away from sport, McGrath's career in the NYPD flourished. He was promoted to sergeant in 1913, lieutenant in 1918, captain in 1926, deputy inspector in 1930 and inspector in 1936, and twice received the New York police Medal of Valour. Matt McGrath died of cancer in St Clare's Hospital, Manhattan, aged sixty-five, on 29 January 1941.

As he lay in hospital, the New York police closed off the street to ensure that a much-loved servant of the city could breathe his final moments in peace.

In his home county, McGrath was never forgotten and in September 2002, statues of three Olympic champions from Tipperary – Johnny Hayes and Bob Tisdall as well as McGrath – were unveiled by Ronnie Delany in Nenagh. In April 2010, a plaque remembering McGrath was unveiled at Boher Parish Hall.

TERRY MCHUGH
Evergreen Olympian

It's probably safe to say that before Terry McHugh arrived on the scene, javelin throwing in Ireland barely existed. While earlier generations had won Olympic and other titles and set world records in the hammer and 56lb disciplines but also in the shot and discus, the javelin was the poor relation of Irish throwing, although there had been a few ripples. Dominating the event in the 1920s was Sean Keavy with a best of 49.2m at the National Championships of 1927 in Croke Park, Dublin. In 1958, John Lawson had finally brought Ireland into the 60 metre club with a throw of 61.849m in Santry. Denis Twomey improved that to 65.735m in 1964 and Pat Moore threw 67.41m in 1974.

On a chilly wet afternoon in April 1982, McHugh moved Irish javelin throwing into a new dimension when he threw 71.30m at the old UCD track in Belfield. Later he would become Ireland's first, and so far, only 80 metre thrower. With 48 international appearances to his credit, accumulated over twenty-three years, McHugh is also Ireland's most capped athlete ever.

Quite where McHugh's interest in javelin throwing came from is unclear. With his father Frank a miner from County Donegal, who had met and married his wife while working in the mines of Scotland at Perth, the family moved frequently while the young Terry was growing up. First stop was Wicklow, where Frank worked with Avoca mines, with the family then moving to the Silvermines mines in north Tipperary and later to Tara Mines in County Meath.

In Tipperary, where McHugh was born on 22 August 1963, the family also moved from house to house several times before settling in McDonagh Street in Nenagh. While in Nenagh, Terry, with his older sister Shirley, his two brothers and his cousins, joined Nenagh Olympic, the local athletic club, where he was coached by Sean Naughton. At first, he competed mostly in sprinting and hurdles and in June 1974 came his first athletics victory when he won the boys' under-11 hurdles race at the county juvenile championships. He went on to compete at national juvenile level and at the Community Games where he would win a silver medal in the U-16 discus – his first throws medal.

After seven years in Nenagh, the McHugh family moved to Navan, County Meath in the summer of 1974 where Terry continued developing as an athlete while a student at St Patrick's Classical School and, as a member of Navan AC, won the Irish under-15 javelin title in 1978 with a throw of 48.16m. He returned to Nenagh in August 1979 to win the under-16 national pentathlon title, although by this stage, he was already specialising in the javelin. He would later credit his shot putting older brother James with 'sponsoring' his first javelin. In 1980, McHugh won the Irish under-17 javelin title in Navan, with a throw of 59.16m using a 700g spear.

Disaster struck in 1981 when a serious back injury requiring surgery almost ended McHugh's career before it had properly started; two screws in his back are a legacy of that operation. He was soon back in training, and his first senior record in the javelin came on 24 April 1982 when, at the age of eighteen, he smashed both Pat Moore's Irish senior record of 67.41m and his own junior mark with a throw of 71.34m in Dublin. By this time, McHugh was working in Dublin and in the evenings, studying for a diploma in industrial engineering at Rathmines College of Commerce.

In July 1984, and by now a member of Dublin City Harriers, McHugh competed in the Irish Athletics Championships for the first time, winning the javelin and beginning a world record sequence of twenty-one consecutive titles that ended only with his retirement in 2004. During this time, McHugh also won the national javelin title in Switzerland in 1999 and 2000, holding championship records in both countries. His throw of 82.75m set at Crystal Palace London on 5 August 2000 remains the national javelin record although in a match between Ireland, England and Russia on 14 June 1991 at the University of Limerick, McHugh had won the javelin with a throw of 84.54m. Counting as an Irish record at the time, the rough-tailed javelin he used, then legal, was replaced at the end of that year, annulling the mark.

With Dan Kennedy as his coach, McHugh competed at his first Olympics on 24 September 1988 in Seoul, South Korea finishing twenty-second in the javelin. It was to be the first of six Olympic Games, summer and winter – Seoul 1988, Barcelona 1992, Atlanta 1996 and Sydney 2000 in the summer games and Albertville 1992 and Nagano 1998 in the winter games where he competed in the bobsleigh.

His best international performances came at the 1993 World Championships in Stuttgart, Germany, where he finished tenth with a 76.22 effort and at the 1994 European Championships in Helsinki, Finland, where he finished seventh with a throw of 80.46m. His final international outing came at the European Championships of 2002.

In 1992, McHugh competed in both summer and Olympic Olympics in the same year – a unique achievement in Irish sport and one that will never be eclipsed since it was the last time summer and winter Olympics were held in one year.

He had been recruited for the bobsleigh at the Seoul Olympics in 1988 by the rower Pat McDonagh where the pair were both competing. After much adventure, his winter Olympic debut four years later in Albertville, France, only came after he had fractured his kneecap while training with McDonagh. The pair worked around the injury and finished 32nd of 46 sleds – ahead of Yugoslavia and both 'Cool Running' Jamaican sleds. Although the Irish Olympic Council refused to entertain the idea of an Irish sled competing at the next Games in Lillehammer 1994, they relented four years later for the Nagano Games, where McHugh carried the Irish flag in the opening ceremony and, with sprinter Jeff Pamplin as his brakeman, finished 27th in two-man bob and 29th in the four-man bob; the first, and so far only, time an Irish four-man bob has competed at the Olympics.

Demonstrating his versatility, McHugh also played Olympic handball at international level for Ireland as well as national league basketball.

After 1998, McHugh concentrated on athletics again and was Irish track and field captain for 1999. He never shied away from controversy, outlining the increasing difficulties throwers faced in a nation where, at the time, middle distance running reigned supreme. 'In 2000 I had to fight tooth-and-nail to be allowed throw javelin in Santry because they were using it as a football pitch. There is still no suitable training centre for field events in the country which helps explain why our standards are so low,' he would say. *Plus ça change*.

Until 1999, McHugh had been a member of every squad for a major championship since 1987 but fell more than three metres short of a B qualifying standard for the World Championships of 1999 in Seville with a best throw of 74.24 metres.

McHugh, now aged 37, was a surprise inclusion in the Irish team for the 2001 World Championships having failed to achieve a qualifying mark of 82.50; his 82.75 metres from a year earlier which had qualified him for the Sydney Olympics was considered.

He competed for the last time at the National Championships in 2004 winning the javelin with a throw of 67.27m

After he retired from competitive athletics, McHugh, by now based in Lucerne, Switzerland, with his Swiss wife Daniela and their son, turned his hand to coaching and the Swiss federation duly appointed him national javelin and discus coach in 2005. A year later, McHugh became the first non-Swiss citizen to be awarded the Swiss Coach of the Year award. One of his charges, Simon Wieland, won the men's javelin at the 2019 European U20 championships with a mighty 79.44m throw and is a three times national champion. Aside from his coaching duties, McHugh, is also the director and manager of the annual international Lucerne athletics meeting. He occasionally picks up a javelin with a respectable effort of 58.79 dating from 2012 when he was 48.

In 2022, Athletics Ireland gave McHugh a special recognition award. He remembered those who had helped him along the way – his brother James, his first coach Sean Naughton, Dan Kennedy, his coach for twenty-five years, British coach John Trower and fellow Olympian Nicky Sweeney. In 2022, the Irish men's javelin title was won with a throw of 64.55 by 20-year-old Conor Cusack of Lake District AC in County Mayo, with five of the fifteen entries throwing over 50 metres and a couple now throwing over seventy metres.

Has McHugh's successor arrived?

CATHERINA MCKIERNAN
Marathon Supremo

By a strange twist of fate, Irish marathon record holder Catherina McKiernan was born on 30 November 1969 in County Cavan – just two days after her great contemporary Sonia O'Sullivan. Yet their backgrounds couldn't be more different. O'Sullivan, brought up in Cobh in County Cork would use the steps and steep climbs of her town when training; for McKiernan her initial training ground were the grassy fields of the family's 90 acre farm at Cornafean, about ten miles outside Cavan town.

McKiernan was the youngest of seven children, growing up with three sisters and three brothers. Her mother, originally from Longford, baked her own bread and kept hens and turkeys, with the family well fed thanks to its own milk, beef and vegetables. McKiernan's father John was a member of the local beagle hunt, with his children often joining him on tramps around the local hills.

Growing up in rural Ireland, the boys played football and the girls camogie as well as any sport that featured on the television at the time, as McKiernan would later relate. While at Loreto Cavan, she became a mainstay of the school's camogie team, helping it to an intermediate championships title and running around the family fields to keep fit. Only in her late teens did the possibility of running races come up and at the 1987 All-Ireland Schools Cross-Country Championships held at Mallusk, outside Belfast, McKiernan's latent talent became clear when she finished ninth in the senior girls' race. Sonia O'Sullivan was the winner that day.

In the meantime, an athletics club had started in Cornafean and McKiernan began training for athletics in a more structured manner. A year later, she had to make the tough choice between running and camogie when the Ulster Schools Cross-Country in Belfast took place on the day before an Ulster Camogie semi-final. She opted for the cross-country, winning the title and qualifying for the All-Irelands which were to be held in Dungarvan that year.

That race would remain one of her happiest memories – her father collecting her from school on Friday evening and seeing her off from Cavan Bus Station to stay with a sister in Dublin. Early on Saturday morning, her brother Peadar drove her to Dungarvan, taking numerous photographs of his sister with his new camera when, running barefoot, she won the race. The delighted pair then headed home.

McKiernan's win inevitably attracted the attention of an American university, but ever the home-bird, she was determined to stay put. After she left school later that year, she completed a secretarial course and then worked in a solicitor's office before moving on to Cavan County Council. Her coach by this time was Joe Doonan, a primary school principal based nearby in County Leitrim. She became a familiar figure locally, now putting in the miles on Cavan golf course.

Success came swiftly. In 1989, at the age of nineteen, McKiernan finished third in the Irish Senior Cross-Country Championships, which saw her selected for the World Cross-Country Championships in Stavanger, Norway, where she finished 73rd. She steadily learned her trade, finished 40th at the World Cross of 1990 and 76th in 1991. In 1992, on a snow-covered course in Boston, she finished runner-up, just two seconds behind the American Lynn Jennings. With Doonan and her brother Peadar, she had stayed with John Treacy in Rhode Island and benefitted from his sage advice. Her silver medal placing brought her victory in the World Cross-Country Challenge and a cheque for $10,000.

McKiernan, by now the pride of Cornafean, arrived home to a rousing reception. Never a woman who liked a fuss, she quickly returned to work at the Cavan County court-house. Later that year, she competed in the 3000m at the Barcelona Olympics. Although she did not make it out of the heats, she was happy enough with her run and time of 8 mins 57.81 secs. When she travelled to Amorebieta in Spain's Basque Country for the 1993 World Cross, a small army of Cavan supporters travelled to cheer her on. Doonan had adjusted her training to cater for the expected fast pace and she finished a determined second behind Portugal's Albertina Dias, beating Jennings into third place. Later that year came the World Track and Field Championships in Stuttgart when blisters forced her to drop out of the 10,000m final.

She returned to cross-country that winter, beating Dias in her opening race at Mol in Belgium. In January 1994, she lost out to an up-and-coming British athlete called Paula

Radcliffe at Mallusk but bounced back with wins in Seville and at the Almond Blossom race in the Algarve. At the World Cross in Budapest, the Kenyan Helen Chepngeno made the early pace and went on to win the race. In the chase for the line, McKiernan caught first Dias and then her Portuguese teammate Conceicao Ferreira, finishing second for a third consecutive year. Also, for a third year, she won the Cross-Country Grand Prix title.

By now, a committed professional athlete, McKiernan took leave from her job and travelled to Albuquerque for altitude training in preparation for the 1994 track season. Initially, it paid off when McKiernan set an Irish record of 31:19.11 for 10,000m in the Europa Cup at Santry. However, by the time the European Championships in Helsinki came around, she was distinctly off form and again forced to drop out of a 10,000m race.

Her target now was the inaugural European Cross-Country Championship scheduled for the 10 December 1994 at Alnwick in Northumberland. At just 4.5km, the distance was shorter than the then standard 6km and the course was far from the manicured golf courses or dead flat racecourses that had become the norm. McKiernan ran an assured race and with the finish line in sight sprinted past the Spaniard Julia Vaquero for a thrilling victory.

She undertook another spell at altitude before travelling to Durham for the 1995 World Cross-Country Championships. This time, she was thwarted by the east Africans and for a fourth year in a row finished in the silver medal position, with Derartu Tulu of Ethiopia the winner. It was to be her final individual medal at the competition but not the last time she would take a cross-country medal. In 1997, when the race was held in Turin, she led Ireland home in seventh place and with Sonia O'Sullivan ninth, Valerie Vaughan 23rd and Una English 25th, helped Ireland to team bronze.

Of course, there was more to McKiernan than cross-country, although she did not have much luck when it came to the track. In June 1995, she improved her own Irish 10,000m record to 31:08.41 but was forced to pull out of the World Championships in Gothenburg with a foot injury. A year later, the Atlanta Olympics proved another disappointment. McKiernan reached the 10,000m final but, suffering in the heat, could only manage eleventh place. A fortnight later, she ran a personal best 14:19 for 5000m in Cologne, Germany.

Now an experienced athlete with a ten-year career behind her, McKiernan decided to move up to the marathon, with the Berlin Marathon on 28 September 1997 her target. Her winning time of 2:23:44 in Berlin proved the fastest ever by a first time female marathon runner and broke Carey May's 1985 Irish record of 2:28:07.

She followed it up the following April by becoming the first Irish athlete to win the London Marathon in a time of 2:26:26 despite a toilet mishap along the way. A few weeks earlier, she had won the Lisbon Half-Marathon in a super time of 67 mins 50 secs, although the time wasn't ratified as a national record. Later that year, on 1 November 1998, she ran a personal best time of 2:22:23 when winning the Amsterdam Marathon which had been set up as an unofficial tilt at the world record. McKiernan finished just

92 seconds off the then world record. On 24 October 1999, she would run one further marathon in Chicago finishing 12th in 2:35:31. With the wisdom of hindsight, she realised that after running three hard marathons in thirteen months, she was exhausted mentally and physically by the time she reached Chicago.

McKiernan's final major race was the Great North Run in September 2004, after which she announced her retirement from competitive running. Her daughter Deirbhile was born in 2002 and her son Patrick four years later. While rearing her two children she continued to run regularly around Dublin's Phoenix Park near the family home. When the children were older, she again began entering road races, enjoying the buzz and picking up occasional age-group prizes. Later she started her own business giving classes on Chi running to groups all over the country.

'For me, running is simple, and running should be pure and enjoyable,' she would say, despite her clear will to win and her considerable achievements. That's Catherina McKiernan in a nutshell.

JAMES MITCHELL
Simply the Best

In the pre-Olympic days, from 1885 to 1896, James Sarsfield Mitchell, the original 'Irish Whale' dominated hammer throwing first in Ireland and the UK and then in the USA, notching up seventeen national titles in Ireland and eight successive USA titles after he emigrated. Along the way were also numerous world records. Incredibly, he made his Olympic debut at the St Louis Games in 1904 six months after celebrating his fortieth birthday. While he didn't feature in the hammer, he took a bronze medal in the 56lb weight throw, which was briefly an Olympic event in the early days of the Games.

Mitchell had come to the USA as part of the GAA's 'Invasion Team' which toured north-east America in the autumn of 1888. In all, forty-eight Irish hurlers, athletes and officials visited New York, Boston, and numerous other towns. Mitchell was one of several athletes who opted to remain in the USA after the tour ended.

Two rival athletics associations existed in the USA at the time and Mitchell competed in the National Association of Amateur Athletes of America championships on 13 October 1888 winning the 56lb one-handed throw in a new USA record. Two weeks later, he set two more American records in variations of the 56lb event.

After the touring party returned to Ireland, Mitchell, with his name slightly adjusted to 'Mitchel' continued competing. Initially banned by the AAU as a professional after joining the Manhattan Athletic Club for whom he worked, he was reinstated in March 1889 and later transferred to the New Jersey AC before joining the New York Athletic Club in 1890.

Mitchell was born at Bartoose, Emly, County Tipperary on 26 January 1864, the eldest of seven children and, like many of his athletics contemporaries, came from a comfortable farming background. A studious pupil, the young Mitchell was a voracious reader, and his favourite author was Charles J. Kickham whose novel *Knocknagow* featured a 'sledgehammer' throwing character called Matt the Thrasher.

At his first athletics competition in 1878, the 14-year-old Mitchell entered the quarter-mile as well as the long and high jumps. He would clear 5' 10" (1.78) in the high jump at the age of seventeen but after breaking both ankles in 1882, turned his attention to the throwing events. Between 1885 and 1888, the GAA All-Ireland championships were his personal fiefdom. He won the hammer, 14lb and 56lb throwing events at the first GAA championships in Tramore on 6 October 1885 and would amass seventeen national titles across a range of events including the hammer throw, the shot put and throwing the 7lb, 14lb, 28lb and 56lb weights. He also won the IAAA shot put title in 1887.

During the same period, he established an international reputation by winning three successive hammer titles from 1886 to 1888 and two shot put titles in 1886 and 1887 at the AAA championships. During this phase of his career, he also established two world best throws in the hammer throwing 36.40m in Limerick on 19 June 1886 and 36.50m almost a year later 9 June 1887 also in Limerick.

After Mitchell moved to the USA, he proved equally dominant, not only winning eight successive hammer titles from 1888 but also 56lb weight for distance titles from 1891 to 1897, and the 56lb weight for height title in 1893. From his New York base he extended the world best mark in the hammer throw on nine occasions between 6 November 1888 when he threw 39.62m and 8 October 1892 when he threw 44.28m.

He was the original member of the Ireland-born group of American weight throwers known as *The Irish Whales* which dominated American and International throwing events between 1896 and 1920. John Flanagan's arrival in the USA ended the Mitchell era of dominance and the great Tipperary-born athlete retired. This proved a temporary abdication. He returned in 1900 and collected another 56lb weight title and in the process established another USA record at the State Fair Park in Milwaukee. In 1903, he added another pair of USA titles to his collection in the hammer and 56lb. He then travelled to Montreal, where he won the Canadian hammer and discus titles.

After his appearance at the St Louis Games, Mitchell won his final USA title, the 56lb weight throw, in 1905 and remained in training with the intention of competing in the stone throwing event at the 1906 Intercalated or 'in-between' Games in Athens, Greece. In the USA trials, he threw the stone over 22m making him favourite for the title in Athens.

It was not to be. Mitchell departed for Athens with the USA team from Hoboken, New Jersey aboard the North German Lloyd steamer *Barbarossa* on 3 April 1906. Just over a day later, a huge wave hit the liner and several athletes were badly injured including Mitchell who was thrown down several flights of stairs dislocating his right shoulder and sustaining other injuries. This prevented him from competing in Athens, where the stone throw event was won with a throw of just short of twenty metres, well below Mitchell's best.

Until the emergence of John Flanagan, Mitchell was undoubtedly the greatest performer in the weight events the world had seen, and a single bronze Olympic medal was poor reward for the athletics pioneer from Tipperary, who won over eighty national and regional weight event titles in Ireland, England, Canada, and the USA.

Mitchell finally retired becoming a well-known sportswriter and author. He would write several books on polo, rowing and athletics and was special correspondent for the *New York Herald* at the Stockholm Olympics in 1912. His book *How to Become a Weight Thrower* featuring photographs of several Irish-born throwers and as well as their advice, gives a fascinating insight into the origins of the various throwing disciplines.

On the shot and the hammer, he argues that 'The first authentic mention of stone putting, and hammer throwing appears in the "Book of Leinster" in connection with the Tailtin Games.

Throwing the hammer 'was termed the *roth chleas*, which means wheel feat, and the first great champion was Cuchulainn, who excelled all the men of his time ...'

He argued that putting the stone 'through centuries of turmoil and strife remained a favourite pastime of the Celt.' As sport became formalised, the need for uniform weights and shapes became more urgent and 'in the annual "College Races" of Dublin University, in 1860, an iron 16-pound shot was used'.

The hammer underwent some transformation too, 'from the old iron head with stiff spade-tree handle to the lead head with piano wire handle and a loop at the extreme end for the hands'.

Technique also changed. 'Nobody then thought of whirling the hammer around his head before executing the body spin, although that style had been introduced in 1867 or thereabout by Donald Dinnie, the Scotch professional. The amateurs contented themselves with holding the hammer out at arm's length, letting it drop down behind, after which they began to spin around. Soon afterward, however, and one by one, they began to wind the missile over the head, and at once the improvement in distance was noticeable.'

He modestly admits that it was he 'the writer' who designed 'the present loop with the link attachment to the head, and the verdict the world over is that there is hardly room for improvement'.

Mitchell became something of a father-figure for USA weight throwers, among them Matt McGrath and Pat Ryan, and his influence was recognised by no less than James E. O'Sullivan, a founding member of the AAU: 'Many of the present day ideas in the hammer and shot were modelled from suggestions advanced and tried out by Mr Mitchell, and to his study of the weights and his remarkable athletic career is undoubtedly due the interest in this branch of track and field events in America.'

On 3 July 1921, after three months in Roosevelt hospital, New York, Mitchell died from heart disease aged only fifty-seven. He never married. At the time of his death, he had been connected with the sporting staff of *The Sun* and the *New York Herald* newspapers for almost two decades. In contemporary newspapers, he was credited with seventeen Irish, five AAA, twenty-six American, twenty New York Metropolitan and fourteen Canadian titles although this may not be entirely accurate.

The *Nationalist* newspaper in Tipperary paid him a fitting tribute: 'Like many true and faithful sons of dear old Emly, he sleeps now by the shores of the mighty Hudson, but his memory lives and may it stimulate the young Gaels of Ireland to go and do likewise in the field of prowess.'

WALTER J. NEWBURN
First Twenty-four Footer

On 16 July 1898, a 24-year old Mayo athlete set a new world record when he cleared 24ft 0½ins in the long jump. The previous record of 24 foot exactly, set by an Englishman, John Howard in 1951, had stood for forty-seven years.

The record breaker was Walter Newburn, born in Ballinrobe, County Mayo on 8 December 1873. Soon after, the family moved from Mayo to Westmeath after his father was appointed clerk to the Petty Sessions of Killucan and Tyrrellspass.

Coming as he did from a Church of Ireland background, Walter Newburn was educated at Farra School, Bunbrosna, County Westmeath, one of six schools under the patronage of the Incorporated Society for Promoting English Protestant Schools in Ireland. His first recorded appearance in an athletics arena was in the annual school sports at Farra when he finished second in the senior boys' 220 yard race. In an interview in the *Irish Athletic and Cycling Record* of August 1898, he explained that he first began jumping when he was a lad at school: 'Some half a dozen of us used to adjourn to a neighbouring field every day the moment school was over, and it was there that I first took the fancy for the pastime…'

In 1896, the lanky Newburn emerged as a major figure on the national athletic stage when winning long jump titles at the IAAA and the GAA championships with relatively modest jumps of 6.57m and 6.56m respectively. He also tied for first place in the high jump (IAAA) but lost the toss for the title. In 1897, he won the 100 yards and the long jump with a 6.84m effort at the IAAA championship and represented Ireland against Scotland at Edinburgh where he won the long jump with a leap of 6.78m, a distance that broke Tom Kiely's Scottish all-comers record. He also finished third in the 100 yards. In August, he improved his long jump best to 7.01m in Dundalk.

Such a performance became routine for Newburn in 1898 – his *annus mirabilis*. He began the season on 19 May at the Mardyke in Cork where he set a new Irish record of 7.12m. At the IAAA championships, he shocked N. D. Morgan to win the 100 yards title, and also took the long jump title with 7.04m on a day when the weather was reported to be 'all against big jumping.' At the Postal Sports on 18 June, he opened with two fouls but went on to break 23 feet in four successive jumps, the best of them 7.24m.

The AAA championships were next up and a winning leap of 7.18m set a new English all-comers and championship record. According to the *Scottish Sport* report: 'The divil (sic) himself was looking out of him as he would gallop like a fire-engine horse up to the take-off mark, spring upwards and the next instant 6' 4" (1.93m) of the finest Irish blood and bone curled up like a ball and literally flew in mid-air landing with a whack just 23' 7" from where he started'.

The Sport was a bit more sober. The report simply pointed out that Newburn's jump was 'magnificent considering it was against a hurricane'. A week later, Newburn cleared 7.17m at the Dublin Transport Sports to record his fifth winning jump beyond 7.01m of 1898. On 16 July 1898, the 24-foot (7.31m) barrier was finally broken, and Walter Newburn secured his place in athletics history with a jump of 24' 0½" (7.32m) in the international match with Scotland at Ballsbridge. The *Irish Athletic and Cycling Record* reported that the mark 'was likely to stand for many years, unless of course, it should be beaten by its creator who appears to have no limit'.

Two days later, in Mullingar, Newburn smashed through the 24-foot barrier again, this time jumping 24' 6¾" (7.48m) even though it was reported that the 'ground was rough and there was a slight cross wind'. However, this jump was never ratified as a record.

At the GAA long jump championship, Newburn again flew six inches beyond the 24 foot (7.46m) mark. At Dundalk on 4 August, he again won the long-jump clearing 7.22m. A week later he reportedly jumped 7.33m at the Irish National Foresters' meeting from a turf take off. Newburn then made his first trip to the north of Ireland in mid-August to compete at the Cliftonville Sports. In the long jump, he cleared 7.16m at his first attempt but unfortunately for the attendance this time, there was no miracle jump.

In this season of greatness, one more challenge awaited Newburn. The record for the long jump from a grass take-off was held by Pat Davin since August 1883 when Davin cleared 7.06m at both Monasterevin and Portarlington. Newburn beat Davin's mark by one inch at Monasterevin, where the original record was established. This ended Newburn's spectacular season. He would never again reach the same standards of consistency despite a strong early start to the 1899 season.

In 1899, he completed his standard 100 yards and long jump double at the IAAA championships, beating Peter O'Connor in the long jump. At the Limerick RIC sports at the Markets Field, before an attendance of 10,000, he was a winner with a jump of 7.25m from a grass take off. From this point on things began to go wrong. Injuries and illness are the nemesis of the highly tuned athlete and Newburn's injury-free gallop came to an end in July 1899.

He successfully defended his AAA title at Wolverhampton with a moderate jump of 6.75m in atrocious weather conditions and suffered a serious injury in the process. After considerable persuasion, he travelled to Scotland to represent Ireland and having unexpectedly won the 100 yards, broke down in the long jump. In August, he travelled to Glasgow to compete in the Celtic Sports at Parkhead on 12 August again suffering an injury and losing to Pat Leahy. The GAA long jump title won in Navan on 15 August 1901 with a leap of 7.08m was his final jumping title.

Some have suggested that Newburn's decline after 1899 was due to the pressure created by the improved jumping of Peter O'Connor, who set a world record of 7.54m at the IAAA Championships of May 1901. That long-distance psychoanalysis makes no sense. Walter Newburn had professional and family commitments that took precedence over his sport. For Newburn, long jumping was simply a recreational activity and never an all-consuming passion. He was a man of many talents: an outstanding goalkeeper in Leinster association football, playing with Richmond Rovers, Shelbourne and good enough to gain representative honours with Leinster. Yet in April 1899, he passed on the opportunity to represent Leinster to participate in a Theatre Royal variety show at which he performed a long jumping display.

He also played rugby and hockey on occasion and was involved in athletics administration as president of the Cross-Country Association of Ireland. He acted as a judge at the Irish championships and on one notable occasion on 27 May 1912, he took time out from his judging duties, wandering across to the throwing area and taking his last athletics title in the 56lb weight without follow competition with a throw of 8.07m.

Newburn's profession as an assistant teacher at the Claremont Institute for the Deaf and Dumb in Glasnevin, a boarding school for Church of Ireland children, curtailed his athletics involvement and limited his income. For the 1895-96 term, he earned a salary of £50; a salary on 'which he found it very hard to live'. Newburn resigned his position in February 1901. Following his resignation, he taught at the Private Oral School for the Deaf, St Winifred's at Sandford

Place in Dublin and founded the Castlewood College for the Deaf and Dumb based at Castlewood House, Rathmines in 1905, where children of any denomination were welcome.

Newburn's large family would also have influenced his priorities. He had married Elizabeth Meredith, also a teacher, in 1896 and was the father of seven boys and two girls. He died in London in February 1919 at the age of forty-five, after which his widow emigrated to the USA.

PAT 'THE DOC' O'CALLAGHAN
The Great All-Rounder

In a detailed report on the 1927 England v Scotland v Ireland athletics match, held in Manchester, the correspondent of the *Irish Times* noted that Bill Britton had 'seldom thrown more consistently, each of his efforts being near 150 feet (45.72m)', but that the surprise was a young doctor called Patrick O'Callaghan. 'He did splendidly... and his 151'5½' (46.16m) suggests that in a couple of years he will be a certainty for the event every time he throws'.

'The Doc', as he would become known, had announced his arrival on the athletics' scene.

Patrick O'Callaghan was the second of three sons born to Paddy and Jane O'Callaghan in the townland of Knockanroe, near Kanturk, County Cork, on 28 January 1906. Sport was in his DNA; his father Paddy was a noted thrower in the pre-First World War years and his maternal uncle, Tim Vaughan a sprinter and Gaelic footballer with Cork. O'Callaghan's eldest brother Seán also played football and won a national hurdles title, while his other brother Con was a gifted runner, jumper and thrower who competed in the decathlon in the Olympics of 1928 when Pat took his first hammer medal.

The young Pat would prove the best of them all – a runner, thrower and jumper as well as a fine hurler and footballer for two local GAA clubs. When he began studying for a medical degree at the Royal College of Surgeons, at the precocious age of aged only sixteen, he was introduced to the sport of rugby.

He soon began to focus on athletics as his main sport, with the weight throwing events his special interest. At home in Cork for the summer of 1925, the nineteen-year-old O'Callaghan picked up an old cannon ball from Macroom Castle, had it drilled and fitted with a handle and wire at a foundry, and began training with it at the family farm. About six months later, he discovered this improvised implement was heavier than the standard hammer, making it easier for him to throw the lighter implement.

Such was O'Callaghan's attention to detail that to improve his movement around the circle, he knocked on the door of a local ballet teacher and asked for tuition. Until then, the custom of hammer throwers was to turn twice in the circle before release. The light-footed O'Callaghan would introduce a third – and then, towards the end of his career, a fourth turn. A next door neighbour, J.J. Carey, initially helped the young Pat with his training and technique, with J.J.'s younger brother, the 1912 Olympian Denis Carey, continuing the work in Dublin.

At the age of twenty, O'Callaghan graduated as one of Ireland's youngest ever doctors in 1926. Over the next four years, he would pursue postgraduate studies in University

College Cork (UCC) and hold numerous temporary positions, including stints with the Royal Air Force (RAF) medical corps at Halton, Buckinghamshire, and in hospitals in Dublin, Cork and Killarney.

In 1927, he won his first national hammer title with a throw of 43.36m gaining selection for the two international competitions that year. In 1928, he retained his national hammer title with a 49.53m effort on the same day as his brother Con won the national decathlon title, with the brothers then selected to represent Ireland at the Amsterdam Olympics.

Before they departed, O'Callaghan threw a personal best of 50.88m at the Royal Ulster Constabulary Sports in Belfast and then set off for Amsterdam with his two brothers, all paying their own way.

After the preliminary round of the hammer, O'Callaghan was lying third behind Sweden's Ossian Skiöld. Using the Swede's hammer for his second effort, O'Callaghan recorded a mighty throw of 51.38m. It was 10cm further than Skiöld could manage and won him the gold. At the medal presentation, a hastily located Irish tricolour was flown and the Irish national anthem heard in an Olympic arena for the first time.

After Amsterdam, O'Callaghan further enhanced his reputation. In 1930, he won five Irish Championship titles on the same weekend and surpassed this in June 1931 when he took 'half a dozen' titles winning the hammer, shot, high jump, discus, 56lbs for distance and 56lbs over the bar at the GAA's Irish Championships in Croke Park.

At the 1930 Garda Síochána sports in Mallow, County Cork, the chain on O'Callaghan's hammer snapped while he was throwing, flinging the head into the crowd where it hit a fifteen-year-old boy, fracturing his skull. The matter would haunt him for years and eventually bankrupt him after the boy's parents sued O'Callaghan in June 1934, with the matter only settled in 1936 when a jury awarded £2,500 damages against him.

He had continued throwing and at the 1931 Swedish international games in Stockholm on 11 July, he set a European record for the hammer with a throw of 54.48m. Earlier in the year, he had been appointed assistant medical officer in St Luke's Mental Hospital, Clonmel.

His appearance in the revived 1931 international match against Scotland in Croke Park later that month was the stuff of legend. After winning the shot with a 14.24m effort, O'Callaghan retired early from the high jump, with his leap of 1.78m good enough for runner-up spot, to concentrate on the hammer which he duly won with a 53.90m throw. He then broke his own European record by throwing 56.06m at Clonmel, County Tipperary on 9 August also setting a world record for the 56lb weight of 27' 11" (8.51m).

O'Callaghan once commented that the standard of hammer throwing in Ireland was the equal of anywhere in the world at the time and, at the 1931 international match against France, held in Croke Park on 15 August, he was proved correct when he tied for first in the high jump and won the shot but was beaten by George Walsh in both the discus and the hammer.

O'Callaghan was still a student at UCC and at the Inter-Varsity Championships in College Park, Dublin, he, added another story to his legend. After stumbling over the fourth hurdle and knocking the fifth in the high hurdles, he gathered the remaining five hurdles under his arm and completed the race. He was later disqualified.

By the time the 1932 Olympics came around, O'Callaghan weighed a hefty 118kg and was regularly throwing the hammer over 52m. After some controversy, he was granted three months leave from his hospital job to prepare for the forthcoming games. Shortly before departing on the 6,000-mile boat and train journey to Los Angeles, O'Callaghan collected a fifth hammer title at the National Championships. The three-week trek across the United States included a stop off in Philadelphia where he hobnobbed with Jack Kelly, a famous Irish-American rower, although not quite as famous as his daughter Grace would become. At the Games opening ceremony, O'Callaghan was flag bearer for the Irish team.

For the hammer, fourteen competitors had entered with the top six after the first three throws getting a further three efforts. O'Callaghan was lying second after the first three rounds to Finland's Ville Pörhölä but well clear of Peter Zaremba in the bronze position. He threw 51.81m and 51.85m before unleashing a massive throw of 53.92m in the final round to win his second gold. Earlier in the day, Bob Tisdall had won the 400m hurdles on what was perhaps Ireland's greatest ever day at the Olympics.

After the long trek back home, Ireland was eagerly awaiting its two Olympic heroes and an estimated quarter of a million people turned out on Dublin's streets to welcome the team home.

O'Callaghan went on to win the American and British hammer throwing titles in 1933 and in 1934 respectively and broke his own European record with a throw of 56.91m at Enniscorthy, County Wexford, using his experimental four-turn technique.In 1934 he married Kitty O'Reilly and set up a general practice at 'Roseville' in Clonmel, also working as a dispensary doctor in Emly.

By this time, O'Callaghan was regarded as the world's top hammer thrower and, among others, German athletics coaches visited Ireland to study his technique. In 1934 Ireland's National Athletic and Cycling Association (NACA) refused to accept the International Amateur Athletic Federation (IAAF)'s decision to recognise Northern Ireland as part of the UK for athletics purposes. The NACA was suspended from international athletics and no Irish team went to the 1936 Berlin Olympics. O'Callaghan watched from the stands as Germany's Karl Hein won the hammer with an Olympic record throw of 56.49m, using the heel and toe turn O'Callaghan had pioneered.

At Fermoy in 1937, O'Callaghan threw 59.54m, more than two metres ahead of the world record set by Paddy Ryan in 1913. Because the meeting was organised by the NACAI, this record was not ratified by the AAUE or the IAAF. In May 1938, O'Callaghan left for America to take up a professional wrestling contract, which he hoped would help pay the debt remaining from the 1930 accident. Although he took part in over forty bouts, he made little money and returned to Clonmel in October where, despite being declared bankrupt on 25 November 1938, he would live a long and happy life. Pat O'Callaghan, Ireland's greatest Olympian, died on 1 December 1991.

PETER O'CONNOR
Ireland's Peerless Grasshopper

Peter O'Connor's place in Irish athletics history was sealed on 5 August 1901 at the Royal Irish Constabulary (Depot) Sports, Ballsbridge, where he jumped 24'11¾" (7.61m), which in 1913 was adopted as the inaugural long jump world record by the IAAF. It would become the longest standing Irish athletic record lasting at 89 years and 301 days until finally broken in 1990.

Peter O'Connor was born on 24 October 1872 in Millom, Cumberland, England, where his father Edward was working as a shipwright. In 1880, Edward was appointed supervisor of the newly completed Wicklow waterworks at Ashtown on the outskirts of Wicklow and the family returned to Ireland. It was here that Peter O'Connor set himself a daily challenge of doing a hop, step and jump (triple jump) from the doorstep of the waterworks lodge across a gravel path to reach a grass margin. He left school at the age of fourteen taking up a job as a clerk with his cousin Michael Judd, who ran a skinners' business in Dublin.

In May 1894, Peter O'Connor moved to Clifden, County Mayo, to work in a solicitor's office and made his athletics debut in the annual regatta and sports at Cleggan. Competing in his socks, O'Connor won the three jumping events and became a sporting hero in the Clifden community. In early summer 1896, after he had moved to a solicitor's office in Galway, he competed in nineteen events at five sports meetings in County Galway, winning thirteen of them – 100, 220 and 440 yard handicaps as well as the long and high jumps.

In the summer of 1897, he competed in fourteen events over four sports meetings, winning all eight long and high jumps. At the Tuam Sports, he placed second in the Connaught 100 yard championship. In September, while competing at a sports meeting in Mullingar, he learned of a vacancy as managing clerk in a solicitors' office. He applied for the job and got it.

While based in Mullingar, O'Connor made his national IAAA championship debut on 31 May 1898 in the long and high jumps but was outside the medals in both. Between June and September, he competed in thirty-seven events at ten sports meetings, winning thirteen jumps, two sprint hurdles and retaining the Connaught 100 yard title. In the long jump, his best mark was 6.76m at the Crooked Wood Sports in Mullingar. In November 1898, he moved to Waterford as managing clerk at Daniel Dunford solicitors and there he joined Urbs Intacta Harriers Club; Urbs Intacta (the untaken city) is the motto of Waterford.

At the IAAA championships in May 1899, O'Connor won the 100 yards handicap (off 7 yards). In the long jump he strained himself on the soft ground, placing second with 6.73m. At the end of June, he won the long jump at Durrow Sports with a personal best 7.06m. His results were enough to give him a place on the Irish team facing Scotland in the annual match held in Edinburgh that July, where he placing second in both the long jump with 6.98m and high jump with 1.78m. Between July and September, he competed in twenty-seven events at seven sports meetings, with the highlight the GAA Championships in Thurles on 17 September where he won his first national titles in four events – 220 yards, high jump, long jump and triple jump.

O'Connor built on those successes in 1890 competing in forty-six events at nineteen sports meetings. Among his thirty-two victories was one in a handicapped 16lb shot. In the long jump, he exceeded seven metres on fourteen occasions, with three winning jumps over 24ft or 7.31m. Potential Irish records of 7.43m at Ballinasloe and 7.39m in New Ross were both disallowed because of slight inclines on the run-ups. After he jumped 7.51m in an 'exhibition' at New Ross, the sports committee presented O'Connor with a gold medal to mark his prowess.

At national level, O'Connor won the IAAA long jump championship with 7.18m and tied for first in the high jump with Pat Leahy on 1.78m. At the Ireland v Scotland international in Belfast, he won the long jump with 7.14m and again tied in the high jump with Pat Leahy, this time at 1.79m. For the first time, O'Connor travelled to London for the AAA championships at Stamford Bridge, then regarded at the most prestigious athletics meet in the world. He finished second in the long jump with 6.81m to the American Alvin Kraenzlein who jumped 6.96m. Following this performance, O'Connor was invited by the English AAA to compete at the Paris Olympic Games for Great Britain. He declined the offer.

The year 1901 proved even better. At the IAAA championships in the RDS Showgrounds, Dublin on Whit Monday 27 May, Ballsbridge, O'Connor leapt 7.54m in the sixth and final round. It was an Irish and world long jump record. He retained the high jump crown with 1.77m, this time beating Pat Leahy by one centimetre. Over the summer, he extended his world long jump record three times: to 7.60, at the Kilkenny GAA Sports, 76.05m at the Annacurra Gaelic Festival and 7.61 at the RIC Sports in Dublin. In a separate long jump competition at the RIC Sports, he set a world record of 7.27m from a grass take-off and later placed second to Denis Murray, the IAAA champion, in the Leinster IAAA 100 yards championship. In Glasgow, O'Connor won the long jump and high jump at the annual Ireland v Scotland match, and at the AAA Championships in Huddersfield, won the long jump and finished second in the high jump. At the Maryborough (now Portlaoise) Sports he jumped 7.63m on a non-level run-up and in the 100 yards, placed second by a yard to Denis Murray in the GAA Leinster Championship. To mark his long jump achievements in 1901, Peter O'Connor was presented with an inscribed 18-carat gold watch by his numerous friends and admirers in Waterford.

In August 1901, O'Connor sailed to New York at the invitation of the Greater New York Irish Athletic Association (GNYIAA) to compete in the long jump under its banner. At a chaotic GNYIAA Games on 2 September when the spectators stormed the in-field, he could manage only 6.92m and strained tendons in his jumping leg on his final attempt. On 7 September, in considerable pain, O'Connor won the long jump with a 6.84m effort at the so-called World Championships held in conjunction with the Pan American Exposition in Buffalo but exacerbated his leg injury. Despite medical advice, he competed twice more, at the New York AC Fall Games on 5 October and the GNYIAA Games on 20 October, with disappointing results.

In subsequent years, O'Connor limited his competitions. He did not compete at the 1902 IAAA championships because the funeral of his close friend Frank Furlong took place the same day. He refused to compete at IAAA championships because of a dispute and consequently, was not selected for the annual Ireland v Scotland matches between 1902 and 1905. Despite that, he retained his AAA long jump title for those five years. His victory with 7.25m at Stamford Bridge in 1905 remained a championship record until 1925.

At the GAA Leinster Championships held at Wexford in August 1902, he won the triple jump title, with a 14.45m leap. A year later, in July at the Waterford RIC Sports, he spiked himself on landing his first long jump, which ended his athletic season. In 1904, he won the GAA long jump title and placed fourth in the triple jump, also winning the GAA Leinster long jump, with a season's best 7.26m, as well as the high jump and triple jump (14.27m). In 1905, he again won the GAA long jump.

O'Connor's most notable day came at the Intercalated Olympic Games in Athens in 1906. In the long jump on 27 April, he jumped 7.02m to finish second behind the American Myer Prinstein who jumped 7.20m in controversial circumstances; O'Connor claimed not only that his best jump had been declared a foul, but that Prinstein had been allowed to compete out of order to avail of a smoother runway, aided by the sole official judge who was an American.

When the Union Jack was flown to represent Ireland at the medal ceremony, O'Connor climbed the 20ft flagpole and unfurled a green flag with the words '*Erin Go Bragh*'. Three days later, O'Connor jumped 14.07m to win the triple jump. In July, he won his sixth consecutive AAA long jump title at Stamford Bridge, also winning the long jump at the Ireland v Scotland international match in Belfast. His final competition was at St James's Park, Kilkenny on 12 August where he won the long jump with 7.37m, his best mark since 1901.

In 1912, O'Connor qualified as a solicitor, and he bought Dunford's practice in 1920. He remained involved in athletics all his life. He was a founder member and first vice-president of Waterford Athletic Club and attended later Olympics both as judge and spectator. He married and had nine children. Peter O'Connor died on 9 November 1957.

FRANK O'MARA
World Indoors Double

At the inaugural IAAF World Indoor Championships held in Indianapolis in 1987, Irish expectations were high when Frank O'Mara and Paul O'Donovan lined out in the men's 3000m. Marcus O'Sullivan had already taken the gold medal in the 1500m, and O'Mara was the fastest indoor miler in the world that year.

Despite a long tradition of Irish athletes competing indoors going back to Tommy Conneff running in Madison Square Gardens a century earlier, Ireland had returned empty-handed from the Bercy Stadium in Paris two years earlier at a prototype World Indoor Championships.

Marcus O'Sullivan had already ensured that would not happen on this occasion, running a personal best of 3:39.04 to head off Spain's José María Abascal and Han Kulker from the Netherlands in the 1500m.

Now it was Frank O'Mara and Paul O'Donovan's turn to enter the dry, rarefied air of the Hoosier Dome, the new home of the Indianapolis Colts. As the ten-man field came under starter's orders, O'Mara, although he was the fastest indoor miler in the world that year, looked tense. After the gun, he was the first to move to the front and led the field through an opening kilometre in 2 minutes 55 seconds, a similar pace to the women's race earlier in the week. O'Donovan took over the pace on the sixth lap but did not measurably increase the pace.

Great Britain's Mark Rowland struck the front on the sixth lap but he too failed to inject any pace as O'Mara slipped down the field. Rowland still led at two kilometres in 5:35 before with four laps to run the USA's Doug Padilla moved towards the front of the field, although Rowland was still leading with six hundred metres to run. Padilla struck with two laps remaining and at the bell, it was Ireland versus America with the American Terry Brahm joining his compatriot in the chase for gold.

O'Mara was not to be out-done, flying past Padilla with 150 metres left and sprinting away to take the gold medal in 8:03.32. In an almighty scramble for the minor positions, O'Donovan pipped Brahm for the silver right on the finish line as Padilla faded to fifth. Ireland's one-two in a world championship is never likely to be repeated. Two gold and a silver put Ireland fourth on the medal table – will we ever see that again?

Two years later, O'Mara would seek to defend his title in Budapest but ran into what was probably the hottest field ever in the event. Morocco's Said Aouita took the gold in a championship record of 7:47.94; Spaniard José Luis González was second in 7:48.66 and Germany's Dieter Baumann third in 7:50.47. O'Mara finished seventh in 7:52.21. Both Aouita and Baumann would later take Olympic gold medals over 5000m.

Undeterred, O'Mara kept training and was again selected for the World Indoors of 1991 in Seville. It was a different

Frank O'Mara who lined up this time after keeping the other nine starters waiting while he finished a last-second stride out down the home straight. Admonished by an official for not having his foot behind the start line, he was the first to show as the race got under way but unlike four years earlier, he was not allowed to lead as Hammou Boutayeb of Morocco took the initiative.

Boutayeb set such a blistering pace that with three laps to go, the race was down to him and O'Mara. The Limerick man kicked with 300m to run and when Boutayeb was unable to respond, O'Mara came home well clear in a championship record and career best of 7:41.14, less than two seconds outside the world record. Boutayeb held on for second in 7:43.64 with Great Britain's Rob Denmark winning the sprint for third in 7:43.90.

Frank O'Mara, born on the 17 July 1960 and growing up in Limerick, started athletics, like many Irish children, at the Community Games. He won the Limerick 400m, earning the dream trip of all juvenile athletes of the time to Mosney, County Meath for the national finals, where he finished third. After attending John F. Kennedy Memorial School on the Ennis Road, he started at St Munchin's College in 1972, and although he played rugby, he always had more affinity with athletics.

At the end of the school year in 1976, O'Mara was packing up and looking forward to spending the long summer holidays at home, when he got word that his father, also called Frank, had suffered a heart attack at 64 years of age and was in the Limerick Regional Hospital. Back then, children were not allowed in intensive care wards, so Frank wrote his father a letter, promising him that he would win the Irish Schools' Intermediate 1500m the following year. He did this hoping it would give his father, an avid sports fan, the motivation to recover and regain full health.

Unfortunately, it would be the last communication they would have as his father died a week later. That did not stop Frank keeping his promise and the following year, he won the schools' 1500m in a record time of 3:58.4 and added the 3000m title for good measure. Those victories helped St. Munchin's win the Intermediate boys' team competition for the first and, to date, only time.

In 1978, he followed in the footsteps of his schoolmate, the late Niall O'Shaughnessy, to the University of Arkansas, after John McDonnell came to his home to recruit him. McDonnell, from County Mayo, was the Razorback head coach for thirty-one years, winning forty-two NCAA team titles during his stewardship which made him the most successful college coach in US sporting history.

For O'Mara, it was arguably the best decision of his life, and he spent eleven years at the Fayetteville campus, earning a civil engineering degree at undergraduate level and an MBA in business administration. Staying on as assistant coach to McDonnell, he then attended law school, passing the Arkansas bar exam while at the same time competing internationally at four European and seven World Championships (indoors and outdoors) and three Olympic Games. O'Mara's best Olympic performance came in 1992 when he made the semi-finals of the 5000m, finishing fourth in 13:38.79.

In 1983, he became only the third Irish male athlete to win the 1500m at the NCAA Championships, following in the footsteps of Eamonn Coghlan and Ronnie Delany. Also, that year, he helped Arkansas overcome Villanova at the acclaimed Penn Relay Championship of America in Philadelphia in 1983, anchoring both the distance medley and 4 x 1500m, and winning the Athlete of the Meet award. In 1986, O'Mara ran a time of 3:51.06 for the mile in Rome, still the fifth fastest ever by an Irishman. His career best time for 1500m was 3:34.02 set in Brussels a year earlier in 1985.

After qualifying as a lawyer, O'Mara was first engaged by his former athlete management company KIM as general counsel and advisor before moving on in 1998 to become vice-president of Alltel Telecommunications, one of the largest phone companies in America. Alltel was sold to Verizon in 2009 and it was at that time that O'Mara experienced the first symptoms of what was to become the greatest challenge of his life. When his left foot started hitting his right calf while he was running, he did not realise at first that it might be symptomatic of something more serious. It forced him to stop running and still troubled him when he reverted to walking. After seven months, he was diagnosed as suffering from Parkinson's Disease at the age of forty-nine.

O'Mara was determined to continue in business, taking beta blockers to prevent shaking in meetings. In September 2009, he was appointed CEO of Allied Wireless, with that company, through a series of transactions, buying back Alltel. O'Mara sold Allied Wireless to AT&T in 2014 and, in the same year, was diagnosed with Lyme disease which can display similar symptoms to Parkinson's Disease. A device was fitted in his chest to allow for intravenous antibiotic treatments three times each week. By now it was a struggle just to walk.

His condition continued to deteriorate including neck cramps affecting his ability to breathe. Exactly ten years after his first symptoms, O'Mara travelled to the Mayo Clinic in Minneapolis for Deep Brain Stimulation surgery, a five-hour operation in which the surgeon places thin metal wires in the brain. These then send electrical impulses to the brain to help control some of the Parkinsonian symptoms. Thankfully this procedure has proved relatively successful and, now in his sixties, O'Mara can enjoy a well-deserved retirement.

In 2023 O'Mara's autobiography *Bend, Don't Break: A Memoir of Endurance* was published. In this inspiring book, he recounts his battle with Parkinson's. At first in denial, he eventually found the strength that made him successful as an athlete and in business – using determination, and humour to weather the worst phases of the disease. He learned to face each hurdle as he came to it: to bend, but not break.

DERVAL O'ROURKE
Queen of the Hurdles

At the age of seven, Derval O'Rourke, born 28 May 1981, began running competitively with Douglas Athletics Club in her native Cork. When the club folded, she moved to the Leevale club joining the club's sprint group where she was coached by John Sheehan and started hurdling under the supervision of Seamus Power; two men with very different coaching styles, as she would later write in *Leevale: Home of Champions*.

The influence of the Leevale Club proved to be defining: 'From the moment I joined Leevale AC., I dreamed about going to the Olympic Games. The club had a strong history in Olympic representation, and I wanted to join the list of names of athletes who went to the Olympics to represent Ireland ... Leevale really instilled belief and a massive competitive streak into me.'

O'Rourke's finest moment would come in March 2006 when she won the 60m hurdles at the World Indoors in Moscow in a new national record time of 7.84 seconds. It was the first time an Irish female athlete had ever won a sprint world title. Later, in 2009, she finished just out of the medals in fourth place at the World Championships in Berlin, Germany with a time of 12.67 secs.

Her success had been a long time coming. In 1999 when aged just seventeen, she had won the national 60m hurdles indoors title in Nenagh with a time of 7.78 secs, winning again in 2000 and 2001. In 2001, came her first success outdoors in the 100m event. From 1999 to 2011, she would win eleven indoor and nine outdoor titles.

Her potential as an athlete was evident and she was awarded a sports scholarship to University College Dublin. She graduated with an honours BA degree in sociology in 2003 followed by followed by a Business Management masters at Smurfit Business School in 2005.

O'Rourke had set her first national record in 2003, when she ran a time of 12.96 secs when finishing fourth at the European Under-23 championships at Bydgoszcz, Poland becoming the first Irish athlete to break the 13.00 second barrier for the 100m hurdles and making the A qualification time for the 2004 Olympics in Athens. She also competed in her first World Championships in Paris that year, going out in the heats.

O'Rourke's Olympic debut was compromised by illness. A month before the Games, O'Rourke had been hospitalised in Thessaloniki, Greece with appendicitis and food poisoning. She ignored medical advice to withdraw and produced what she considered to be one of the most disastrous performances of her career, going out in the heats.

It inspired O'Rourke to reassess her career. Back home, she gathered the backroom team she felt she needed for what she called *Team Derval: Operation World Domination*. The first recruit was the nutritionist, Andrea Cullen followed by the husband and wife coaching team of Sean and Terri Cahill, both former international athletes; Sean in the hurdles and Terri in the long jump.

Sean Cahill saw that while O'Rourke had basic speed, her hurdling technique needed work. 'I couldn't believe how raw she was, how little she knew about hurdling ... she hasn't a clue basically and she can run this quickly. If you could show her anything, it was going to make a massive difference,' he said. In 2007, O'Rourke, would split with her previous coach Jim Kilty to work solely with the Cahills.

Within six months, O'Rourke was looking like a possible championship winner. When, in her *Irish Examiner* column of 24 June 2014, she announced her retirement, she identified Sean and Terri Cahill as having 'turned my dreams and ambitions into reality. It seems unfair to have my name alone alongside the medals and records when they were such a massive part of every single one. Their coaching and high-performance expertise has been phenomenal ... they are truly the best out there.'

The first fruits of the relationship came in 2005 when O'Rourke made the semi-finals of the 100m hurdles at the World Championships in Helsinki, Finland. One week later, she won the bronze medal in the 100m hurdles at the World University Games in Izmir, Turkey and was a member of the bronze medal winning Irish 4 x 100m relay team at the same games. At home, she won her fourth national title in 12.95 seconds, a championship best time that has yet to be surpassed.

Following her victory at the 2006 World Indoors, O'Rourke set her sights on the European Championships of that year scheduled for Göteborg in Sweden. After missing a few weeks through injury, she showed that she was right back in form when she improved the national record first in Lausanne on 11 July when she ran 12.92 and again fifteen days later in Helsinki when she knocked over half a second off that time when running 12.85. In Göteborg she ran a sensational race to take silver in another new national record time of 12.72, firmly establishing her credentials as world-class athlete. At the same championships, she ran the first leg for the Irish 4 x 100 m relay team which set a new national record of 44.38 secs.

Following a frustrating season in 2007 when she sidestepped the indoor season and could only manage eighth in the semi-finals at the World Championships in Osaka, Japan, although she did manage to run a time of 12.88 in Bochum, Germany in mid-August. In 2008, O'Rourke made the radical decision to move to Bath where she would work with the British sprints-hurdles coach Malcolm Arnold while maintaining close links with Sean and Terri Cahill. In her own words, it proved an 'idiotic decision'; she was lonely and miserable. Her form that year was inconsistent, and she did not compete at the World Indoors, where she was the defending hurdles champion. At the Beijing Olympics, she trailed home sixth in her heat in 13.22. There was some good news. On the journey home from China, she met sailor Peter O'Leary; the pair hit it off and would marry in 2013.

Better days were to come over the next two years. In 2009 O'Rourke finished third in the 60m at the European Indoors in Turin in a time of 7.97. Later in the year came her fourth place in the 100m hurdles at the World Championships in Berlin, Germany. O'Rourke ran a season's best of 12.86 secs to qualify for the semi-final where she improved that time to 12.73 secs and booked herself a place in the final as a fastest loser. Her time in the final was yet another Irish record time of 12.67, the fastest time by any European woman in 2009.

A minor injury kept her out of the 2010 World Indoors and her focus turned to the European Championships scheduled for Barcelona, Spain. In the semi-finals, she qualified for the final with a season's best time of 12.71 secs. In the final, she set her sixth national record of 12.65 secs when she finished second place: just 0.02 of a second behind Nevin Navit from Turkey. This earned O'Rourke a place on Team Europe for the 2010 IAAF Continental Cup held in Split Croatia, only the fifth Irish athlete and the second female athlete after Sonia O'Sullivan to achieve a similar distinction. For Team Europe, she finished fifth in the 100m hurdles in 12.99.

Injury again interrupted O'Rourke's training for the 2011 European Indoor Championships in Paris. She still managed to finish second in her heat in 8.07 and ran a season's best 7.98 to come third in the semi-finals. In the final, she finished fourth in another season's best 7.96. In July, she clocked a time of 12.84 at La Chaux-de-Fonds in Switzerland, also running on an Irish 4 x 100m team, and then won her ninth – and final – Irish outdoor title. In late August, she headed for the World Championships, where she finished second in her heat but was then forced to withdraw from the semi-finals with an injury.

At her third Olympic Games in London in 2012, O'Rourke, now aged thirty-one, at last made it out of the heats but in the semi-finals, her time of 12.91 was only good enough for fifth place and she did not progress. Her last major championships appearance was the 2013 European Indoors in Gothenburg, Sweden, where she finished fourth in 7.95 secs behind her old rival Nevin Yanit from Turkey. When Yanit was later disqualified for drug violations, O'Rourke was upgraded to third place.

O'Rourke retired from athletics in June 2014, giving birth to her daughter Dafne in August 2015 and a son Archie in April 2019. She has worked as a player development manager for Munster rugby, an athletics pundit on RTE, a coach on the RTE reality TV show *Ireland's Fittest Families* and a weekly columnist in the *Irish Examiner* newspaper. She has written two successful cookery books *Food for the Fast Lane* and *The Fit Foodie* and maintains a website where she offers advice on health and well-being.

GILLIAN O'SULLIVAN
World Champion Race Walker

While Kerry has produced quite a few male Olympians, race walker Gillian O'Sullivan holds the unique distinction of being Kerry's very first woman Olympian. With a career beginning in 1994, O'Sullivan would represent Ireland at European and World Championships as well as at the Olympics in the 20km race walk. She became the first Irish race walker to win a medal at global level when taking silver at the 2003 World Championships. Her records for 3000m on the track and for 5km, 10km and 20km on the roads still stand.

Born in Killarney on 21 August 1976, O'Sullivan began walking in her early teens and at the age of sixteen met coach Michael Lane from Mullingar. Around that time, Jimmy McDonald finished seventh in the walk at the 1991 World Championships and sixth the following year at the 1992 Barcelona Olympics inspiring many others, including O'Sullivan to take race walking seriously,

Her first international appearance came in July 1994 when she was picked to compete in the 5km walk at the World Junior Championships in Lisbon, Portugal. She finished 22nd in 24 mins 19.38 secs, improving that time to 23:53.25 a year later in Nyíregyháza, Hungary. In 1996, representing University College Cork, where she was a student at the time, O'Sullivan won the National 10km road title with a time of 50 mins 19 secs and retained the title the following year in a faster time of 48:59; both times were slower than Deirdre Gallagher's record of 48:45 set in 1995. At the 1997 European Under-23 Championships in Turku, Finland, she finished ninth in the 10km in 50:19 and a year later, was 23rd in her first outing at the European Championships in a solid time of 48:24.

O'Sullivan's first national track title came in 1998 when she won the 5000m in a championship record time of 21:57.22. That same year, on 1 August, she set a national record of 45:28.75 secs for the 10,000m track walk in San Sebastian, Spain. A year later, she won the first of five consecutive national 20km titles on the roads with a time of 1 hr 43 mins 42 secs. Her winning time of 1:29:12 from 2002 remains a championship best. At home, she won her third of four national 5000m titles.

Having moved up to the 20km, which was the only Olympic distance for women in the walks at the time, O'Sullivan had a busy year in 1999. She clocked a time of 1:36:44 at Leamington in March 1999 and was the winner of the inaugural Irish 20km championships in 1999 with a time of 1:43:42. In her first appearance at the World Race Walking Cup in Mézidon-Canon, France, O'Sullivan she finished well down the field in 72nd place with a time of 1:42:20, while in Seville, Spain, she made a first appearance at the World Championships improving her 20km time to 1:40:33 and finishing a respectable 32nd.

In 2000, O'Sullivan set a personal best of 12 mins 13.19 secs for 3000m on the track in Castleisland, County Kerry on 11 June, followed by a personal best time of 43 mins 28 secs for the 10km walk in Dublin on 15 July. Over 20km, she finished a creditable 14th in a new best time of 1:31.31 at the European Race Walking Championships at Eisenhüttenstadt in Germany.

Her only Olympic appearance would come at the Sydney Games later that same year, and her tenth placing in the 20km in 1:33:10 was enough to convince O'Sullivan that it was time to give full and undivided attention to her sport. She quit her job as a history and geography teacher in Ballincollig, Cork and began training full time.

O'Sullivan, by this time a member of Kerry club, Farranfore Maine Valley, started her 2001 season in the best possible way when for the first time she dipped under ninety minutes for the 20km with a personal best 1:29:57 in Douglas, Isle of Man on 17 February. At the 2001 European Race Walking Cup in Dudince, Slovakia, she finished ninth in 1:31:13. Competing in her second World Championship at Edmonton, Canada on 9 August, she was one of fifteen athletes disqualified in a race that saw Olimpaida Ivanova of Russia set a championships record of 1:27:48 and her Irish teammate Olive Loughnane finishing 13th in 1:35:24. Ivanova had been banned for two years for a doping offence in 1997.

On 7 August 2002 O'Sullivan took Irish race walking to a new level when she finished fourth in a personal best 1:28:46 at the European Championships in Munich, Germany. Only in the chase for the finish was she overtaken for the bronze medal by the Italian Erica Alfridi. Less than a month earlier she had set a personal best time of 20 mins 02.60 secs for the 5000m walk in Dublin; a championship record that stands to this day.

In a 3000m track race in Belfast on 15 February 2003 O'Sullivan set an unofficial world indoors best for the distance of 11 mins 35.34 secs when winning her fifth of seven Irish titles at this distance indoors. Clearly on top of her game that year, she then travelled to Tijuana, Mexico for the Pan-American Race Walking Championships, where on 9 March, she won the 20km in 1:29:55. At a race in Milan, Italy on 1 May, she took nearly a minute and a half off her previous 20km best when clocking an outstanding time of 1:27:22 and then recorded a time of 20 mins 11 secs for the 5km walk in Kraków, Poland on 14 June. At home, she took her fifth 20km Irish title in 1:29:2.

All came together at her third World Championships in Paris, France, on 24 August 2003, when she finally made the medal rostrum taking the silver medal in a time 1:27:34. In a race requiring supreme concentration from the start, she finished over a half minute behind Russia's Yelena Nikolayeva but over half a minute ahead of Valentina Tsybulskaya of Belarus, who finished third. Had she enjoyed the experience? 'Not really. It was not until the last sixty metres or so that I could relax a little and enjoy the moment. You are under tremendous mental and physical pressure, and I had to keep concentrating so hard.' She remains one of only five Irish athletes to have won a World Championships medal.

O'Sullivan's final year on the international circuit was at the 2004 World Race Walking Cup, held in Naumburg, Germany on 2 May, where she placed eighth in 1:28:01. She knew by then that she was 'not right' with a left hamstring requiring constant physio treatment to keep her going. She still hoped to make the Irish team for the Sydney Olympics later that year, but when she went to France for altitude training, found that her technique had broken down irretrievably. Her left knee was not 'locking out' properly; a weakness she had first noted in 2001. With her coach Michael Lane, she was working hard to correct the problem 'and it was absolutely wearing'.

With great reluctance, O'Sullivan accepted that she would not make the Irish team for her second Olympics at Sydney later that year, where she had looked like one of Ireland's best hopes of a medal. She kept going for a year or two more and clocked 46:28.0 for the 10km at the Isle of Man on 15 October 2006. After winning a 3000m at the indoor track in Nenagh in January 2007, she followed that up by taking her final Irish title in the 3000m at the Irish Indoor Championships in Belfast a month later.

In April of that year, O'Sullivan announced her retirement at the relatively young age of thirty, accepting that she would never again reach the heights she had attained in 2002 and 2003. She had no regrets; for her, becoming a professional athlete had been a dream come true. 'It's a great lifestyle and you're doing something that you love. Among the places I got to visit included Australia, France, Spain, Germany, Italy, Mexico, Russia, Canada, and South Africa'.

Since 2008, O'Sullivan has worked as a qualified personal trainer in Cork, working with clients ranging from complete beginners to competitive athletes of all ages from 16 to over 60.

MARCUS O'SULLIVAN
Sub-Four Minute Mile Centurion

As a student atColáiste Chríost Rí in Cork city and with the Leevale club, Marcus O'Sullivan's initial involvement in athletics provided little indication of future greatness and no offers of an athletic scholarship arose when his secondary education was completed. 'I was very small, very light, but I had willpower to do something well. I wasn't sure what it was going to be, but I knew I wanted to be the best at something,' he told the *Irish Examiner*.

In the year following his Leaving Certificate, O'Sullivan, born on 22 December 1961, worked as a sail maker while Donie Walsh's twelve month plan of intensive training put him on the path to becoming 'the best at something'. The investment proved worthwhile when O'Sullivan, now aged eighteen, sliced 20 seconds off his best 1500m time and won the BLE junior 5000m title in 1980. When O'Sullivan ran a 3:47 time in the 1500m, a recommendation from Donie Walsh to Villanova University's legendary coach Jumbo Elliott quickly followed.

O'Sullivan turned out to be the last athlete recruited by Jumbo Elliott to the Villanova programme. Success was not immediate, and O'Sullivan would later admit that he made several foolish mistakes. 'I threw away those first three years of my scholarship at Villanova. I lost sight of what I should be doing, and what I really set out to do when I first left Cork,' he explained in an *Irish Runner* interview of July 1986. 'I did a certain amount of training and study, but never reached the maximum of my capabilities. During that time, I never got the results which other athletes, of less potential, managed to achieve.'

Although he managed to break the four minute barrier for the mile the first time on 22 January 1983 at Chapel Hill, North Carolina, he had little else to show for his first three years in Villanova. In the summer of 1983, when back home in Cork, Donie Walsh gave O'Sullivan a talking to, reassessing his training and pointing out that the worst thing in life was not failing but not trying. It proved a defining moment for O'Sullivan. On 13 July 1983, after just two months of intense training, he ran a time of 3:56.65 for the mile at the Cork City Sports.

O'Sullivan returned to Villanova a changed athlete and in the 1984 NCAA 1500m final, he finished second behind the Brazilian Joaquim Cruz in a career best time of 3:37.4, which secured qualification for the 1984 Olympic Games. After coming home, he ran another personal best for the mile at the Cork City Sports with a time of 3:56.11. He then outsprinted Paul Donovan in Santry Stadium to win his first and only national 1500m title. In Los Angeles, O'Sullivan finished third in the heats of the 1500m, winning a place in the semi-finals where a ninth-place finish in 3:39.40 ended his interest in the event. In the 800m, he made the quarter-finals, where an Irish record time of 1:46.21 was not good enough to see him progress. Taking the gold was Cuba's Joaquim Cruz.

He returned to Villanova in early 1985 supported by a New Balance contract and combined a career as a professional athlete with post-graduate studies. When Tom Donnelly was recruited as his regular coach, training was again intensified, and the results were immediate. He pushed South African-born athlete Sydney Maree all the way to the line at the Cork City Sports on 9 July ending up with a mile time of 3:52.64, over three seconds better than his 1984 time.

O'Sullivan went on to win the AAA 1500m title, producing another lifetime 1500m best of 3:37.20 and smashed his own national 800m record with a more than respectable 1:45.87 in Berlin on 25 August. He was then recruited by GOAL charity's John O'Shea for an attack the world 4 x 1 mile relay record at UCD's Belfield track on 17 August 1985. The mission succeeded and Eamonn Coghlan, Frank O'Mara, O'Sullivan and Ray Flynn combined for a time of 15:49.08, shattering New Zealand's existing world record of 15:59.57. O'Sullivan's 3:55.3 leg was the fastest of the four.

In 1988, O'Sullivan qualified for the 1500m final at the Seoul Olympic Games as a fastest loser. In the final, he helped set the early pace and ran comfortably during the middle part of the race but when the chase for home began, he missed the crucial break, struggling to an eighth-place finish in a time of 3:38.39. Winner was the Kenyan Peter Rono. O'Sullivan admitted that the Seoul experience was 'a perfect example of not getting it right when I could've'.

Four years later, at the Barcelona Olympics, O'Sullivan was eliminated from the 1500m when finishing eighth in his semi-final with all seven athletes ahead of him qualifying for the final. In 1996, O'Sullivan was again selected to run the 1500m for Ireland at the Atlanta Olympics, becoming the first Irish athlete to compete in the same event at four successive Games. He travelled to the Games buoyed by a 1500m personal best of 3:34.09 but, in the heats, his time of 3.38.16 was fractionally too slow to allow further progress.

O'Sullivan was introduced to indoor running in the USA and was immediately smitten. His low centre of gravity was ideal for negotiating the tight bends of the indoor arenas and he became one of Ireland's greatest indoor runners. At the European Indoor Championships held in Athens in 1985, he won his first major medal when he finished second behind Spain's José Luis González in a time of 3:39.75. Between 17 January and 28 February in 1986, he dominated the indoor circuit in the USA, winning nine successive mile races including first-time victories in the Wanamaker Mile and the USA indoor mile championships and beating Eamonn Coghlan on four occasions. At the Wanamaker Mile, then held in Madison Square Garden, he took on the seven fastest indoor milers in history including Coghlan who was attempting to win an unprecedented seventh title. In their final lap duel, O'Sullivan edged Coghlan to win in 3:56.05. O'Sullivan also won the race in 1988, 1989, 1990 and 1992.

At the first World Indoor Championships held at the Hoosier Dome, Indianapolis in March 1987, O'Sullivan out-sprinted José Abascal of Spain in the 1500m final to win the first of his three world titles. Two years later, he travelled to the 1989 championships in Budapest, Hungary, having set a world indoor record of 3:35.6 for 1500m on 10 February 1989 at the Meadowlands Arena in East Rutherford, New

Jersey. On 5 March, he comfortably defended his world title in a championship best time of 3:36.64. Two years later in Seville he could manage only fourth place in 3:44.79, but at his fourth World Indoors in Toronto, Canada in 1993, he qualified for the final without difficulty and in a slow, tactical race, collected his third gold medal after a last lap sprint of 26.14. His time was 3:45.00. His fifth and final outing at the 1995 World Indoors came in Barcelona, where he finished tenth in 3:47.02.

By 1992, when O'Sullivan was contemplating retirement, a new challenge presented itself after he discovered the trophy from his first sub-four minute mile in the basement of his New Jersey home. It inspired O'Sullivan to chase the dream of becoming only the third man to record a century of sub-four minute miles. On the recommendation of Limerick-based physical therapist Gerard Hartmann, he trained with a heart rate monitor, keeping every effort in a highly specific zone.

On 13 February 1998, Marcus O'Sullivan joined New Zealand's John Walker with 124 sub-4 minute miles and Steve Scott of the USA with 136 sub-4-minute miles in one of athletics' most exclusive clubs when he finished third in the Wanamaker Mile recording a time of 3:58.1. To be certain he had made the century milestone, he travelled to Melbourne in Australia, where on 25 February, he ran a mile in 3:56.35 to notch up his 101st sub-four minute time – fifteen years and one month after his first sub-four mile on 22 January 198. Of those, fifty-four were run outdoors and forty-seven indoors.

After he retired in 1997, O'Sullivan was appointed head coach of Villanova men's cross-country and track and field teams. He still ran occasionally, and on 26 January 2002, aged forty, could run a time of 8:09.13 for 3000m at the Penn State Open. Indoors of course!

SONIA O'SULLIVAN
Queen of Distance

Sonia O'Sullivan first came to national prominence in February 1987 when she won the national senior cross-country title on a muddy course at Killenaule County Tipperary. Aged just seventeen years and eighty-six days, she was the youngest winner of the race ever, male or female. Dick Hooper writing in the *Irish Runner* described the victory 'as far and away the shock of the day' before adding that 'rarely has there been such a display of raw talent at this level'.

That raw talent was quickly refined, and the promise fulfilled. A few months later, having completed her Leaving Cert examination, O'Sullivan recorded her first significant track victory when in the 3000m at the Cork City Sports, she beat Scotland's Liz McColgan, then a big star in the athletics world, in a time of 9 mins 01.8 secs.

O'Sullivan who was born in Cobh, County Cork on 28 November 1969, began her athletics career as a ten-year-old when she ran a mixed race around the field of the Ballymore-Cobh athletic club attracted by a promise of lollipops after the race. By 1985, helped by her coach Sean Kennedy, she was winning 3,000m titles at the Munster, Irish, Tailteann Games and International Schools (SIAB) championships.

Later in the year, she followed the well-worn path of Irish middle-distance runners and accepted a scholarship from Marty Stern at Villanova University as its first Irish female recruit. Because of a stress fracture, she arrived at the college on crutches and her first two years proved frustrating. Determined to make an impact, she trained alone, running loops around a grass field to protect her fragile limbs.

By 1990, she was fit again, and won both the NCAA cross-country and 3,000m titles. She followed that up in 1991 by becoming the first Irish athlete to complete the grand slam of NCAA championships when she won the indoor, track, and cross-country titles also leading Villanova to an undefeated cross-country season. Her five NCAA titles makes Sonia Ireland's most successful college athlete ever. In January 1991, she had become the first Irish woman to set a world record when running the 5000m in a time of 15:17.28 at the Terrier Classic indoor meet in Boston. After graduating from Villanova, O'Sullivan returned to Cobh where she continued to be coached by Sean Kennedy, the man who had supervised her transition from talented schoolgirl athlete to world class competitor.

She had displayed her potential on an international stage for the first time at the 1990 European Championships in Split, Croatia, when she finished a fighting eleventh in the 1500m. Learning from the experience, in 1991 she won a fiercely contested gold in the 1500m ahead of China's Qu Junxia at the World University Games in Sheffield, where she also took silver in the 3000m.

Inexperience deprived O'Sullivan of a medal at the 1992 Barcelona Olympics where she had to be content with fourth place in a tactical 3000m. From 11 to 21 August on the post-Barcelona Grand Prix circuit, a determined O'Sullivan smashed five Irish records, the highlight probably being a time of 14 mins 59.11 secs for 5000m in Berlin which reduced her own record by more than twenty-seven seconds. By season's end, O'Sullivan was firmly established as an athlete to watch, placing second behind the USSR's Yelena Romanova in the women's world ranking list for 3000m compiled by *Track and Field News*.

Leading up to the 1993 World Championships in Stuttgart, Germany, O'Sullivan was hot favourite to win the 3,000m title. In July, her status as the leading runner over the distance was confirmed at the Bislett Games in Oslo where she notched up a superb victory in 8:28.74 – a personal best and the fastest time by any athlete since the 1988 Seoul Olympic Games.

These were the championships where a group of Chinese female athletes, coached by the enigmatic Ma Junren and little known before the event, took the top three places in the 3000m causing awe and disbelief in the world of international athletics. Winner was Qu Yunxia in 8:28.71, with a shocked O'Sullivan relegated to fourth place. She quickly recovered and qualified for the 1500m final where on 22 August, eight days after her 3000m disappointment, she finished second to Liu Dong, also from China, with a time of 4:03.38.

O'Sullivan's good form continued into 1995. She set a new 2000m world record of 5:25.36 in Edinburgh on 8 July and a week later smashed the ten-year old European 3000m record at Crystal Palace, London, with a time of 8:21.64, the then fastest non-Chinese time in history. She also ran fast times in the 1500m, the mile and 5,000m, before suffering three successive losses. By the time she arrived in Helsinki for the European Championships, looked a tired athlete. Despite that, she qualified for the 3000m final with ease and on 10 August, made another piece of Irish athletic history by becoming the first Irish athlete to win a European title in a time of 8:31.84.

By now, O'Sullivan was making Melbourne in Australia her base for the European winter before returning to Teddington in London for the Northern Hemisphere summer. Prior to the 1995 World Athletics Championships in Gothenburg, she accumulated several victories in preparation for the women's 5000m which was included in the programme for the first time. In the final, Gabriela Szabo of Romania, the world junior champion, took the field through the first four laps at world record pace but failed to crack the field. O'Sullivan's crucial move was made 200m from the finish and a final sprint gave her a comfortable victory in a championship record time of 14:46.47.

In races after the World Championships, O'Sullivan proved almost unbeatable. In twenty-two races she lost just once; that was to Britain's Kelly Holmes over 1500m in Gateshead. She was honoured as the IAAF's Woman Athlete of the Year and made the cover of the January 1996 *Track and Field News* as the magazine's Women's Athlete of the Year and its first to be ranked at No. 1 in the 1500m, 3000m and 5,000m events in a season.

Her good form continued into 1996. She performed superbly in the weeks prior to Atlanta Olympics and completed her preparations at the Crystal Palace Grand Prix with victory in the 5000m in 14:48.36, her fastest time of the season. Unfortunately, at the Games, it soon became clear that Sonia O'Sullivan was exhausted and weakened by illness. In the 5000m final, her invincibility evaporated in the Atlanta heat when she sensationally dropped out of the race with two laps remaining.

While the 1997 season was largely disappointing by her own sky-high standards, O'Sullivan did win a silver medal in 3000m at the World Indoor Championships 3000m in Paris, France, where Szabo was the winner. Around this time, O'Sullivan left her old coach, the agent Kim McDonald, and linked up with Alan Storey, whose more laid back approach saw O'Sullivan winning not only the classic 8km race at the 1998 World Cross-Country Championships at Marrakech, Morocco, but then also winning the shorter 4km race for her best cross-country results ever. Later that year, she made her 10,000m debut in the European Championships, held in Budapest, Hungary, sprinting home for gold 200 metres from the finish and clocking a time of 31:29.33.

By now a mother, with her daughter Ciara born in 1999, O'Sullivan comfortably qualified for the 5000m final at the 2000 Sydney Olympics, and, on 25 September 2000, finally secured the Olympic medal she so richly deserved after a last lap battle with her old Romanian rival Gabriele Szabo. In the sprint for the line, the diminutive Romanian just made it ahead of O'Sullivan in an Olympic record time of 14:40.79. O'Sullivan's time of 14:41.02 was a personal best and an Irish record. Five days later, on 30 September, O'Sullivan finished sixth in the 10,000m in 30:53.37.

In the post-Sydney years, Sonia O'Sullivan continued to perform with distinction. She made her marathon debut, winning the Dublin Marathon in a time of 2:35:42 on 30 October 2000. In 2002, after the birth of her second daughter Sophie in December 2001, she helped the Irish team to bronze at the 2002 World Cross-Country Championships. Later that year, O'Sullivan showed some of her old form when finished second in both the 5000m and 10,000m at the European championships in Munich. At the 2003 World Championships in Paris, O'Sullivan qualified comfortably for the 5000m final from the heats, where she ended up 15th with a time of 15:36.62.

Sonia O' Sullivan departed the Olympic stage in 2004 when she qualified for a fifth Olympic final at her fourth Games in Athens. She made the 5000m final as a fastest loser in 14:59.61, her second fastest time of the season, but in the final, drifted backwards to finish last to a standing ovation from the large crowd of Irish supporters.

O'Sullivan continues to be a prominent figure in Irish athletics, writing a weekly column for the *Irish Times* and always willing to help upcoming athletes among them her daughter Sophie who, in 2018, took silver in the 800m at the European U18 Championships and in 2023, won the European U23 1500m title in Espoo, Finland. In 2024, Sophie qualified to represent Ireland in the 1500m at the Paris Olympics.

MARY PETERS
Golden Girl of Munich 1972

Munich 1972: the Games of swimmer Mark Spitz's seven gold medals, of gymnast Olga Korbut's elfin charm and of the massacre of the Israeli team. This was the year the Olympic Games finally lost any semblance of innocence.

This was also the year of gold medal pentathlete Mary Peters from Belfast, representing another few acres of the world torn apart by hatred and bigotry. Peters, with her flowing blond hair and huge smile, showed that there could be a positive side to life in Northern Ireland and people duly took her to their hearts. She was the epitome of the girl next door; the hometown athlete, who, at the age of thirty-three, finally came good.

Mary Peters, born 6 July 1939, has not a drop of Irish blood in her, as she readily admits. Her parents were both English and she only moved to the North at the age of eleven. Yet she is a Belfast woman through and through. So strongly is she attached to her adopted city that even after a threat on her life around the time of the Munich games and later, the murder of four men in the house next door to hers, she refused to budge.

Peters, like a few other Northern Irish athletes, also managed to compete for both Britain and Ireland. In 1964 the athletics bodies ruling the sport north and south of the border were speaking to each other – for once. That September, a combined team was sent to Brussels to compete in a match against Belgium and Scotland. Ireland beat both, helped in no small part by Peter's wins in the 80m hurdles and the high jump. Just a month after competing on that rare, combined Ireland team, she was back in her British vest at the Tokyo Olympics, where she finished fourth in the pentathlon.

She agreed that the situation was strange. 'I remember being in Mexico City in a bus, hanging on to a strap with some of the boxers who lived very close to me in Belfast, but who were competing for Ireland. Do you know them, someone asked as we were getting off. I said yes, he lives down the road. It did seem a bit ridiculous that we were competing for two different countries.'

When she could, Peters travelled to England for a competition, although in the pre-budget airlines era, this was expensive and forced her to take the occasional year off competition. 'When I was a British international athlete, we would have been away every weekend and sometimes midweek also and because I was working, it was very difficult for me to take time off. I always had to earn my living.' In retrospect, she felt the breaks helped her and account for her lengthy career as an international. 'I would still train but not drastically and then focus again on an Olympics or Commonwealth Games.'

At the start of her career, athletics was an easy going sport, with training more of a social occasion than anything else. Even when selected for her first Commonwealth Games in Cardiff in 1958, Peters regarded it as little more than a wonderful holiday. Although she went out at 1.46m in the high jump and finished eighth of nine in the shot, she was still quite pleased with her efforts.

Not so impressed by the Northern Irish performance in Cardiff was weightlifter Buster McShane, and when they all returned to Belfast, he invited the athletes he had met to start weight training with him. When Peters accepted the invitation, she quickly discovered that she loved gym work. McShane was equally fascinated by athletics. 'Buster always read up a lot on other sports and how they trained and one day he said that he'd like to come with me to the track and see what I was doing in the shot. So down we went and immediately he could see mistakes I was making. Within a short time, I was putting the shot a lot further.'

Her association with McShane caused friction in the small world of Northern Irish athletics. A year in limbo began when Peters decided to leave the Ballymena Athletics Club, which had been founded by Maeve Kyle and her husband Sean. Marea Hartman, for many years the power behind women's athletics in Britain, stepped in. 'She was involved with Spartan Ladies in London and myself and Maeve had already gone with them to Holland in 1961. So, I decided to compete with them in the year I wasn't allowed to compete here.'

By 1970, Peters had already competed in two Olympic Games, finishing fourth in one and frustrated by injury in the other, and she knew she was coming close to the end of her career. Deciding to put in one last effort, she started training for the Commonwealth Games in Edinburgh. Exactly one year to the day after she had begun her training, Peters won the pentathlon at the 1970 Edinburgh Commonwealth Games. Her score of 5,148 points was a British and Commonwealth record. She also won the shot with a put of 15.93m and came fifth in the 100m hurdles. At the age of 31, she at last had struck gold.

By now her ambitions were firmly focused on Munich 1972 and every move for the next two years was calculated and planned. 'My coach was very astute. He used to set me very high standards and I always did what he said I could do, even to almost 1.82m in the high jump.'

As it turned out, it was Peter's huge improvement at the high jump that would win her that gold medal in the Munich Olympics. 'I was losing too many points in the high jump. I could only clear 1.67m and I knew that I hadn't enough in the other disciplines to make up the deficit. So, at the end of the 1971 season, we went to Crystal Palace and watched a group there doing the Fosbury Flop. We took a film of me and of the others there and played it again and again, forwards and backwards on the office wall, to see what they were doing. I went away and tried it and jumped higher than I had ever done before.'

Flexibility was a problem: 'I was very unsupple – still am – so we did a lot of mobility and flexibility exercises to get my back hyperextended. Fortunately, it all worked out for me.' Indeed, it did. On a twilight evening in Munich after the other women went out of the competition, buoyed by a fanatical crowd waving the Union flag and chanting her name, Peters jumped higher and higher. She went over the bar at 1.77m, and then 1.82m, fifteen centimetres higher than she had managed the previous year.

Her superb performance had come after a long first day of competition. Heide Rosendahl, the bespectacled West German with the stripy knee socks, already the long jump champion, was always going to be the biggest threat. But Peters was pulled to a brilliant time of 13.29 secs in her 100m hurdles heat by the East German, Christine Bodner. In the other heat, Rosendahl could manage only 13.34. Next was the shot, Peter's strongest event. She won with a throw of 16.29m, her best in a pentathlon, and went into the lead for the first time.

After that magical high jump, she was still topping the points table, but had she done enough? That night she tossed and turned while she thought of what was to come in the long jump and the 200m, which were Rosendahl's two strongest events. The German was lying fifth after the first day, but she could more than make up for that in the long jump alone. This she did, jumping an astonishing 6.83m, five centimetres further than her winning jump in the long jump competition itself, to move up to third position. Peters with 5.98m did enough to keep a narrow overall lead. It would come down to the final event, the 200m.

After an agonising wait, the starter called, and it was tracksuits off. From the gun, Peters had a brilliant start, maintaining her form around the bend. With 70m to go, the efforts of two long days finally caught up with her. She felt her legs turn to lead. 'Arms! Arms!', she recited frantically, pumping and pulling herself across the line.

The clock on the infield showed she had run faster than ever before in her life, but was it enough? Only when Rosendahl came over to give her a congratulatory embrace did she realise that she had won. Her final total of 4801 was a new world record. Rosendahl on 4791 was just ten points behind. Had Peters run one-tenth of a second slower, she would have lost the gold.

Back home in Belfast, Peters received a rapturous reception, despite a bomb scare which turned the victory celebration into a major security headache. It changed her life utterly. Olympic gold medal winners have many demands on them, but Peters still found time for a campaign to help the young athletes of her adopted city. She began a special fund to give Belfast its first tartan track. Today, it still stands in a glorious natural bowl on the outskirts of the city. As she says herself, that is her monument.

MARY PURCELL
'I Always Wanted to Do Better, Be Better.'

In the late 1960s and early 1970s, an emerging number of Irish women were putting in the miles and starting to compete in cross-country and endurance races. Among them was Peggy Mullins, Ireland's first ever female cross-country champion in 1966, followed swiftly by Deirdre Nagle, Emily Dowling and Kathryn Davis.

In such distinguished company, Mary Purcell was the shining star. She was born Mary Tracey on 22 May 1949 and grew up in the Dolphin's Barn area of Dublin, where she learned to be quick on her feet. Her parents operated a pharmacy on Dublin's Eden Quay (which is still in the family), and Mary would carry on the family tradition by studying pharmacy at UCD.

As a sporty youngster, Purcell had won interprovincial caps for hockey before she started to take running seriously around 1971. By then she was already in her early twenties. She would claim that she only became interested in athletics because she rather fancied a young chap called Peter Purcell, then a coach at the Guinness athletics club which was based at the Iveagh grounds in Crumlin.

Tracey's raw talent quickly became obvious and, on a bleak June evening at Santry in 1972, she hit the headlines when running a time of 2 mins 04.2 secs for 800m, which qualified her for the Olympic Games in Munich later that year. Over 1500m, she ran an Irish record time of 4:18.14, also in Santry. Before heading for Germany, she won the 800m title at the WAAA Championships on 8 July at Crystal Palace in an Irish record time of 2:02.98. Later that month, she travelled to Banteer in north County Cork for the Irish Championships where she lined out in the 1500m and won her first Irish title, beating her Guinness AC clubmate Deirdre Foreman Nagle, who would become a perennial rival. Her time was 4:20.8.

Tracey, unbeaten on home soil from 1972 to 1976 and notching up thirteen national titles, would become Ireland's first truly world-class female athlete, winning several British titles as well as competing at the Olympic Games of 1972 and 1976 and racing at invitational races all over the world. Germany, the Netherlands, Bulgaria, Poland, Finland and even South Africa were among the countries she visited.

A notable success came in 1975 when she beat the reigning Olympic champion and world record holder Lyudmila Bragina of the Soviet Union over 1500m at the Golden Spike Meet in Ostrava. She would compete in the 800m and 1500m at the 1972 Olympic Games in Munich and over 1500m in Montreal four years after. Typically, she was deeply disappointed by her performances in both Games, blaming a 'lack of adventure' for her failure to make it out of the heats.

In 1974, Purcell won her only title over 3000m, a distance which had been added to the athletics schedule for women two years earlier; 5000m was evidently considered a step too far. Her time was 9:51.4. She was setting Irish records almost every time she ran this distance; her best official time of 8:53.10 would come in Dublin in August 1978. She had also improved her own Irish 800m record to 2:02.8 by 1974 and was remarkably consistent over this distance, regularly going under 2 mins 6 secs.

Throughout this time, Purcell continued to work full time as a pharmacist, most notably with Leo Laboratories in Crumlin, where on one occasion, everyone gave 10p per pay cheque towards a fund to enable their star employee to train and race at Crystal Palace in London.

By 1975, Purcell was married to Peter Purcell and running 70 miles a week in training, which was unusual for a woman at the time. She ran an Irish 1500m record of 4:08.63 at the Montreal Olympics, finishing fifth in her heat, which was still not enough to see her progress. She became one of the first Irish athletes to train at altitude, travelling to St Moritz in Switzerland. It is worth recalling that this was the era of East German and Russian state-sponsored dominance in women's athletics. Purcell, as a pharmacist, was aware of what was going on at a time when testing for performance enhancing drugs was rare and the extent of the problem not acknowledged, although the tell-tale signs were everywhere.

With few women in Ireland capable of pushing her to faster times, Purcell's only option was to race against men, which, of course, was frowned upon officially. On one memorable evening at the track in UCD Belfield in the summer of 1978, she took matters into her own hands, lining out in a men's 5000m, aiming to drop out at 3000m. Officials threatened her with a ban from athletics and a few of the male runners objected, but Purcell, typically, held her ground. Her unofficial time that evening was 8:51.4 – the fastest ever by an Irishwoman over this distance, which was added to the Olympic schedule in 1984.

In total, Purcell would represent her country internationally twenty times. At the 1974 European Championships in Rome, she set an Irish record of 2:02.8 in the 800m qualifying for the semi-finals, where she finished sixth in 2:04.0. In the 1500m, she ran 4:15.1, another national record, but did not progress from the heats. Four years later, in August 1978, she ran the 3000m at the 1978 European Championships a year after giving birth to her daughter Kara. She finished 15th in 9:11.9. Earlier that season, she had clocked a time of 4:30.52 for the mile at Gateshead.

Away from the track, at the 1979 World Cross-Country Championships in Limerick, Mary finished a magnificent sixth in the women's race behind the late great Grete Waitz from Norway. Her achievement was eclipsed only by the victory of a certain John Treacy in the men's race.

In those days, cross-country was what distance athletes did to keep fit over the winter and although not her favourite discipline, Purcell had taken her first national cross-country title in 1973 and on St Patrick's Day, 17 March 1973, had finished 17th in the women's 4000m race at the inaugural World Cross-Country Championships held in Waregem, Belgium.

Only later in her career did Purcell venture indoors, travelling to the USA and Canada for races, and taking bronze in a closely-fought 1500m at the 1980 European Indoor Championships in Sindelfingen, West Germany; it was her only international medal.

She opted out of the 1980 Moscow Olympics, disillusioned by the rampant drug taking and the politics afflicting the sport. As well as competing indoors earlier that year, she had won a second Irish Inter-Club cross-country title and competed at the World Cross-Country Championships in Paris. Outdoors, she won the 1500m national title. By this stage, the Guinness club had dissolved, and Purcell had joined a strong women's squad at Crusaders Athletic Club.

After the birth of her second daughter Jan in 1981, Purcell's focus changed. The longer distances were opening up to women and that included the marathon. In 1982, Purcell won the second (official) national women's marathon championship held in Limerick with a time of 2:38:49. It was her final national title, and that time would remain her fastest for the distance. Later that year, she finished sixth in the Dublin Marathon. In June 1983, she finished seventh in the inaugural Dublin Women's Mini Marathon with a time of 35 mins 49 secs; later in the year, she won the Dublin Marathon in 2:46:09. It was her final outing as a competitive athlete and a fitting end to an outstanding career.

It was not just in sport that Purcell proved a high achiever. In the early 1980s, attempting to juggle work, training and a growing family, she set up a company called SEQ, which is a regulatory affairs consultancy for the pharmacy industry.

A move to the tranquillity of the Isle of Man followed in 1993. Daughters Kara and Jan now run the company which employs a staff of fifteen in Douglas, Isle of Man and five in Ireland.

Purcell kept fit and in 2013, ran the London marathon with Jan to raise funds for the Bliss charity, which had supported Jan after the premature birth of her daughter Hope. After a break of thirty years from racing, Jan reported that her mother was as competitive as ever, even in training. 'I always like to be in front!' Mary admitted.

She was inducted into the National Athletics Awards Hall of Fame in 2018, a fitting recognition for a woman who had proved as competitive and committed as any man in her sport, inspiring a generation of women, and paving the way for so many others.

PADDY RYAN
The Late Developer

Whether now or over a century ago, one of the accepted truths of athletics is that athletes in strength-based events generally do not reach their prime until their late twenties.

In this respect, Paddy Ryan, of Pallasgreen, County Limerick, born 20 January 1883, was quite an exception, competing at national level when only eighteen years of age in the shadow of his older brother Con, himself a double Irish weight-throwing champion. In the GAA 28lb weight event in 1901, Paddy finished runner-up to Con.

A year later, when he was all of nineteen, came Ryan's first big breakthrough. In the Market's Field, Limerick, he finished in the minor placings behind Con in two 56lb events but produced two remarkable victories in the then current versions of the hammer. He won the standard event from a nine-foot circle by eighteen inches and a second event, with an unlimited run and follow-through, by just short of ten feet. Finishing behind him in both was Tom Kiely, then probably the most famous athlete in Ireland. Ironically, five years previously, a young Ryan had been inspired to take up weight throwing after witnessing Kiely win seven events in an Old Pallas sports meeting.

Ryan went on to win a total of eleven Irish hammer titles up to 1909, his best distance coming that year – 47.06m in the GAA championships. Ryan dabbled in other weights events but concentrated in the main on the hammer. While this may have limited the number of national championships he could have won, the 1906 GAA ban, which prevented Ryan from competing in both GAA and IAAA championships annually had a bigger impact.

Ryan opted to remain with the GAA, which meant that he could not be considered for the Great Britain and Ireland team at the 1908 Olympics or enter future IAAA or English AAA championships, although he did represent Ireland twice in the annual international against Scotland. Even more unfortunately, the standard of competition in GAA hammer throwing was declining and he won the 1908 GAA hammer title by a whopping 17 feet 6 inches (5.33m). A reporter for *Sport* reflected on the lack of progress Ryan was making:

'Ryan has been hovering around 150 feet (45.72m) for years – why he does not improve we cannot understand. We thought when he appeared a few years ago he would run up big things in the hammer.'

He 'was one to speedily turn his trainer grey-haired' athletics historian Bill Dooley wrote in his book *Champions of the Athletic Arena*, 'What John L. Sullivan was to boxing Ryan was in athletics, almost to the letter.'

All changed after 1910 when Ryan decided to try his luck abroad emigrating to the USA. In New York, he joined the Irish-American Athletic Club and got a job as a supervisor with the Edison Energy Supply Company.

Although sometimes referred to as a 'former New York policeman', he never actually joined the New York Police Force, preferring to work 'as the foreman of a gang of Italian labourers,' according to the *New York Times*. As one sportswriter of the day put it, 'Ryan found lots of time to train in this post, hurling laborers from one job to another…He has a pugnacious face and is of the fighting type when aroused.'

As early as October 1910, better competition, improved training methods and more technically advanced hammer equipment saw Ryan going well beyond 50.29m at an I-AAC meeting. By 1911, Ryan went within inches of 180' (54.86m) at another I-AAC meeting.

Although he played second-fiddle to the new great of hammer throwing, Matt McGrath, Ryan was improving all the time. Beneath a casual attitude to training and lifestyle, he showed himself a keen student of the sport and was a fast learner, quick to realise that hammer-throwing was all about finding the balance between strength and speed. He wrote about this at some length.

'The balancing of the swings and the timing of the turns is the main secret of hammer throwing… The main hinge of the secret is to strike a medium between the too fast and the too slow swing of the hammer at the start… There should be one thing before the man's mind, first, last, and all the time, and that is a vicious, snappy finish, with every ounce of weight working. Keen judges of the game tell me that I appear around half my natural size at the finish of my best throws. That suits me, for I know when I look like that, I am getting in all my strength and pulling for every ounce of power in my body,' he is quoted as saying.

Unfortunately, Paddy Ryan was unable to obtain US citizenship in time for the 1912 Olympic Games in Stockholm, although his throws at that stage put him second on the US lists and he beat Matt McGrath for the New York Metropolitan title in 1912, throwing 55.77m. McGrath would win that year's Olympic hammer title with ridiculous ease with a throw of 54.74m.

The following year, Ryan was all-conquering. He won the American hammer crown at Grant Park, Chicago, at 54.14m, a championship record. That first US hammer title set in train a series of victories that lasted until 1921, interrupted only in 1918 when Ryan was abroad on army duty. Soon after, Ryan threw 57.77m at the Eccentric Firemen's Games at the I-AAC grounds in Celtic Park to break McGrath's world record of 57.09m.

This, the first official IAAF world record for the hammer, was to stand for twenty-five years and remained a US record until well after the Second World War. Ryan went on to break several other weights records in non-IAAF recognised events, both outdoors and indoors, before the year was out.

Ryan would dominate American hammer throwing for the rest of that decade and gained a couple of US 56lb titles into the bargain, with his career interrupted only during that period from 1917 to 1919 when he joined the US Army and saw service in the First World War. During that tour of duty, he became life-long friends with a fellow recruit, the boxer and future heavyweight champion of the world, Gene Tunney.

While on leave from the army, Ryan managed to return to Ireland and win the hammer and 28lbs throw at the 1919 IAAA championships at Lansdowne Road. The irony, of course, was that he had been prevented from competing in previous IAAA championships because of his GAA affiliation. Now, as world record holder and with the IAAA in serious decline, there was no problem. Ryan also won a few military titles while in the US Expeditionary Forces.

In his book *How to Become a Weight Thrower*, published in 1916, James Mitchell used Pat Ryan as his model for the hammer, using photographs of him at the start of the first turn, after the first turn, spinning on left for the second turn, landing on second turn, in full swing on last turn and finally delivering the hammer after three turns.

In 1920, Ryan's Olympic opportunity finally came when he was selected to compete for the USA at the Antwerp Olympics. A great hammer contest between Ryan and Matt McGrath was anticipated, but anticipation turned to disappointment when McGrath picked up an knee injury after just two throws and ended up in fifth place. Ryan won the event with ease, throwing the hammer 52.73m feet in miserably wet conditions, although he had gone over 54.86m in practice. A distant second with a throw of 48.43m was Carl Johan Lind of Sweden. Among the others was Scottish thrower Tom Nicholson who had beaten Ryan twice when the pair met in the annual Ireland v Scotland matches years before. Now, Ryan was over six metres ahead of the Scot, even though both, in their late thirties, were at an age when modern athletes would have been well retired.

Three days after his hammer victory, Ryan went close to a second gold medal, losing the 56lb weight throw to Pat McDonald by a foot. Since this was the last time the event was held at the Olympics, McDonald's 11.265m throw was an Olympic record and has remained so. Ryan threw 10.965m for second place.

In 1924, Paddy Ryan moved back to Ireland to take over running the family farm in Bunavoy, Pallasgreen. He and his wife raised five daughters: Josephine, Bernadette (Bernie), Mary, Catherine and Christine. Ryan died aged eighty-one on 13 February 1964. In 2004, his daughters were thrilled when Ronnie Delany unveiled a beautiful memorial to their father in the centre of Pallasgreen. Bernie's son, Ryan O'Dwyer, was a prominent hurler with both Tipperary and Dublin for many years.

MARTIN SHERIDAN
Bohola's Hero

Although Martin Sheridan was born in County Mayo, he never competed as an athlete in Ireland after emigrating to the USA in 1897 at the age of eighteen, where his brother James was already living. Born in Bohola in 1881, Sheridan was the second youngest in a family of seven. When Martin was barely a teenager, one of his brothers, Richard, emigrated to the USA achieving considerable fame as a weight thrower. Between 1898 and 1902, Richard won the AAU discus title four times, which must have inspired the young Martin to try the same event when he took up athletics. Martin, already a striking figure at 6 ft 3 in (1.91m) tall, followed his brother to New York in 1897, joining the Pastime Athletic Club after he found a job as a streetcar driver. With American training, challenging competition and a good diet, his talent blossomed.

In September 1901, four years after his arrival in New York, the *New York Times* reported that 'M.J. Sheridan of the Pastime Athletic Club of this city made a new world's record in the discus throwing at the games of the Entre Nous Athletic Club at Patterson NJ, yesterday afternoon, throwing the missile 120' 7¾" (36.77m).' Sheridan improved that record to 38.71m a year later and would break it at least five more times, before finishing the 1902 season with a staggering throw of 40.71m at an event on Long Island, where he beat his brother Richard.

In 1903, Martin Sheridan left the Pastime club and joined the burgeoning Greater New York Irish Athletic Association (GNYIAA), based at Celtic Park in Long Island City. Within a short time, this club changed its name to the Irish-American Athletic Club (I-AAC), the name by which it is best known historically.

Sheridan's arrival coincided with the club becoming the most successful in the USA. He was joined by hammer great John Flanagan and the group of Irish weight throwing athletes who became known as the 'Irish Whales'.

The I-AAC attracted many athletes who would not have been welcomed in more 'upmarket' clubs. Among Sheridan's clubmates were John Baxter Taylor, who became the first African-American to win an Olympic title, and Meyer Prinstein, the first Jewish-American Olympic champion. Sheridan came from a staunch Irish nationalist background and felt very much at home when Celtic Park hosted athletic fundraisers for the Irish Republican Brotherhood and Irish nationalist causes.

When the GNYIAA, aided by Sheridan, won the AAU title, the rival New York AC accused Sheridan of being a professional athlete since he was then earning a living as an athletics instructor in Pelham Bay. Sheridan contested the claim and won his case on the basis that he was the administrator of the Pelham Bay grounds and had a civil service recognised certificate to prove it.

As the AAU discus and shotput champion in June 1904, Sheridan was selected for the US team at the St. Louis

Olympic Games. He finished fourth in the shot and four days later won a titanic discus struggle following a throw-off against another American team member, Ralph Rose after both men had thrown 39.28m. Given a further three throws, Sheridan won with a throw of 38.25m to Rose's 36.74m.

Sheridan was by now a serious all-round athlete and, in 1905, won the US all-round title, the first of three such wins in his career, with the others coming in 1907 and 1909. His record-breaking in the discus continued at the same time, with the *Washington Post* noting in October 1905 that 'Martin J. Sheridan of the IAAC all-round champion of America beat all records at throwing the discus today establishing a new world's record of 42.13m...' Sheridan beat his previous record twice, his first throw being 41.17m and on his third attempt he made the longer distance.

Both the Olympic Games of 1900 in Paris and of 1904 in St. Louis had suffered badly when run in conjunction with long drawn out World's Fairs. In 1906, the core Olympics idea was rescued at the Intercalated Games held in Athens, Greece, to celebrate the tenth anniversary of the first modern Olympic Games. These well organised Games did much to provide the template for subsequent Olympics.

In Athens, Sheridan competed in seven events. He won the discus (freestyle) yet again in a world record 41.46m. He also won the shot put and showed his versatility by taking second places in the stone throw, standing high jump and standing long jump events, all three now long discontinued, and fourth in the Greek-style discus, where the implement was thrown from a stand. He was favourite for a new pentathlon event but was forced to pull out with a knee injury. Even though these were easily the highest standard Games held to date, the International Olympic Committee has refused to recognise the 1906 Games as proper Olympic Games. Most members of the International Society of Olympic Historians continue to contest the IOC's view.

At the 1908 London Olympics, an intense and acrimonious athletics battle broke out between the American and British teams. At the opening ceremony, the American flag bearer controversially failed to dip the Stars and Stripes in front of the royal box. Sheridan, as star performer and *de facto* captain of the US team, also wrote a daily column for an American newspaper and in this, he berated the British team and its mentors for its alleged lack of sportsmanship. Away from the controversy, Sheridan won two more gold medals in London. In the freestyle discus an Olympic record throw of 40.89m gave him a narrow 5.5 inch victory over the American Merritt Griffin. In the Greek-style discus, thrown from a stand on a pedestal that sloped forward, he set another Olympic record of 38m. It was his ninth Olympic medal. He was also the non-pulling captain of the United States tug-of-war team which controversially lost to Liverpool Police in the first round, with the Americans making a complaint about the Liverpool team's footwear. Liverpool, with a team that included Irishman James Clark, then volunteered to take on the Americans in their stockinged feet. The USA team withdrew from the competition.

When Sheridan visited Ireland after the Games of 1908, he was warmly greeted in his native Bohola and enjoyed a well-attended GAA-led celebration in Dublin. He took part in various exhibition events around the country, including a draw against Tom Kiely at Dungarvan. Seen as one of the pin-up boys of Irish nationalism in the USA, his various utterances in public while in Ireland reinforced that impression.

Like several other Irish-American athletes, Sheridan also earned money from endorsing sporting goods, particularly those of the Spalding Company.

Sheridan broke the world discus record at least fifteen times, and set world marks each time he won the American all-round title. Yet, before he had even reached thirty, he told *The Brooklyn Daily Eagle* on 20 February 1910 that he was thinking of retiring. 'Simply, when a man has been competing for ten years, and I started in 1900, he gets tired of continually running, jumping and hurling weights. You know I am a heavy man, and it is hard work to keep in shape…

In 1910, Sheridan made the news for non-sporting reasons when he arrested Jack Johnson 'the champion world heavyweight pugilist of the world' after an altercation in New York with an actress called Emily (or Annette) Cooper. The case was dismissed as a publicity stunt.

Sheridan suffered severe blood-poisoning and mastoiditis during 1912 and underwent an operation to tackle a growth on his spine in 1913. His NYPD career saw him promoted from patrolman to detective sergeant and, as 'the strongest and biggest man in the detective bureau', he served as personal bodyguard to the state governor whenever he visited New York. After 2008, he never returned to Ireland, missing the marriage of his brother Joe to Kitty Collins of Clonakilty, sister of the future IRA leader Michael.

Sheridan's fame was used to encourage recruitment and good citizenship. He was asked to review a body of troops heading for the First World War, shaking hands with hundreds of young soldiers. Within days he was stricken by what was thought to be pneumonia. He died days afterwards on 27 March 1918, an early victim of the Spanish Flu pandemic. It was just one day before his 37th birthday. He was buried in Calvary Cemetery in Queens, New York near his beloved Celtic Park.

If Sheridan's 1906 Olympic medals were accepted by the IOC, then his nine medals would place him fourth in the all-time list of US medal winners behind Michael Phelps, Carl Lewis and 'standing' jump expert Ray Ewery. Even if 'only' the four won at St. Louis and London are counted, he still has a very strong claim to being most successful Irish-born Olympian of all time.

JASON SMYTH
The Usain Bolt of the Paralympics

It is not often that a World and European Champion lines up for the Ulster Schools' Athletics Championships at Antrim Forum. Add in three World Para records and you know that there is a special athlete on the track. But that is exactly what happened in May 2006 when the 18-year-old Jason Smyth defended his Ulster Schools' titles at both sprint distances.

Twelve months earlier, Smyth was almost unheard of outside his native County Derry. Double gold at the European Paralympics August changed all that. Despite dreadful conditions in Espoo, Finland, he raced to world records in the T13 category for the visually impaired at both the 100 and 200 metres with 10.96/21.84 clockings.

Later, in March 2006, he added a third world record to his growing collection when he won the 60 metres at the inaugural World Indoor Championships for the Disabled. His 6.92 seconds timing in Bolinas, Sweden also shaved a hundredth of a second off Jeff Pamplin's 14-year-old Irish Junior (U20) record. Unfortunately, his limited vision was to curtail an indoor career, since he was unable to distinguish clearly the lane and finish lines.

Jason Smyth, born in Derry on Independence Day 4 July 1987, was brought up in a Mormon family and diagnosed with Stargardt's disease when just seven. The condition affects the central vision meaning that he only has 10% of what is considered normal sight. When he attended Limavady Grammar special arrangements were made to facilitate his education. It was there that the school's PE teacher noticed his speed and recommended that he should join a local athletics club. And it was there he became acquainted Stephen Maguire.

The Strabane, County Tyrone man who had been a triple jumper but whose athletics career had been cut short by injury and illness. He had switched to coaching and would become trainer, mentor and much more to Smyth who because of his disability needed transporting to and from training. Maguire also had to accompany the athlete to training camps and competition. The relationship would also benefit Maguire's own coaching career to the point that he would be hired on a full-time basis by UK Athletics and was credited with the success of the British sprint relay team that claimed gold medals at the 2017 World Athletics Championships in London. His input was recognised when he received a share of the BBC Sports Personality of the Year coaching award later that year.

Meantime Smyth, then aged just twenty-one, had announced himself fully on the global stage when he won both the 100m and 200m at the 2008 Beijing Paralympics in China, setting world records in both. His runaway victories made him the poster boy of the Games. On his return home, he and Maguire found themselves inundated with invitations from all parts of the globe for track meetings during the upcoming indoor season and the following summer. That would become a pattern as the years progressed.

Instead of joining the jet set, Smyth concentrated on his training, and his decision was justified when in 2010 he made history by becoming the first Paralympian not only to compete in an able-bodied European Championships, but reaching the 100m semi-finals where he narrowly missed out on qualifying for the final when finishing fourth behind the eventual gold and silver medal winners. His impressive showing saw him selected by Northern Ireland for the Commonwealth Games in Delhi, India that autumn, although he was forced to withdraw from the team because of a back injury. Throughout his career, his back would prove to be a problem and at one point required surgery.

Smyth's next goal was to qualify for the 2012 Olympics and Paralympics in London. To do this, he and Maguire joined Lance Brauman's elite sprint group in Clermont, Florida which included, among other world class sprinters, the 2007 world sprints champion Tyson Gay. Modest as ever, Smyth revealed nothing of disability nor of his Paralympics achievements to his new training partners. When the group found out, they taunted Gay, pointing out that he did not have as many medals as the man from Northern Ireland. Gay, as you would expect, took it in good spirit and a special bond developed between the two speedsters. Maguire also used the time wisely absorbing Brauman's coaching methods, which would prove to be vital since his own career advanced in leaps and bounds as was appropriate for a former triple jumper.

In May 2011, the gamble of working with world class sprinters paid off with Smyth running a lifetime best of 10.22 seconds in Clermont which fell agonisingly only four-hundredths of a second outside the Olympics qualifying standard. Even at the time of writing, that mark remains the Northern Ireland record. Undaunted by coming so close and yet so far from making the Irish Olympic team, Smyth still was there to do the business at the Paralympics. There he proved one of the icons of the Games, successfully defending both his titles in breath-taking fashion.

He opened his account with a comfortable victory in the 100m in a Paralympic record 10.54 mark, winning by a massive four-tenths of a seconds. A week later he added a further gold in the 200m cruising to what would prove to be the second fastest time of his career; a time of 21.05 seconds. With the longer sprint dropped subsequently from the programme both in Rio and Tokyo, it would be the last time he had the opportunity to do the double at the Paralympics.

His career continued at full speed. After two further world titles in Lyon in 2013, he was dropped down to the T12 category in 2014, allowing him to take two European golds in that grade in Swansea, before being reinstated as a T13 for another World Para Championships gold in Doha the following year. In between times he made his long-awaited Commonwealth Games debut in Glasgow where he was eliminated in the first round of the 100m.

Another year and after the 2016 Paralympics in 2016, another gold medal was displayed in the Derry man's trophy cabinet followed by two more from the 2017 World Para

Championships in London and another sprint double at the 2018 European Para Championships in Berlin.

By now Smyth's body was starting to show the strain of battle over many years and the preparation for every event had to be planned minutely. Despite this, a hectic 2019 season was capped by a successful defence of his World Para 100m title in Doha. When the world closed for the Covid-19 pandemic, it gave Smyth a chance to rest from the demands of competition and prepare for his fourth Paralympics Games which were postponed until 2021.

Faced by Algeria's Skander Djamil Athmani, an opponent who was younger and faster that season, Smyth dug deep into his muscle memory and competitive juices for the final, producing one of his best starts ever and maintaining the narrowest of advantages all the way to the finish line. He would take gold by a mere one hundredth of a second.

Although now in his mid-thirties and married with two young daughters, Smyth had intimated that he would continue until the Paris Paralympics in 2024. It came as quite a surprise when he announced his retirement from Para Athletics in March 2023. He could look back on an unparalleled career that spanned three decades and included four Paralympic Games from Beijing in 2008, through London 2012 and Rio de Janeiro 2016 to Tokyo in 2021. Smyth retired undefeated in Paralympic competition, winning six gold medals at the Paralympic Games in the 100m and 200m events, eight titles at World Para Championships and six gold medals at European

Championships plus that often overlooked 60m gold at the World Indoor Para Championships at the start of his career.

In mainstream competition, the Derry Track Club sprinter won three national 100m titles in 2009, 2011 and 2016, represented Ireland at three European Athletics Championships, the World Athletics Championships, and numerous Europa Nations Cup matches. He was first ever Paralympian to compete in those events.

'I think now is the right time for me to step away from competitive Paralympic Sport,' said Smyth. 'I lived and fulfilled the dream and now I hope to support the next generation of para-athletes on their journey. I have loved my time with Team Ireland, and I have had many incredible memories that I will really treasure from my time as an athlete.'

Happily, Ireland's Usain Bolt has not been lost entirely to the sport as he took up the role of strategy manager with Paralympics Ireland which will allow the country's up and coming Paralympic athletes to benefit from his experience and vast store of knowledge.

'I feel that I have a lot to offer thanks to my experiences as an athlete and as someone who has been in the Paralympic and Disability sporting environment since my youth.'

While that is certainly true, it may be a while before Ireland finds someone to fill Jason Smyth's shoes on the Paralympic stage. In a fitting recognition of Smyth's contribution to Paralympic athletics, he was inducted into RTE's Sports Hall of Fame in December 2023.

TIM SMYTHE
Cross-Country Supremo

On 28 March 1903, the first International Cross-Country was held at Hamilton Park Racecourse, southeast of Glasgow. Although over the years, it would grow to become the unofficial world championships, it started life as a contest between the then four Home Nations of the United Kingdom and Ireland. France was admitted in 1907 followed by other continental European countries in the 1920s.

In that first historic race, Galway City Harrier John J. Daly finished third. It would take another twenty-eight years before a remarkable Irish man stood at the top of the individual podium.

Timothy Smyth (no 'e') was born to Cornelius and Mary Smyth on 12 April 1905 at Gurraun, Feakle, County Clare. It is not clear when the 'e' was added to the family name. His father was a farmer.

After the death of his mother on 6 July 1909, his father married Mary Margaret Tuohy on 19 July 1910 but only lived a further eight years himself. At that point, the thirteen-year-old Timothy moved to Clonloum, O'Callaghan's Mills, County Clare, where he was reared by his aunt Norah Lenihan, a sister of his father's.

A traumatic accident as a young man when he was crushed under a fallen horse and cart resulted in him being left him with a leg one and a half inches shorter than the other. Despite that, Smyth was determined to pursue an athletics career and in May 1925 at a sports meeting in Feakle he finished second in both the 880 yard run and one mile and third in a bicycle race. In 1926, he won several races at one and four mile distances including a double over the two distances at the Limerick Garda sports.

The following year of 1927, Smyth started training and competing with Limerick Athletics Club and was introduced to cross-country running. In the All-Ireland Junior championship at Baldoyle Racecourse, near Dublin, he finished tenth behind Paddy Coyle of Navan. His club made little impact in the team race, finishing fifteenth in a competition dominated by Dublin City Harriers, which may have prompted him to join the Ryan Athletic Club in Thurles.

During the subsequent track season, he won the Munster three and five mile championships as well as lifting numerous prizes in local events. Yet in the 1928 Junior Cross-Country, again at Baldoyle Racecourse, Smyth finished nineteenth and his Tipperary club a lowly ninth in a race dominated by army teams from the Limerick Depot and Dublin Metro.

Later that year, Smythe (at this point the 'e' was added) was one of the founder members of the O'Callaghan's Mills club in his hometown. During this time, his trainer was Patty O'Halloran who was seen frequently accompanying him on training runs around the roads of County Clare. That training paid off when he finished second in the 1929

Irish Junior Cross-Country at Limerick Junction behind Private Kinsella of the Army Metro club. A third place in the Senior Championships two weeks later saw Smythe gain his first selection for the International Cross-Country to be held at the Hippodrome de Vincennes in France.

He made a creditable debut, finishing second of the Irish behind national champion Tom Fanning in 44th spot, with the team ending up seventh of the record ten competing countries. Further international recognition was to come his way later in the year when he was selected to take part in the four miles at the annual track and field triangular match with England and Scotland.

In 1930, Smythe won his first All-Ireland Cross-Country title and once again was chosen for the international hosted by England at Leamington Spa. In a race won by England's Tom Evenson. Smythe finished outside the Ireland scoring six in fiftieth place.

A year later, Ireland was hosting the international cross-country at Baldoyle. After retaining his Irish title, Smythe became the first ever Irish athlete to win the International Cross-Country individual title in front of his home crowd Making the most of the poor underfoot conditions, Smythe went into an early lead that he was never to lose, winning by nineteen seconds from England's Jack Winfield with defending champion Evenson another five seconds back in third.

It was an historic first victory for Ireland although Irish athletes had previously been runners-up on three occasions. In a halcyon year for the 28-year-old, he would also finish first in the Irish ten-mile championship that summer as well as winning the 5000m in the Ireland v France match, although it must be pointed out that in the absence of French representation, only Smythe and compatriot T. Kinsella had contested the race.

'The moral of Smythe's success is complete,' wrote the respected journalist of the day, P. J. Devlin in the *Sport* newspaper. 'It is that we have the material for success for the highest achievement in plenty and must give it a chance. I have never known a successful athlete so averse to publicity as this Clareman'.

'He is as immune to flattery as he has been to the disparagements which would have disheartened many another. We must, however, reap the fruits of the endurance and self-confidence he has shown by holding these qualities up for emulation by the athletic manhood of the entire country.

'Smythe profited by his early mistakes. He knew his own resources of strength and stamina and has now reached the peak of achievement for which he set out. Not only did he complete his own preparation aloof from all the adjuncts now regarded essential for athletic success, but he created an atmosphere around him which give us the junior championship team (O'Callaghan's Mills), and which should provide us with a future senior and international champions."

While serving as a Garda in Dublin, Smythe won the Irish Senior Cross-Country title again in 1932, running as an individual and not part of the O'Callaghan's Mills team that picked up silver medals. In the international, he could manage only 42nd behind Evenson who picked up his second individual gold after his victory two years earlier. Later in the year, Smythe won the Irish four-mile championship as well as defending his ten-mile title. Smyth's club O'Callaghan's Mills won its first Senior Inter-Club the following year kicking off a four in a row. It was also the year that teams organised by the National Athletics & Cycling Association (NACA) were barred for political reasons from taking part in the International Cross-Country.

By a vote of ten to two, O'Callaghan's Mills left the NACA in 1937 to join the fledgling Amateur Athletics Union (of Éire). Smythe was appointed delegate to the new body despite having finished second in the NACA senior cross-country earlier that year.

Although he only finished sixteenth in the Irish Championship, Smyth was selected by the AAU to take part in the 1938 International held in Belfast. For the first time teams from both the Irish Free State (Éire) and Northern Ireland competed at the championships. Smyth, in his final appearance at the event, justified the faith of the selectors by finishing 49th, fourth of the southern Irish who ended up seventh in the team listings, one place behind their Northern cousins.

Smythe continued to compete until he was a mature forty-nine years old by which time, he had also entered the world of politics. A founder member in Clare of Clann na Poblachta (The People's Party), he was first elected to Clare County Council in 1950 on a Clann na Poblachta ticket. After the party was dissolved, he stood as an independent, topping the poll in three subsequent elections. He was a member of Clare Council until 1974 when he retired from politics.

From 1959 to 1963, Smythe was treasurer of the Clare County GAA Board and a member of Éire Óg hurling club in Ennis. He trained the Ennis Faughs team that won the County Intermediate Championship in 1945, while his innovative training methods also helped Éire Óg win senior titles in 1956 and 1957. In addition to his athletic and political interests he was a keen huntsman and rode out with the Old Mill Street Harriers, Ennis, every Sunday morning well into his sixties.

He was married to Ennis-born Maura Duggan, and they had ten children. Two of his sons carried on the family sporting tradition, Barry being a regular member of the Clare hurling squad while Michael was a prominent player and official in London Irish Rugby Football Clubas well as an inter-provincial player with Connaught.

In 1982, Smythe took his leave of this world following a brief illness, aged 77 years, in Cahercalla, Ennis. In his honour, the fair green in Ennis was renamed the Tim Smythe Park in 1985. He is also commemorated by a plaque at the entrance to the Doonaille housing estate beside St Patrick's National School in O'Callaghan's Mills.

ROBERT 'BOB' TISDALL
The Irish Wonder

When Bob Tisdall crossed the finish line in the 400 metres hurdles final at the Los Angeles Olympics on 1 August 1932, he became only the second athlete to strike gold officially in the green of Ireland. His victory capped an amazing chapter in the life of one of the country's greatest and most remarkable athletes.

Robert Morton Newburgh Tisdall was born on 16 May 1907 in Ceylon, now Sri Lanka, although the family, initially minus his father, returned to Ireland when he was just five-years-old. Born to an Anglo-Irish family, Bob, as he was always known, considered himself one hundred per cent Irish. His father William was an All-Ireland sprint medal winner in 1887 over both 100 and 220 yards while his mother was selected to play hockey for Ireland, although a family bereavement prevented her taking up the selection. By all accounts she was also a formidable golfer.

Inspired by the acrobats on a visit to circus as a young boy, Tisdall developed an interest in physical culture that was to last all his life. For weeks afterwards he spent his free time doing cartwheels, walking on his hands, and using the branches of tree as a trapeze. It was in prep school at Mourne Grange, standing in the shadow of Slieve Donard in County

Down, that he first found a gym that enabled him to develop the skill, balance and poise that was eventually to take him to the top place on the winner's podium in Los Angeles.

After Mourne Grange, he went to public school at Shrewsbury where, by the age of 14, a fascination for hurdling had already gripped him. He excelled at the school, which would later produce 1956 Olympic 3000m steeplechase champion Chris Brasher, winning an unprecedented seven events at one sports day.

After leaving school, Tisdall went to work in an office in London where, after only ten months of city life, an x-ray showed he had deposits of soot in his lungs. He was advised to live in the country, and it was only then that a university career was considered although he had no formal qualifications from his school days. When Oxford refused him a sports scholarship – a decision the university's athletics club would come to regret – he took and passed the entrance exam for Cambridge in 1928.

A remarkably successful athletics career followed. In 1931, his final year, Tisdall was elected CUAC president with responsibility for selecting the team to compete in the annual match against Oxford. As the team's captain, he played a key role in driving his team to an 8-3 victory in the match held at Stamford Bridge. Tisdall himself won four events – 120 yards hurdles, shot put, long jump and 440 yards – within thirty minutes, a feat not equalled for sixty years. He could have won a fifth in the 220 yards hurdles, which was his strongest event, but stood down so that a friend would have the opportunity of winning a full 'blue'.

With his background of Shrewsbury and Cambridge, the English athletics establishment assumed that Tisdall he would go on to represent England in the international arena. He quickly corrected them in no uncertain terms: 'These friends of mine thought I would probably run for England,' he said during an interview for the documentary *A Golden Hour*. 'But when it came down to it, I said I can't do that. Although I'm qualified, I'm proudly an Irishman and I can't do that.'

Early in 1932, he wrote an impassioned letter to the President of the Irish Olympic Council, General Eoin O'Duffy, asking to be considered for the Irish team representing Ireland at the Los Angeles Olympics later that year. O'Duffy was so taken by the tone of the letter that he immediately invited the Nenagh man to run in Ireland's Olympic Trials at Croke Park. To pursue his Olympic dream, Bob promptly left his job and moved with his wife to Sussex where he lived in a disused railway carriage set in an orchard and trained by running around the rows of trees.

Although Tisdall failed to make qualifying time at the trials, he was invited to a training camp in Ballybunion, County Kerry with the other Irish Olympic hopefuls. The hard work was rewarded when, given another chance by O'Duffy he won the 400 yards hurdles in a national record of 54.2 seconds, well inside the 55.0 seconds standard, at the Irish Championships, also at Croke Park. It was only his third time racing in the event. After another two weeks at the Irish Olympic training camp, he and rest of the Irish team faced a gruelling fourteen-day journey to California, seven days by Atlantic liner to Boston and seven days across America by train.

According to contemporary accounts, the temperatures crossing the deserts of Nebraska and Colorado registered more than 118°F (53°C). Tisdall whose normal racing weight was 11st 11lb (75kg) lost seven pounds (3.5kg). He also slept badly during the journey, worrying about his lack of 400m hurdling experience. In Los Angeles, he lost another three pounds and then amazed everyone with his unusual preparations.

'I went to bed to start to recover from the journey. I spent up to sixteen hours every day in bed. I had a couple of hurdles on the grass, and I used to jump over those. I was my own trainer, and I knew what my body wanted. And that was rest after that trip, you see. So, I took a chance and did that.'

Even more surprisingly, he never put on a running shoe or ran a yard. Three days before the heats, he tried a jog but discovered that a foot injury sustained twelve months previously had recurred. He attributed his symptoms to nerves. He opened his account in Los Angeles by winning his preliminary round heat in 54.8 seconds before leading home the competitors in the second semi-final two hours later in 52.8 seconds, 1.4 seconds faster than his personal best for the 440 yard hurdles and equalling the Olympic record.

Drawn in lane four with his main rivals outside him for the final, Tisdall enjoyed a narrow advantage in the early part of the race and was well ahead when the field entered the home straight. In the dash to the line, he brought down the final hurdle making him stumble for five or six strides and allowing the American Glenn Hardin to get within a yard of him at the tape.

'I had a feeling I was in front and about halfway round the bend there was this pole with loudspeakers on top of it and it bellowed out enormous noises. "Tisdall is leading," I heard that, and it upset me, as a matter of fact, but I recovered and got round. I reached the last hurdle and I thought I'm going to jump it like it was a four foot hurdle, but I hit it with my left calf.'

Tisdall did not waste any time celebrating his success but immediately made for the throwing area to support and encourage his friend and teammate Dr Pat O'Callaghan who was competing in the hammer. With his last throw of the competition, O'Callaghan nailed down Ireland's second gold medal of the day. It completed Ireland's greatest ever hour in the Olympic Arena in only the country's third Olympic Games.

Tisdall's victory came as a major surprise since, as previously stated, he had only run the 400 metres hurdles (or equivalent) three times before arriving in Los Angeles. He was denied a world record of 51.7 seconds under the rules at the time because he knocked down the final hurdle. Instead, a world record of 51.9 was attributed to Hardin who had finished second. Four days later, Tisdall finished eighth in the decathlon.

Later, Tisdall lived in South Africa, where he ran a gymnasium which he converted to a nightclub in the evening. He moved to Tanzania and grew coffee before moving on to Australia, where he raised cattle. He claimed to have run his last race at the age of 80 and took part in the Sydney Olympics torch relay. Although he had visited Ireland at the age of ninety in 1997, Tisdall was not present in Nenagh in 2002 when a statue was unveiled honouring him and the town's two other Olympic champions, John Hayes and Matt McGrath.

At the age of 96, Tisdall had a serious accident, falling down a steep set of rock stairs, rupturing his spleen, breaking a shoulder blade and fracturing several ribs. Within a short time, he was back on his feet – only a minor setback for a man who had conquered the world all those years ago. Bob Tisdall died peacefully at his home in Australia on 27 July 2004, aged 97. At that time, he was the world's oldest living Olympic track and field champion.

JOHN TREACY
Deise Distance King

From an early age, John Treacy, who would go on to win two world cross-country titles and take silver in the marathon at the 1984 Los Angeles Olympics, was a runner.

Born 4 June 1957 in Villierstown, County Waterford, where his father Jack was a well-known greyhound breeder, John and his twin sister Liz followed in the footsteps of their older brother Ray when taking up athletics as teenagers.

From his early teens, though often and happily sharing the limelight with his siblings, Treacy came to the notice of local and then national athletics organisers, winning everything from the Community Games 'marathon' to national titles at schools' level. A highlight of those early years was his 1974 victory in the Irish Senior Schools Championships when, representing St. Anne's in Cappoquin, Treacy won the 5000m in a record time of 14 minutes 17 seconds. His training routine in those days included a run between school and home every evening, with his schoolbag travelling without him on the school bus. The distance from the Treacy home, then the post office, shop and bakery in Villierstown, to St. Anne's in Cappoquin was almost exactly five miles.

Treacy made the leap to junior international competition in the mid-1970s. In 1974, aged sixteen, he finished third in the junior men's race at the World Cross-Country Championships held in Monza, Italy. He followed that up with another third place at the 1975 event in Rabat, Morocco, with his strong run helping the Irish junior team to an unprecedented second place.

After his Leaving Certificate, Treacy snapped up an athletics scholarship to Providence College in Rhode Island, USA, and there his development continued. After a few years in the USA, a stronger John Treacy made a spectacular transition from the junior to the senior ranks when winning the men's senior 12.3km race at the 1978 World Cross-Country Championships in Bellahouston Park, Glasgow. He hadn't yet reached his 21st birthday. Later that year, at the 1978 European Athletics Championships in Prague, Treacy he finished a creditable eleventh in the 10,000m and an excellent fourth in a slow and tactical 5,000m, where he crossed the line just three tenths of a second behind the third placed runner, Aleksandr Fedotkin of the Soviet Union.

From 1976 onwards, Treacy and his Waterford Athletics Club teammates would dominate the national inter-counties cross-country championships, winning the team title six times in nine years, and Treacy winning the individual title in both 1976 and 1977. With Limerick racecourse already selected to host the 1979 World Cross-Country Championships, an Irish athlete would be defending a world title on home soil.

On 25 March, in front of close to 25,000 fans, Treacy certainly didn't disappoint. In the senior men's 12km, he ran brilliantly through mud and encroaching crowds to win his second World Cross-Country title, beating the great Polish

Olympian Bronislaw Malinowski into second place. The day was crowned when the Irish team (which included Ray, John's brother) won an unheard-of second place, marshalled and led by the ageless Danny McDaid.

John Treacy, whether he liked it or not, was fast developing a reputation as a 'mudlark'. This was a fallacy, as shown by his repeated winning of the Irish 5000m title between 1978 to 1984 and the 10,000m title in 1985 and 1987. His track prowess was also shown internationally, not least in the 1980 Moscow Olympics, where in the 10,000m, Treacy collapsed with only 200 metres left in the race, a victim of heat paralysis and dehydration. A few days later, he placed seventh in the 5,000m final, three places behind his teammate Eamonn Coghlan.

At Crystal Palace a few weeks after those 1980 Games, Treacy confirmed his undoubted ability as a track runner in a classic 5000m which had been billed as a homecoming race to celebrate Steve Ovett's 800m win at the Moscow Olympics a week earlier. With Ovett leading the race and waving to the crowd with 100 metres to go, Treacy caught him on the line, surprising both Ovett and the BBC commentator, who still referred to him as a 'mudlark' after he had won.

Treacy's determination was demonstrated when for a period of six months in the early 1980s, he was forced to wear a back brace for 23 hours a day. He still managed to run every day, and included a 14 minute 5,000m run among his achievements during that time.

For his second Olympics in 1984, at Los Angeles, Treacy was selected to run the 10,000m and finished ninth in that race. He had also persuaded the Irish selectors to take a chance on him for the marathon, an event he had never raced before, although he had frequently run the distance in training with fellow distance runner Jerry Kiernan. Few had any expectations.

Lining up in the marathon that day were seven athletes with times of under 2:09:00. A group of six African runners set the pace in the early stages, with a lead of about ten seconds over a larger group which included Treacy, and the pre-race favourite Rob de Castella from Australia. After the 30 km mark, a group of four, which included Portugal's 37-year-old 10,000m specialist Carlos Lopes, led another group of five by just one second. In the group of five were Treacy and Jerry Kiernan, a fantastic sight for the Irish supporters watching the race on television at home through the night. Not since Jim Hogan took on Abebe Bikila in 1964 had an Irish runner been so well placed so far into an Olympic marathon.

At 37km, Lopes, Treacy and Charlie Spedding of Britain were battling it out in front. When Lopes turned on the pressure, neither Treacy nor Spedding was able to go with him. By the time Lopes entered the packed stadium, he had a 200m lead and crossed the line in an Olympic record time of 2:09:21. Treacy swept past Spedding on that last lap to take second in an Irish record of 2:09:56 with Spedding two seconds behind for third. Finishing ninth in 2:12:20 was Jerry Kiernan.

There was a symmetry about Treacy's Los Angeles medal. When he won his two World Cross-Country titles, the great Norwegian athlete Grete Waitz did likewise in the women's event. Their parallel lives would continue in Los Angeles when Treacy won the men's Olympic marathon silver and Waitz the women's silver.

Treacy did not win any further major international championship medals, with his best result a sixth in the 10,000m at the European Championship of 1986.

In 1983, with his athletics career seemingly stalled, mainly due to injury, Treacy packed his belongings and moved back to Providence with his wife Fionnuala and their daughter, Caoimhe and remained in the USA for ten years where three more children arrived. Treacy had been reluctant to make a serious move to the marathon, but in 1978, the Boston Marathon organisers came to him with an offer he couldn't refuse. Even better, Boston was only a fifty minute drive away. He trained flat out for six weeks in Phoenix, Arizona, but on the day it all fell apart on Heartbreak Hill at twenty miles. He dropped out soon after. He came back to finish third in both 1988 and 1989, with his 1988 time of 2:09:15 still an Irish best time.

Treacy finished third in the 1988 New York Marathon and second in the Tokyo Marathon two years later. In 1991, he lined out in Boston again but was forced to drop out when a pulled hamstring troubled him in the later stages of the race. Returning to Los Angeles in 1992, he won that city's marathon eight years after his Olympic silver. While the Olympic marathons of 1988 and 1992 did not go according to plan, Treacy nonetheless achieved the remarkable feat of competing at four Olympics.

At the age of thirty-six, John Treacy rounded off his marathon career in the best possible way with victory in the 1993 Dublin Marathon

His final race was in his hometown of Villierstown in 1995, where he was joined by Carlos Lopes and Charlie Spedding, his fellow medals winners from Los Angeles.

Treacy and his family returned to live in Ireland, where John was appointed chief executive officer of the Irish Sports Council, now Sport Ireland. He held the job with distinction until his retirement in 2022.

CLAIRE WALSH
A Trail-Blazer and 'Morton Marvel'

In October 1963, Billy Morton of Clonliffe Harriers invited women who were interested in athletics to attend a meeting in Moran's Hotel, Dublin. At a time when athletics clubs in Ireland were strictly men only, Crusaders AC had revived its women's section and Clonliffe Harriers was about to follow its lead. Thanks to Morton's genius for publicity, the meeting attracted a large number of aspiring young female athletes and as a result about forty women turned up in Santry for training soon after.

About six weeks later, on 16 December, a short race of about 600 yards race was organised for 'the girls' on Santry Avenue. The winner was Claire Dowling (later Walsh).

Dowling, born 27 May 1942, started as a sprinter. 'I knew from playing games at school that I could run fast, and I suppose I thought I'd have a go,' she said later in an unpublished interview. Growing up in Templeogue, Dublin, Dowling had learned to ride horses as a young teenager and that had kept her strong and fit. In Clonliffe Harriers, the new recruits were encouraged to try everything – throws, jumps, pentathlon – which Dowling enjoyed, although there was little competition for women at the time.

All changed in 1964 when between May and September of that year, Dowling competed in thirty-one events at thirteen athletic meetings, winning twenty of them. She represented Ireland in two international matches; against Scotland at Ayr where she placed second in the 880 yards and against Belgium and Scotland at the Heysel Stadium, Brussels, where she placed fourth in the 200m with a time of 25.8 secs and along with Jackie Spence, Lorna McGarvey and Maeve Kyle was a member of the 4 x 100m relay team that set an Irish record of 47.7 secs.

In 1965, women at last were admitted to the Irish Track and Field Championships at Santry where Dowling became the inaugural women's champion at 220 yards, 440 yards and long jump also finishing second in the 80 yards hurdles and third in the 100 yards and high jump. Inevitably, she was selected for the England v Northern Ireland v Ireland international match at Aircraft Park, Belfast on 18 August, where she finished fourth in the 80m hurdles, 440 yards and long jump, and was a member of the 4×100m relay team that placed second to England.

With Jackie Spence, Lorna McGarvey and Arlene Hunniford, Dowling set an Irish 4×110 yard relay record of 47.1 secs at the Clonliffe International Meeting on 5 July, and then on 4 September, was runner-up in the inaugural national pentathlon with 3,885 pts, just 50 points behind Maeve Kyle. Later that month, she married Brian Walsh.

Now called Claire Walsh, she did not compete in 1966 or 1967, having moved to Collooney, County Sligo in 1967, where Brian Walsh worked as an accountant. Their daughter

Patricia Mary was born in 1966 and a sister, Niamh, a year later.

When Walsh resumed her athletic career, she joined Calry AC and ran for the club at the Connacht cross-country championships at Tuam in February 1968, training on the road outside her home. A few months later, at the Connacht Track and Field Championships in Ballinamore she won the 100 yards, 880 yards and long jump. A week later at the Guinness Sports in the Iveagh Grounds, Dublin, she won the 100 yards in 11.9 seconds and at the national championships she took both 100 and 220 yard sprint titles and won silver in the high jump.

By 1969, Walsh was back with Clonliffe Harriers and at the national championships in Santry, where metric measurements were at last making an appearance, she won the 100m, 200m and 400m titles. In invitation events for women at a men's international match against Spain held at Santry, she finished second in the 100m, 200m and 800m. Other wins came in the 880 yards at both the Limerick City Sports and the Galway City Sports in late summer. In November, the Clonliffe quartet of Ann O'Brien, Ursula O'Brien, Rita Keogh and Walsh won the 4×880 yards relay at Blackrock AC's 25th anniversary road races. In December, she won the Clonliffe Harriers women's Oaks Road race at Santry over six furlongs (1320 yards) in 3:34.

The year 1970 proved special for Walsh. At the women's AAA Championships in June, she finished second in the 800m, setting an Irish record of 2:07.0 in the heats and improving that to 2:04.9 in the final. Competing at an indoors athletics meeting in Berlin on 4 December, she won the 800m in 2:10.9, beating the German champion, Hildegard Falck.

Even busier was the following year with Walsh competing in the 800m at both the European indoor and outdoor championships. Sofia in Bulgaria was the location for the indoor championships in March where Walsh placed third in her heat in 2:07.4 – the third fastest time overall of the three heats. Unfortunately, only the first two from each heat qualified for the final. In August, she travelled to Helsinki, Finland, in the form of her life. After finishing second in her heat in 2:06.1, she set a national record of 2:03.4 in her semi-final. Her hopes of a medal in the final were dashed when West Germany's Hildegard Falck and Gunhild Hoffmeister of East Germany tripped each other up right in front of Walsh, who was caught on the wrong leg.

'I couldn't sidestep them, and I couldn't hurdle over the flying legs so I had to stop and start,' she would remember later. Walsh ran on, almost catching the others and going through 400m in 58.4 secs, but then blew up. 'Over the last 100m-120m, the legs just didn't want to work.' She finished a gallant sixth in 2:08.6.

A month later, she finished second in the 800m at the pre-Olympic test meeting in Munich with a time of 2:05.7 and followed this up with a fifth place in the 800m in 2:04.5 at the ISTAF meeting in West Berlin.

Facing into an Olympic year, Walsh fell ill in the winter and overtrained when she got back on her feet. She did not have a great year. In Munich, she finished seventh in her heat in 2:08.98, which was won in an Olympic record time of 1:58.93 by Svetla Zlateva of Bulgaria. On 5 September, the day two members of the Israeli team were shot and nine kidnapped by Palestinian terrorists, she left the Olympic village early to cheer on the Irish at the rowing competition. Only when she got back did she hear about the raid which had taken place in the Israeli quarters during the night, less than 100 metres from the Irish quarters. 'We didn't know what was happening. I have a camp newspaper from that day which said that the hostages had all been saved – and they hadn't.'

After the 1972 Olympics, Walsh, disappointed with how the 800m had gone for her, dropped back to the shorter distances. At the WAAA championships at Crystal Palace in July, she finished second in the 400m with a time of in 54.4 secs and a day later, set a national record for 100m of 11.9 secs at the Raheny Shamrock Sports. At the National Championships, held that year at the Mardyke in Cork, she set an Irish record of 24.3 secs when winning the 200m, also winning the 100m in 12.2 secs. In September, she had an outstanding run in the 400m at the Coca-Cola International at Crystal Palace, London, placing second in 53.8 secs. She finished her season with a flourish at the Carlsberg International at Aircraft Park, Belfast where she won the 200m in 24.1 secs.

In early 1974, the Walsh family moved back to Dublin. At the WAAA Championships in England, Claire finished sixth in the 400m with her time of 53.9 secs inside the European qualifying standard, although a muscle injury kept her out of the national championships. Now aged thirty-two, she captained the Irish women to victory in a match against Portugal in Lisbon in mid-August, winning the 400m and anchoring the 4 x 400m relay quartet of Aideen Morrison, Padraigin O'Dwyer, Mary Purcell and herself to victory. A week later, she anchored Clonliffe to victory in the national 4×400m relay.

In September 1974, at the European Championships in Rome, Walsh finished sixth in her 400m heat in 54.14 seconds and that was it for her at international level, although she did run in one more Europa Cup. She gave birth to her son Niall in 1975.

In the meantime, her daughters Patricia and Niamh had joined Dundrum South Dublin AC and Patricia was showing some flair for the sprints. In both 1986 and 1987, she won the National 400m title and in 1987, set an Irish record of 53.6 secs for 400m. Claire and Patricia remain the only mother and daughter in Irish athletics to have won national titles and set Irish records.

Claire Walsh died on 23 June 2023. In her distinguished career, this 'Morton Marvel' had set new standards for Irish female sprinters winning fourteen national titles and breaking nine Irish records. With her husband Brian, she was very much involved in the early days of the Dublin Women's Mini Marathon and in her later years, continued to compete in the sport of orienteering. A true legend of Irish women's sport.

APPENDIX 1
Pen-pictures of the seven authors

Tom Hunt from Clonea, Carrick-on-Suir, Co. Waterford is a social and sports historian. He has had a lifelong involvement in the GAA as both a player and administrator. He was awarded a PhD in History by De Montfort University, Leicester in 2005. He has written extensively on social, economic and sports history. His books include *Portlaw, County Waterford: Portrait of an Industrial Village and its Cotton Industry* (2000); *Sports and Society in Victorian Ireland: The Case of Westmeath* (2007); *The Little Book of Waterford* (2017) and *The Little Book of Irish Athletics* (2017)

Kevin McCarthy from Cappoquin, Co. Waterford is a former teacher and inspector of history. He has written textbooks, local histories and undertaken a range of media work on sports history. He holds a PhD from UCC, based on Irish Olympic participation before independence and its links to nationalism; the resulting book, *Gold, Silver and Green: The Irish Olympic Journey 1896-1924* won the International Society of Olympic Historians 'Karl Lennartz' award (2010) and was shortlisted for the 2011 Aberdare Literary Award. McCarthy has also written *Tom Kiely: Erin's Champion* (2020) and ghost-wrote Ronnie Long's autobiography *The Long Road* in 2021.

Malcolm McCausland is an ex-international athlete. He was middle-distance coach to Northern Ireland teams at all levels; also, Irish and Great Britain U19 team. He has been athletics correspondent of *The Irish News* since 2000 and writes a weekly page on athletics under the pseudonym *Inside Track*. He had his first book published in 2020. *Lion For A Day* was a biography of Derry runner Anton Hegarty who won a silver medal in cross-country at the 1920 Olympics in Antwerp.

Colm Murphy from Castletownbere was a senior teacher in Kent. A former athlete, he was heavily involved in the sport as an administrator, organiser and official. He was also a keen military enthusiast and regularly organised tours to the battlefields of both World Wars also acting as guide and historian. He wrote extensively on cricket and athletics with a focus on field events. The four-volume set of books covering the Irish National Championships from 1874 through to 1999 was the first such history of a National Championships. Colm died in October 2022 and his ashes were interred in Donoughmore, County Cork on 23 April 2023.

Lindie Naughton is a Dublin journalist, writer and editor who has been involved in club athletics for over fifty years and is still running and coaching. In 2008, she co-wrote *Faster, Higher, Stronger: A History of Ireland's Olympians* with fellow sports journalist Johnny Watterson. She has written several other books, most notably *Lady Icarus – the Life of Irish Aviator Lady Mary Heath* (2004), *Markievicz - A Most Outrageous Rebel* (2016), *Markievicz – Prison Letters* (2018) and *Herbert Simms: Architect of Dublin* (2023).

Pierce O'Callaghan was an international athlete who represented Ireland at European and World level before embarking on a professional career in sport. He has been a member of the association of Track & Field Statisticians (ATFS) since the early 90s and has compiled numerous lists for Irish Athletics including the winner of every national title since 1873 and every Irish international cap winner since 1876.

Cyril Smyth Originally from Dunoon in Scotland, Cyril Smyth became involved with local athletics as a staff member at Trinity College Dublin, assisting at meets in College Park from the 1980s. He is a long-time member of Bray Runners Athletic Club and an official race starter since 1990. In 2021, Smyth was presented with the Official of the Year award by Athletics Ireland.

www.ingramcontent.com/pod-product-compliance
Lightning Source LLC
Chambersburg PA
CBHW071302110426
42743CB00042B/1143